DECOLONIZING
AMERICAN
PHILOSOPHY

SUNY series, Philosophy and Race
―――――――
Robert Bernasconi and T. Denean Sharpley-Whiting, editors

DECOLONIZING AMERICAN PHILOSOPHY

EDITED BY
COREY McCALL
AND
PHILLIP McREYNOLDS

Published by State University of New York Press, Albany

© 2021 State University of New York

All rights reserved

Printed in the United States of America

No part of this book may be used or reproduced in any manner whatsoever without written permission. No part of this book may be stored in a retrieval system or transmitted in any form or by any means including electronic, electrostatic, magnetic tape, mechanical, photocopying, recording, or otherwise without the prior permission in writing of the publisher.

For information, contact State University of New York Press, Albany, NY
www.sunypress.edu

Library of Congress Cataloging-in-Publication Data

Names: McCall, Corey, editor. | McReynolds, Phillip, editor.
Title: Decolonizing American philosophy / Corey McCall and Phillip McReynolds.
Description: Albany, NY : State University of New York, [2021] | Series: SUNY series, philosophy and race | Includes bibliographical references and index.
Identifiers: LCCN 2020039935 (print) | LCCN 2020039936 (ebook) | ISBN 9781438481937 (hardcover : alk. paper) | ISBN 9781438481920 (pbk. : alk. paper) | 9781438481944 (ebook)
Subjects: LCSH: Philosophy, American. | Colonization. | Decolonization.
Classification: LCC B851 .D33 2021 (print) | LCC B851 (ebook) | DDC 191—dc23
LC record available at https://lccn.loc.gov/2020039935
LC ebook record available at https://lccn.loc.gov/2020039936

10 9 8 7 6 5 4 3 2 1

Contents

INTRODUCTION 1
Corey McCall and Phillip McReynolds

Part One: The Terms of Decolonization

CHAPTER 1
Culture, Acquisitiveness, and Decolonial Philosophy 17
Lee A. McBride III

CHAPTER 2
Without Land, Decolonizing American Philosophy Is Impossible 37
Kyle Whyte and Shelbi Nahwilet Meissner

CHAPTER 3
Decolonizing the West 63
John E. Drabinski

Part Two: Decolonizing the American Canon

CHAPTER 4
Enlightened Readers: Thomas Jefferson, Immanuel Kant, Jorge Juan, and Antonio de Ulloa 83
Eduardo Mendieta

CHAPTER 5
Writing Loss: On Emerson, Du Bois, and America 111
Corey McCall

Chapter 6
Latina Feminist Engagements with US Pragmatism: Interrogating Identity, Realism, and Representation 131
Andrea J. Pitts

Chapter 7
Dewey, Wynter, and Césaire: Race, Colonialism, and "The Science of the Word" 155
Phillip McReynolds

Part Three: Expanding the American Canon

Chapter 8
The Social Ontology of Care among Filipina Dependency Workers: Kittay, Addams, and a Transnational Doulia Ethics of Care 177
Celia T. Bardwell-Jones

Chapter 9
Creolization and Playful Sabotage at the Brink of Politics in Earl Lovelace's *The Dragon Can't Dance* 205
Kris Sealey

Chapter 10
Decolonizing Mariátegui as a Prelude to Decolonizing Latin American Philosophy 229
Sergio Armando Gallegos-Ordorica

Chapter 11
Distal versus Proximal: Howard Thurman's *Jesus and the Disinherited* as a Proximal Epistemology 251
Anthony Sean Neal

Contributors 271

Index 275

Introduction

Corey McCall and Phillip McReynolds

In his justly famous account of colonizer and colonized and the fraught process of decolonization, Frantz Fanon claims that Europe is the creation of the Third World. "In concrete terms," he writes, "Europe has been bloated out of all proportions by the gold and raw materials from such colonial countries as Latin America, China, and Africa. Today Europe's tower of opulence faces these continents, for centuries the point of departure of their shipments of diamonds, oil, silk, and cotton, timber, and exotic produce to this very same Europe. Europe is literally the creation of the Third World."[1] Fanon proceeds from here to argue that simply granting these former colonies their independence and leaving them to their own devices is not sufficient. Just as the individuals and countries most affected by the crimes perpetrated by Germany's Nazi regime have had stolen art returned and reparations paid, these newly independent states are due this same consideration. But what of the United States of America? After all, the nation-states that comprise the Americas were also once colonies of Europe. Actually, Fanon addresses this question in his brief conclusion, which takes up the question of the future, and Fanon is adamant that these former colonies not look to Europe as a model. After all, that mistake has already been made by the United States: "Two centuries ago," says Fanon, "a former European colony took it into its head to catch up with Europe. It has been so successful that the United States of America has become a monster where the flaws, sickness, and inhumanity of Europe have reached frightening proportions."[2] Certainly this sickness and inhumanity affects all aspects of this monstrous nation, including its philosophy. Could the disease also be part of the cure? Might the diseased thought expressed in this monstrous land also be part of the healing process of turning away from Europe toward new traditions of thought, some of which were here all along but neglected by the thinkers who sought to emulate European models of thought?

Ralph Waldo Emerson, in his essay "The American Scholar" also urged American intellectuals not to look to Europe as a model. Indeed, Emerson sought to break free of intellectual vassalage to Europe. Hence, he urged the generation of a new kind of being: the *American* scholar. Emerson, however, was unable to recognize the irony in this call, which includes an act of naming in which a non-European land is named for a European explorer, and then settler colonists are identified with this name. Naming, indeed, as Patrick Wolfe observes, has played a central role in processes of "effacement/replacement" of colonial projects.[3] And, as Jodi Byrd notes, naming subsumes indigenous peoples "within the logics and justifications of U.S. imperial mastery that depend upon racial and political hierarchies to maintain and police hegemonic normativity at the site of inclusion."[4]

What, then, can we say about the naming of "American" philosophy and, by extension, the naming of this volume? We offer the name *Decolonizing American Philosophy* to at once identify and cast into doubt the very idea of American philosophy as a single, unified tradition, as well as to raise the question of whether any such philosophy must be a colonizing force or whether it might also work toward decolonization.

We might ask, What do we talk about when we talk about "American philosophy"? And what systems of domination and histories of oppression are hidden in this question? As has been pointed out repeatedly, the question itself is both a *philosophical* question and also one that is geographically fraught and admits of a number of different answers. What answer one receives seems to depend mainly upon whom is asked. Does American philosophy, if such a thing even exists—no less an eminent American philosopher than Richard Rorty has claimed that it does not—simply mean whatever philosophy is practiced in "America" (typically, if myopically, simply understood as shorthand for "the United States of America") by, one might suppose, professional philosophers? (Whether practitioners need be professional to count and what it means to be a philosopher is another in a long series of questions elicited by the supposedly simple one raised at the outset.) This is the sort of answer one might hear from those in the mainstream of what is commonly called "analytic" philosophy that is practiced and taught in most university philosophy departments in the United States. Another answer, an alternative offered by many members of the Society for the Advancement of American Philosophy, goes something like this: American philosophy is the philosophy of America. It is the philosophy that emerged on American soil and is the product of the encounters of Europeans with new challenges on a newly "discovered" continent: this is, of course, a continent that could only be considered "newly discovered" by the Europeans who first sought to enslave the indigenous peoples found there before forcibly removing them from their ancestral lands. Finally, the memory of these peoples was erased as well, though they still resonate hauntingly in the many place names derived from words in various indigenous languages. On this account, American philosophy renders the American settler experience as something heroic.

American philosophy in this second sense includes various philosophical movements that emerged in this context, including Transcendentalism and Personalism but most notably Pragmatism. This conception presupposes the idea that there is something distinctively if not uniquely *American* about American philosophy and, as such, implies any number of further questions such as: What is distinctive about "the American experience" that could give rise to this set of philosophical movements? What could it mean for a philosophy to pertain to a nation or a people? Who is this nation or people? Who counts as American? What do we even mean by America? Do we mean North America, or could we include South and Central America? Does it just mean the United States of America? Even if we were to limit the term in this way, how should we account for the influence and interactions of a great many philosophical traditions in what is, after all, a large, diverse, cosmopolitan society?

One way that people who self-identify as American philosophers speak of the field that they study and to which they contribute is to call it the indigenous philosophy of America or America's native philosophical tradition. They will hurriedly add that of course when they say this, they don't mean to identify American philosophy with the philosophy of America's indigenous peoples (though many will add that they don't mean to exclude this either). What they mean is the philosophical tradition that came to life out of "the American experience," whatever that might mean.

In this hurried clarification we begin to see something that might count as a distinctive if not unique feature of the philosophies that emerged in the Americas: what is called "American philosophy," both construed narrowly as "classical American philosophy" and broadly as "philosophy of the Americas," as it emerged from the contexts of colonization and settlement. Like other products of this culture, this philosophy bears the scars of a racialized past and present that are the product of a racialized colonialism. "America" in its various meanings is a settler colonial society that bears the imprint of settler logic. American philosophy is, therefore, a colonized and a colonizing philosophy. But we must not stop there, otherwise we run the risk of denying the agency of the peoples who have emerged from and been transformed by this encounter. In talking about the colonial past of the Americas, one can be tempted to view colonization, disappropriation, and slavery as historical events that occurred in the past and necessarily structure the present and the future. However, as Patrick Wolfe points out, settler colonialism "is a structure rather than an event."[5] It will be better to think instead in terms of processes of colonization. Once we have made that move, it is an easy step to notice that processes of decolonization were born with the advent of colonization, and the two have always existed alongside one another. As Gurminder Bhambra notes, "The meaning of modernity does not derive from a foundational event in the past, but from its continual contestation in the present.[6] Decolonization is not simply resistance to structures of colonization; it exerts its own creative force as well. Colonization *is* oppression, and decolonial thought and practices have emerged and continue to emerge as resistance to that oppression. But to focus exclusively upon oppression and resistance is to overlook the tremendous creativity and novelty that has been and continues to be unleashed in this encounter. Understanding decolonization as an ongoing process will enable us to better attend to the distribution of creation in the realm of ideas, no longer identified exclusively with Europe or with US settler culture. Decolonization in philosophy has to be partly about uncovering silences. Thus, as Kris Sealy points out in this volume, the question raised by the idea of decolonizing American philosophy is "how American philosophy might engage with questions pertaining to resistive acts of self-determination, political agency, and alternative futures." Fundamentally, the issue is one of "making newness."

Even so, one principal idea motivating this volume is that since American philosophy is the product of a racist and colonial culture and, insofar as it contains residua of that culture, American philosophy ought to be both deconstructed and reconstructed to weed out its racist and neocolonial aspects from the parts that can be used to fight racism and further the process of decolonization. We might, following Anibal Quijano, call this necessary first move "a decolonial analytic," and it is manifested in various ways in the essays that comprise this volume.[7] While it is a necessary first step, it is by no means sufficient, and many of the essays in this volume show why this is the case as well. Still, if it is to serve useful, moral purposes in the twenty-first century and beyond, American philosophy will first need to be decolonized. This volume is meant to be a contribution to the forensic task of decolonizing American philosophy and, in so doing, follow in the footsteps of works such as McKenna and Scott's (2015) *American Philosophy: From Wounded Knee to the Present* and Dussel's (2013) *Ethics of Liberation: In the Age of Globalization and Exclusion*. One thing that the contributors to this volume set out to do is to identify racist and colonial aspects of American philosophy and, having done so, seeing whether anything of value remains.

However, another aim of this volume is to investigate the claim that this process of decolonization is not only something that needs *to be done to* American philosophy but, more significantly, that decolonization is something that American philosophy *does*, or at least, *can do*. American philosophy, *even understood as a settler colonial enterprise*—an understanding that this volume seeks to challenge—has not only been a tool of colonial and racist oppression but has also at times been a resource for resistance to such oppression. One might take as an example the social and political reforms that lie at the heart of the pragmatism of Jane Addams and John Dewey, the trenchant critiques of racism offered by W. E. B. Du Bois, or the strong anti-imperialism of William James's political philosophy, which Alexander Livingston has recently analyzed in *Damn Great Empires: William James and the Politics of Pragmatism*. Apart from these specific examples, the principal idea here is that because American philosophy, in both the traditional and expanded senses of that term, is and has been a philosophy of reconstruction and transformation, it stands to reason that American philosophy should be able to provide a set of reconstructive and transformative tools that can help advance the cause of decolonization. That is to say, even if one accepts the premise that *the very idea* of "American philosophy" necessarily presupposes colonial hegemony, one might still acknowledge that this tradition could nonetheless offer resources to overcome its own disavowal of thinkers once deemed voiceless and rendered invisible to the tradition. Moreover, as several of the contributors note, once we expand and reconstruct the scope of "American philosophy" in the ways that this volume seeks to do, it begins to reemerge as a transformative enterprise. This happens not least when philosophical expressions of the colonial encounter and thought that preexisted and persisted in spite of and in resistance to colonization give rise to new ways of thinking that reimagine and reconstruct the alleged "givens" of colonization.

This volume is an exploration of some of the possibilities and difficulties of such a reconstruction. The essays in this volume are examples of the decolonization and decolonizing potential of American philosophy. Decolonization is better thought of not as an event or an outcome, upon the achievement of which we might take what William James called a "moral holiday," but a process, an ongoing struggle, and a generative force that constantly reimagines present and future.

There are two aspects to this reconstruction. The first entails an acknowledgment of those voices that have been marginalized or silenced by the myopic view of philosophy as the sole domain of white men. Secondly, this reconstruction demands that we let these voices speak, however belatedly, but also demands an engagement with them on their own terms.

Our goal in this volume is to unite a variety of scholars working in American philosophy and the philosophy of the Americas—as well as in the scholarship of decolonization—to ask what it might mean to decolonize American philosophy. Can American philosophy, the product of a colonial enterprise, be decolonized? Does American philosophy offer any tools or resources for decolonial projects? As such, the titular "Decolonizing" functions as both adjectival subject and adjectival object: What might it mean to decolonize American philosophy? And is it possible to consider American philosophy, broadly construed, as a (part of a) decolonizing project?

It is worth noting that as a *philosophical* project, decolonization as an idea not only aims at a transformation but is also a framing of a complex and historically bound set of phenomena as a problem. That is, by setting up decolonization as an objective, the philosophical project can't help but frame the boundaries of the decolonial subject. In other words, decolonial philosophy, in identifying its subject, necessarily says something about who or what it is supposed to be operating on and on whose behalf it operates. But, of course, many decolonial projects are at least partly the products of colonial cultures, and there's a way in which decolonization can be understood as another form of colonization.

The volume is divided into three parts. Part 1, "The Terms of Decolonization," includes essays that take a critical look at the very idea of the project of decolonizing American philosophy even to the point of understanding the ways in which, as just noted, decolonization can be understood as another form of colonization. Lee McBride takes up this idea in chapter 1, "Culture, Acquisitiveness, and Colonialism." McBride observes that there has been a recent surge in decolonial discourse. Decolonial thought is touted in op-ed pieces and blogs and shared via social media. At university, one is prodded to decolonize the curriculum, the canon, and the faculty. In broader contexts, some suggest decolonizing your diet, your sexuality, and your future. Hoping to dispel superficial and enigmatic evocations, McBride articulates what he takes to be the core features of decolonial philosophy. Decolonial philosophy is described as an oppositional reaction to teleological colonial systems of development designed to promulgate European cultural imperialism and amass capital. In closing, McBride briefly highlights three potentially problematic issues worthy of attention: one dealing with the way decolonial populations are conceived, a second regarding the reciprocity of cultural products, and a third reaffirming the need to challenge the acquisitive tendencies and material conditions of capitalist cultures.

Similarly, Kyle Whyte and Shelbi Nahwilet Meissner challenge the meaningfulness of academic uses of "decolonization" absent consideration of material conditions, literally, on the ground. They note that the word "decolonize" can be employed in ways that are unclear when *land* is not at the heart of event planning and philosophizing. They argue, by contrast, that "decolonization," as we have inherited the concept from Potawatomi, Luiseño/Cupeño, and numerous other indigenous traditions, refers to diverse, land-based political projects and the land-centric philosophies guiding them. Indeed, in these traditions, decolonial practice and philosophizing are already occurring, and land cannot be extricated from these decolonial traditions. In contemporary bodies of work on decolonization, the struggle for collective self-determination and the rematriation of lands is tied to indigenous efforts to protect our futurities. In chapter 2, Meissner and Whyte ask: "What does the connection between land and decolonization mean for philosophy in 'America'?"

In articulating this question, they first note some ideas about how land is understood by indigenous persons. Next, they offer a brief slice of some of the indigenous traditions that center land in both the critique of colonialism and the pursuit of decolonization and indigenous futurity. Indeed, *decolonization* refers to indigenous resistance practices, and the philosophies guiding them, that date back to the arrival of European colonizers. Next, they emphasize the necessary interrogation of the land-based practices perpetuated by American philosophy. Finally, they gesture at steps that would be necessary in decolonizing American philosophy. Ultimately, however, Meissner and Whyte conclude that decolonizing American philosophy is impossible.

Closing Part 1, John Drabinski takes up a similar concern when he explores the meaning of "the West" as a racial, colonial project. In reckoning with the African American tradition and its complex relationship to the history and memory of antiblack racial violence, Drabinski argues that the white West is entangled in that violence. In particular, Drabinski argues that embedding the African American tradition in the same violence expands the idea of the West into diverse space, replacing the notion of a single-rooted tradition with a rhizomatic model. Drabinski concludes, in contrast with the previous chapter, that such a model decenters "the West" and, in that very moment, decolonizes the concept, thus indicating a path toward the decolonization of American philosophy.

Having explored the terms of decolonization in Part 1, Part 2 takes up the project of "Decolonizing the American Canon."[8] In chapter 4, Eduardo Mendieta observes that the eighteenth century was the age of the scientific voyage as well as the Enlightenment. At this time, he explains, a new conception of nature began to take shape, one that was instigated by the emergence of a new type of literature that was partly inspired by the many popular and widely disseminated travelogues of the so-called age of reason. Along with this new literature, a new type of reader was called for: an enlightened reader. This is a reader that is curious, unprejudiced, scientifically informed, and hermeneutically generous. Chapter 4 takes up Thomas Jefferson and Immanuel Kant as two exemplars of readers that lived up to (or failed to live up to) the Enlightenment's motto: *Sapere Aude!* Jefferson was a founding father, a two-term president, a polyglot, and undoubtedly the most well-read member of the young republic. Jefferson, Mendieta notes, was also a bibliophile whose goal was to gather any and all literature dealing with the Americas. Kant, on the other hand, while not a bibliophile due to his lack of means, was known to be an avid reader of travelogues and the scientific voyage literature, which was indispensable for his courses on physical geography and anthropology. In a fascinating and very telling coincidence, Jefferson and Kant read, with different lenses and consequences, a text from this emergent literature: Juan and Ulloa's *Voyage to South America*. Their readings and misreadings of Juan and Ulloa's travelogue proved decisive for their views on slavery and race, showing how the constitution of intellectual traditions relies upon a series of readings and misreadings of thinkers and texts that are often forgotten as these intellectual traditions solidify. Mendieta's essay carefully reconstructs one such episode.

Similarly, in chapter 5, Corey McCall compares the experiences of loss and very different responses of two important American philosophers in terms of how they constitute our nation's democratic *ethos:* Ralph Waldo Emerson and W. E. B. Du Bois. In this chapter, McCall argues that Emerson's sense of loss isn't the same as the one shared by Du Bois: it's a white American sense of loss and not an African American one, which means that it is a disavowal of its pain. Although, McCall explains, both Du Bois and Emerson write their experience of loss into their work, Emerson declares that the loss of his son Waldo wasn't nearly as burdensome as he thought it would be, while Du Bois feels sadness mixed with relief at the death of his firstborn child, relief born of the fact that his son won't have to bear the burden of American blackness or of a life lived behind the veil of race. The second section of the essay focuses on these two scenes of terrible loss before turning to the question of the necessary relationship between democracy and loss. McCall interrogates how these authors' respective responses to deeply personal loss animate their writings on topics such as America, empire, self, and world. What happens to our conceptions of philosophy and American philosophy when we read these two thinkers alongside each other on this topic of loss?

Chapter 6, "Latina Feminist Engagements with US Pragmatism," by Andrea J. Pitts analyzes three Latina feminist engagements with Anglo-American pragmatism and neopragmatism: Jacqueline M. Martinez's Peircean-inspired account of semiotic phenomenology; Paula M. L. Moya's conception of postpositivist realism; and Linda Martín Alcoff's critique of Rortyan antirepresentationalism. Each theorist proposes arguments that effectively place an emphasis on the historically contingent and contested nature of social identities while also seeking to impact political forms of stability and the normative significance of identity-based claims. Accordingly, two goals of the chapter are: (1) to examine how Latina feminist interventions within debates regarding the epistemic and political authority of marginalized social identity categories either augment or critique existing US pragmatist and neopragmatist frameworks and (2) how each approach thereby responds to an existing series of questions within Latina feminism through pragmatist and neopragmatist philosophical insights. The chapter concludes by demonstrating how these three theorists can be located within a broader vein of Latina feminist decolonial theory.

Part 2 concludes with chapter 7, "Dewey, Wynter, and Césaire: Race, Colonialism, and 'the Science of the Word,'" in which Phillip McReynolds seeks to bring into conversation three thinkers who are not often invoked in the same context: John Dewey, Aimé Césaire, and Sylvia Wynter. The reason for bringing these three writers together is to create a space within pragmatism for opening up a genuinely postcolonial approach to race. While there has been some recent work in applying pragmatism in general and Dewey in particular to problems of race, Thomas Fallace's *Dewey and the Dilemma of Race* (2011) brings to light some problems with this enterprise. Fallace shows that far from being an isolated anomaly within his work, Dewey's ethnocentrism is a "weight bearing structure" that any pragmatist concerned about race must squarely reckon with. In light of these problematic issues, Dewey's work is itself in need of reconstruction. Happily, as Westbrook notes, " 'Reconstructing Dewey' has a decidedly Deweyan ring to it."[9]

For Césaire and Wynter, as for Dewey, it is the layered, textured, and thoroughly cultural and encultured quality of human experience that necessitates a new science based on what Susanne Langer called "the forms of human feeling." In noting the layered nature of human experience where archaic structures are never abandoned but built upon and repurposed, Césaire is calling attention to what Dewey called "the principle of continuity." This is important to us now because, according to Wynter, it is the only way of dealing with "the code of symbolic life inscripted by The Color Line."[10] It is the only way of proceeding because of the bodily enacted historical rupture of colonialism, both for colonizer and colonized.

McReynolds notes that pragmatists are sometimes accused of not paying sufficient attention to the past, but for both Dewey and Césaire we cannot go back (and would not want to). Yet at the same time, as a Faulkner character observed, the past is still with us. The only promising way of dealing with the reality of racism and the legacy of colonialism is to engage critically with it. Wynter writes, "With the destruction of these barriers (barriers, in Césaire's terms, between the 'study of nature' and the 'study of words'), the 'narrative order of culturally constructed worlds, the order of human feelings and belief will become subject to scientific description in a new way."[11] This new science of the human, which is not rooted in the deliberate subjugation and dehumanization of vast swaths of humanity, was what Dewey was calling for in his hopes for a "scientific ethics" and is the reconstruction that is needed in order to put pragmatism to work on race and decolonization.

Part 3 represents this volume's attempt not merely to decolonize the American canon as it has been inherited and interpreted by settler logics but to begin to expand the American canon by allowing traditionally silenced voices to be heard. Part of this expansion involves destabilizing geographical verities, which requires our frameworks to be extended into transnational relationships—thus destabilizing a domestic conception of the American self. In chapter 8, Celia T. Bardwell articulates an ethics of care within transnational boundary conditions so as to address the concerns of the Filipina dependency worker. In effect, this analysis generates a transnational public ethos of care situated within the complexities and contradictions of transnational relationships of dependency that serves as the context many Filipina dependency workers must navigate. Bardwell-Jones's approach is to examine Eva Kittay's argument about dependency and the way it generates a public ethos of care known as a doulia principle. On this basis, Bardwell-Jones expands this notion of the doulia principle to a transnational context through Jane Addams's conception of care and dependency in her work with immigrant communities. Finally, Bardwell-Jones articulates a transnational doulia principle that aims to guide an ethics of care to apply to transnational relationships of dependency, which will help improve the lives of Filipina dependency workers.

Kris Sealey's "Creolization and Playful Sabotage at the Brink of Politics in Earl Lovelace's *The Dragon Can't Dance*," offers the theoretical framework of Creolization as a tool through which American philosophical thought might theorize moments of resistance at the everyday level. Her approach is explicitly transatlantic, insofar as Earl Lovelace's *The Dragon Can't Dance* is her anchoring literary text in this endeavor. Lovelace's literary works (particularly *The Dragon Can't Dance*) are ultimately meditations on meaning making and self-definition for black subjectivity in the Americas, given the legacy of the plantation and the lingering forces of neocolonialism. The goal of this chapter is to name such meaning-making practices "creolizing" practices, which she argues has particular significance for how American philosophy might engage with questions pertaining to resistive acts of self-determination, political agency, and alternative futures. In other words, this chapter offers Creolization—its conceptual grid, its organizing frame—as indispensable for understanding emergent possibilities for freedom and empowerment within this historical violence of the Americas.

Although José Carlos Mariátegui has been considered one of the most original Latin American philosophers of the first half of the twentieth century insofar as he articulated an original emancipatory philosophical project blending Sorelian Marxism and indigenous nationalism that influenced subsequent decolonial thinkers such as Anibal Quijano, his works often exhibit a paradoxical treatment of race. Such is the claim made by Sergio Armando Gallegos-Ordorica in chapter 10, "Decolonizing Mariátegui as a Prelude to Decolonizing Latin American Philosophy." Indeed, though Mariátegui argues persuasively in some passages that the notion of race has been used as a tool to divide and oppress populations, in other places he often deploys the notion in ways that bolster racial hierarchies and perpetuate racist stereotypes. Specifically, Gallegos-Ordorica contends that Mariátegui's thought requires itself to undergo decolonization insofar as Mariátegui subscribes to certain claims that stem from the Eurocentric intellectual framework that he criticizes. To show this, Gallegos-Ordorica offers an analysis of the essay "The Problem of Races in Latin America" and claims that Mariátegui subscribes to same division of human beings into races that he criticizes elsewhere, as well as to the view that certain races are inferior to others by virtue of their passivity. In this chapter, Gallegos-Ordorica argues that if we want to use Mariátegui's thought to support decolonial endeavors, it is crucial first to decolonize Mariátegui's thought. Gallegos-Ordorica offers a tentative proposal to carry out this project.

Finally, in chapter 11, "Distal versus Proximal: Howard Thurman's *Jesus and the Disinherited* as a Proximal Epistemology," Anthony Sean Neal offers a careful reading of Howard Thurman's *Jesus and the Disinherited* in order to show how African American philosophy speaks to the particular concerns of African Americans but also is understood as a product of an African American reflective thought. Howard Thurman's work embodies this dialectical relationship between the particular community and thought born from the experiences that constitute it. Thurman's work reflects these experiences, and the version of Christianity he develops represents a critical discourse that serves to decolonize inherited religious forms. Thurman successfully makes the shift from Christianity to the religion of Jesus or love, ushering in a new path for an oppressed religious understanding based on his religious humanist concerns. It was his intent to demonstrate the necessity of a religion that claims to be about love to also be against oppression of any kind. In doing so, he closed the gap between the idea of revolutionary love as he understood it in the message of a historical Jesus and "those who stand at a moment in human history with their backs against the wall."[12]

With the essays that comprise *Decolonizing American Philosophy*, we hope to continue the long-simmering conversations about the various meanings of American philosophy: its scope, its purpose, what it has been, and what it still might become. More importantly, we hope that these essays, taken together, will help us move away from talking about "American philosophy" as a single unified tradition of philosophical thought in the United States to thinking about the many connections between various philosophical traditions of philosophical thought in and of the Americas.

Notes

1. Frantz Fanon, *The Wretched of the Earth*. Trans. Richard Philcox (New York: Grove, 2004), 58.

2. Fanon, *The Wretched*, 236–237.

3. Patrick Wolfe, "Elimination of the Native," *Journal of Genocide Research* 8, no. 4 (2006): 387–409, 388–389.

4. Jodi A. Byrd, *The Transit of Empire: Indigenous Critiques of Colonialism* (Minneapolis: University of Minnesota Press, 2011), 171.

5. Wolfe, "Elimination," 390.

6. Gurminder K. Bhambra, "Postcolonial and Decolonial Reconstructions," in *Connected Sociologies*, ed. Gurminder K. Bhambra (London: Bloomsbury Academic, 2014), 117–140, 123.

7. Anibal Quijano and Michael Ennis, "Coloniality of Power, Eurocentrism, and Latin America," *Nepantla: Views from South* 1, no. 3 (2000): 533–580.

8. This division into parts that takes up the terms of decolonization and actively seeks to further the project of decolonization should in no way be understood as a reification of the theory/practice distinction, which many of the essays themselves criticize and seek to undermine. Rather, the division is offered as an indication of difference in emphasis and is offered to the reader merely as a navigational aid.

9. Robert Westbrook, introduction to *Dewey and the Dilemma of Race: An Intellectual History, 1895–1922* by Thomas Fallace (New York: Teachers College Press, 2011), viii.

10. Sylvia Wynter, "'Genital Mutilation' or 'Symbolic Birth?' Female Circumcision, Lost Origins, and the Aculturalism," *Case Western Law Review* 47, no. 2 (1997): 128, 501–553.

11. Wynter, "Genital Mutilation," 179.

12. Howard Thurman, *Jesus and the Disinherited* (Boston: Beacon, 1996), 11.

PART ONE

THE TERMS OF DECOLONIZATION

CHAPTER ONE

Culture, Acquisitiveness, and Decolonial Philosophy

Lee A. McBride III

There has been a recent surge in decolonial discourse. Decolonial thought is touted (and mocked) in op-ed pieces and blogs and shared via social media. At university, there are calls to decolonize the curriculum, the canon, the faculty.[1] In broader contexts, some suggest decolonizing your diet, your sexuality, your future.[2] But what exactly is entailed in the call to decolonize? In an attempt to dispel straw men and feckless, superficial depictions of tenable decolonial philosophies, I wade into the discussion, articulating what I take to be general contours and goals of decolonial philosophy.[3] I describe decolonial philosophy as an oppositional reaction to teleological systems of (spiritual and material) development devised to serve the imperial and economic interests of the colonizers. And, in closing, I voice my concerns about three potentially problematic issues. First, the move to decolonize can rely upon an overly simplistic conception of decolonial populations. Second, it is historically erroneous and conceptually wrongheaded to see cultural products as things proprietarily owned by one racial or ethnic group. And, lastly, I suggest that decolonial thought is mere window dressing if it fails to address the acquisitive tendencies and material conditions of present-day capitalist cultures.

Colonial Acquisitiveness and Imperialism

Here I am, writing in English. English is readily spoken in many former British colonies: South Africa, Nigeria, Egypt, India, Hong Kong, Papua New Guinea, Australia, Canada, the United States, Jamaica, Barbados, Guyana, and Ireland. French is spoken in Madagascar, the Democratic Republic of the Congo, Chad, Cameroon, Côte d'Ivoire, Senegal, Algeria, French Guiana, Haiti, and Quebec (Canada). Portuguese is spoken in Brazil, Cape Verde, Angola, Mozambique, and East Timor. Spanish is spoken in Mexico, Cuba, the Dominican Republic, Puerto Rico, Guatemala, Nicaragua, Colombia, Bolivia, Uruguay, Argentina, and slew of South and Central American countries in between. It is instructive to think about the influence of the background assumptions and postulates implicit in these western European discursive practices.[4] These culturally specific background assumptions (or *episteme*) influence our conceptual frameworks, our ontologies—what counts as "human," as "discrete object," as "real."[5] These culturally specific background assumptions frame the values, tacit hierarchies, conceivable genders, and sacred/profane cultural practices for a given epoch. In this vein, colonial languages, vocabularies, and basic categories bear implicit values, predilections, and hierarchies. In this sense, colonizers did more than establish colonies to seize land, extract natural resources, exploit cheap labor, and amass capital. They brought with them intervening discursive practices and conceptual frameworks. They brought intervening cultural products, intellectual traditions, and norms. Colonizers established their dominance.

During the fifteenth century, galleons sailed from various western European ports to establish new colonies.[6] The Portuguese, Spanish, Dutch, French, and British were forerunners, establishing footholds in Africa, Asia, and the Americas.[7] Their ostensible purpose was to venture into the heart of darkness to bring light (*Jesucristo*), to save heathen souls; or, to explore the world and claim/expropriate new lands, to establish colonies for the glory of the empire; or, to find mountains of gold, diamonds, and other precious metals and deliver them back to the Monarch; or, to secure cheaper sources of spices, raw materials, and labor, enriching the trading companies that financed their expeditions; or, to allow those of lower station the opportunity to strike out and seize or settle on their own plot of land and have personal property free of religious persecution and feudal serfdom. I do not mean to suggest that there was only one shared colonial vision across western European colonial projects. In fact, the history is complicated, spanning several centuries and numerous geographical sites.[8] Each of the modern colonial projects was likely motivated by more than one of these purposes, especially as empires, alliances, and trading agreements waxed and waned over time.

In 1492, Cristóbal Colón/Cristoforo Colombo (Christopher Columbus) sailed from Palos, Spain, heading West into uncharted ocean, eventually unwittingly "discovering" the West Indies.[9] In 1493, on Columbus's second voyage to the West Indies, King Ferdinand of Aragon supplied him with a letter addressed to the indigenous people that already inhabited those lands (i.e., the Taino/Arawak people). The letter reads:

> In the name of King Ferdinand and Juana, his daughter, Queen of Castile and Leon, etc., conquerors of barbarian nations, we notify you as best we can that our Lord God Eternal created Heaven and earth and a man and woman from whom we all descend for all times and all over the world. . . . [God appointed a Pope to serve as ruler of the world.] . . . The late Pope gave these islands and mainland of the ocean and the contents hereof to the abovementioned King and Queen, as is certified in writing and you may see the documents if you should so desire. Therefore, Their Highnesses are lords and masters of this land; they were acknowledged as such when this notice was posted, and were and are being served willingly and without resistance; . . . Therefore, we request that you understand this text, deliberate on its content within a reasonable time, and recognize the Church and its highest priest, the Pope, as rulers of the universe, and in their name the King and Queen of Spain as rulers of this land, allowing the religious fathers to preach our holy Faith to you. . . . Should you fail to comply, or delay maliciously in so doing, we assure you that with the help of God we shall use force against you, declaring war upon you from all sides and with all possible means, and we shall bind you to the yoke of the Church and of Their Highnesses; we shall enslave your persons, wives and sons, sell you or dispose of you as the King sees fit; we shall seize your possessions and harm you as much as we can as disobedient and resisting vassals.[10]

Indeed, "the Pope must have been drunk, the King of Castile a madman."[11] Ferdinand seems to rely upon a (preposterous) argument from authority: God, through His Pope, has bequeathed this land to the King and Queen of Spain. Their Highnesses have documents verifying this. Recognize colonial reign or suffer the consequences.[12]

John Locke, in 1689, operating from a different social station, penned a different type of justification. In the *Second Treatise of Government*, Locke asserts that God has given rank-and-file human beings reason to make use of the world to the best advantage of life and convenience.[13] He seems to suggest that anyone can acquire private property (i.e., that part of nature one mixes with their own labor). Our claim to private property is only limited by our ability to use it without waste or spoilage.[14] Here, we find a barefaced argument for colonialism. First, Locke asserts that the light of reason tells us that God meant for the world to be subdued/cultivated for the benefit of life. Second, the indigenous peoples of far-off lands do not cultivate the land (in proper European fashion). No fences, no linear row crops—the lands they inhabit are "untamed" and "wretched." In other words, the indigenous peoples are failing to maximize potential yield. They are letting the land (i.e., God's creation) go to waste. Thus, God and reason commands "the rational and industrious" to cultivate these untamed lands (and thereby take possession of it).[15] So, with hard work and initiative, anyone can own property; one only need consider the waste and wretchedness of the Americas, Asia, and Africa.[16] Moreover, Locke believed that nonperishing assets (i.e., capital) could be hoarded without injury to anyone; he believed that "a disproportionate and unequal possession of the earth" was inevitable.[17] Put plainly, God really intended the world to be possessed by the industrious and rational, for their cultivation of the world makes the most of it.

Whether motivated by church, empire, or raw pecuniary ambition, each instantiation of modern colonialism seems to evoke a teleological system prescribing spiritual or material development.[18] That is, the colonial projects arising out of western Europe post-1492 were designed to accomplish an ultimate end—a τέλος (*telos*)—to serve the imperial and economic interests of the colonizers. I find it helpful to think of these systems working at two levels. At one level, colonial development is intended to compel the colonized to think and behave in a particular manner. Colonizers inculcate indigenous populations and (imported) enslaved populations with European background assumptions, values, and character traits, thereby rendering them well disciplined, beholden, subservient—subordinate functionaries, valets, and instruments of production.[19] Or they are erased.[20] At a second level, colonial development treats the land and the subordinated populations as raw or unrefined exploitable materials. The goal is proper cultivation, maximal production, intensified extraction, and the reaping of high yields. In these senses, colonial systems of development were designed to promulgate European cultural imperialism and to amass capital.[21]

Conceptual frameworks and culturally specific prescriptive behavioral pathways were vital in establishing the dominance of modern colonialism. María Lugones writes, "Modernity organizes the world ontologically in terms of atomic, homogeneous, separable categories."[22] Aristotelian categorical logic and dictates of mutual exclusion are employed to establish the oppressive logic of colonial modernity.[23] One is either human or nonhuman, man or woman, Christian or heathen.[24] These particular dichotomies are central to the hierarchical organization of the colonized world. The European, bourgeois, colonial, modern man was (mis)represented as the ahistorical, acultural, archetypal human subject, the truly human: "Man."[25] As such, the bourgeois European man was fit for public life and ruling, a being of civilization, heterosexual, a Christian, a being of reason. Bourgeois European human beings—men and women—were categorized as civilized. The bourgeois European woman thus occupied a civilized gender role as someone who reproduces the race, the docile object of affection for the colonial European man. But colonized people, as nonbourgeois non-Europeans, were categorized as nonhuman (perhaps subhuman, half devil and half child). As such, the colonized were not considered (proper) men or women; they were reduced to the state of beasts.[26] The various sexual practices and modes of gender expression in indigenous and colonized civilizations were met with xenophobic horror and religious zealotry. In this fashion, hierarchical dichotomies functioned as normative tools to damn the colonized; their souls were judged as "bestial and thus non-gendered, promiscuous, grotesquely sexual, and sinful."[27] "Hermaphrodites, sodomites, viragos, and the colonized were all understood to be aberrations of male perfection."[28]

Of course, modern colonialism came with palpable Christian overtones—at first Catholic, later Protestant.[29] Some justified their colonial forays as civilizing missions.[30] Ostensibly, these Europeans came to the Global South to bring salvation to the natives, to convert them to the one true faith. Fanon writes, "The colonial world is a Manichaean world."[31] One is either Christian or not. Moreover, "*Christianity = civilization, paganism = savagery.*"[32] By this logic, the colonized are depicted as unredeemable—impervious to ethics, innately corrosive, agents of malevolent powers.[33] Fanon explains: "The customs of the colonized, their traditions, their myths, especially their myths, are the very mark of this indigence and innate depravity."[34] Thus, it was the obligation of benevolent Christian colonizers to serve as patriarchs, shepherds to "those not elected for salvation" (i.e., the *massa damnata*).[35] Michel Foucault describes these types of power relations as pastoral power relations, whereby "each individual, whatever his age or status, from the beginning to the end of his life and in his every action, had to be governed and had to let himself be governed, that is to say directed towards his salvation, by someone to whom he was bound by a total, meticulous, detailed relationship of obedience."[36] The colonial civilizing mission then becomes an ongoing pastoral project to cleanse the filthy, discipline the unruly, absolve the sinful, and Westernize/civilize the natives. Lugones writes, "The civilizing transformation justified the colonization of memory, and thus people's senses of self, of intersubjective relation, of their relation to the spirit world, to land, to the very fabric of their conception of reality, identity, and social, ecological, and cosmological organization."[37] These colonizing practices justified the erasing of indigenous forms of community, ecological practices, and knowledge of planting, weaving, and the cosmos.[38]

While the modern colonial systems of this epoch began under decidedly pastoral and imperial auspices, they would over time come to bear marks of the new scientific approaches to knowledge: *Novum Organum Scientiarum* (1620); *Discours de la méthode pour bien conduire sa raison, et chercher la vérité dans les sciences* (1637); *Scienza Nuova* (1725), etc.[39] The medieval power relations (based in metaphysical, spiritual redemption) were suffused or overlaid with the Enlightenment's power relations (based in epistemic, mechanistic, material redemption).[40] The modern scientific method directed rational subjects/agents to analytically reduce phenomena to their most basic parts, recognize fundamental laws and properties, then build objective, scientific theories upon these firm foundations. And once these rational agents came to understand Nature's fundamental parts and how these parts worked together, they were able to harness and wield Nature's power.[41] *Scientia potestas est!* (Knowledge is power!) "And what hath ever beene the worke of the best great Princes of the world, but planting of Countries, and civilizing barbarous and inhumane Nations to civility and humanity[?]"[42] Development, so conceived, bound "developing peoples" to Western acquisitive conceptions of progress (focused on maximizing yield and the amassing of capital). According to Vandana Shiva, it is a project "based on the exploitation or exclusion of women (of the west and non-west), on the exploitation and degradation of nature, and on the exploitation and erosion of other cultures."[43] That is, colonial projects superimpose Western patriarchal concepts on women, non-Western peoples, and nature, rendering all three deficient or in need of development. The natural environment, women, and other subordinated groups are thus turned into passive objects—raw materials to be exploited and manipulated by the patriarchal colonial bourgeoisie.[44] Similarly, Sylvia Wynter writes:

> The more material scarcity is ostensibly technologically conquered, the more world hunger increases and the more the crisis of Africa and the underdeveloped world deepens. At the same time, the phenomenon of the debt burden, [qua] *oracular mechanism*, transfers wealth steadily from the South to the North, from the inner cities to the suburbs, and intensifies a systemic misallocation of resources. This accelerates the extension of poverty, and the joblessness-and-casual-labor phenomenon, and leads to overpopulation, the breakdown of all alternative "local cultures" in the Third World, and the overconsumption of excessively affluent life-styles in the First World. The resultant ongoing degradation of our human modes of life is, therefore, inseparable from that of the physical and organic environment. The latter are seen as "natural resources," within our cultural logic, to be ceaselessly exploited, thereby systematically ensuring the ongoing extinction of many other forms of life at the purely organic and, therefore, nonhuman level.[45]

Understood in this light, modern colonialism is teleologically designed to serve the imperial and economic interests of the colonizers. It emphasizes "development" at both a spiritual/ethical/behavioral level and a material/economic/ecological level. It has had deleterious effects for "the undeveloped," seriously impeding their ability to carve out antihegemonic cultures and modes of subsistence.[46]

Decolonization

But "that which is" has not always been. Foucault tells us that power relations and their attending systems of rationality reside on a base of contingent human practices—a precarious and fragile history. "Since these things have been made, they can be unmade, as long as we know how it was that they were made."[47] Other systems of rationality and different power relations are possible. In other words, decolonization is possible.

Decolonial philosophy, as I see it, is an oppositional reaction to modern colonial projects. It is an attempt to critique, contest, and undo modern colonialism: the subordination/reduction of persons, the egregious seizure of land, and the "developed" world's acquisitive exploitation of natural resources and labor in the "developing" world.[48] As such, decolonizing projects will need to expose the genealogies of the extant teleological colonial systems—at both the spiritual/ethical/behavioral level as well as the material/economic/ecological level. Ideally, decolonization will liberate the colonized from those conceptual frameworks, behavioral norms, and institutions that marginalize, dehumanize, or oppress colonized populations. It will undermine hierarchical dichotomies that make class, caste, racial, and gender hierarchies possible. It will historically reorient, contextualize, and critically interrogate European canonical figures and methods, making room for and further legitimizing indigenous and subaltern ontologies, knowledges, and wisdom. It will allow for new conceptions of *anthropos* (human), new ways of articulating identity or self, new modes of self-determination, nascent cultures.[49] Decolonization will recognize the moral, economic, and ecological failings of modern colonialist development (and its ugly twin, capitalistic imperialism). Chandra Mohanty, appropriating Fanon, writes:

> The success of decolonization lies in a "whole social structure being changed from the bottom up"; that this change is "willed, called for, demanded" by the colonized; . . . that "decolonization is the veritable creation of new men." In other words, decolonization involves profound transformations of self, community, and governance structures. It can only be engaged through active withdrawal of consent and resistance to structures of psychic and social domination.[50]

Shedding Colonial Baggage

So, let us drop the colonial baggage. Let us interrogate and eradicate those conceptual frameworks, norms, and institutions that marginalize, dehumanize, or oppress colonized populations. This seems right to me. But I do feel the need to highlight three *potentially* problematic issues.

The first concern has to do with the way decolonial populations are conceived.[51] The rejection of modern colonialism does not necessitate a return to a romantic premodern past, regaining a long-lost indigenous culture free of the taint of European colonial "development." To be clear, Césaire and Fanon saw this.[52] Césaire writes:

> It seems that in certain circles they pretend to have discovered in me an "enemy of Europe" and a prophet of the return to the pre-European past. . . . For my part, I search in vain for the place where I could have expressed such views; where I ever underestimated the importance of Europe in the history of human thought; where I every preached a *return* of any kind; where I ever claimed that there could be a *return*.[53]

Decolonial philosophy need not assume that a homogenous indigenous population existed harmoniously prior to the colonial interference.[54] In fact, before 1492 there were hundreds of disparate indigenous groups on each continent, with competing languages, cultural norms, and forms of governmentality. Of course, the vast majority of these tribes and ethnic groups have been vanquished or assimilated by hegemonic colonial orders, their languages and their distinctive cultures gone. Nevertheless, some indigenous and ethnic groups persist, retaining some semblance of their languages and cultural practices in spite of colonialism.[55] There are various groups with various traditions, differing languages, and differing colonial experiences. Fanon writes:

> During the First Congress of the African Society for Culture in Paris in 1956 the black Americans spontaneously considered their problems from the same standpoint as their fellow Africans. . . . But gradually the black Americans realized that their existential problems differed from those faced by the Africans. The only common denominator between them was that they all defined themselves in relation to the whites. But once the initial comparisons had been made and subjective feelings had settled down, the black Americans realized that the objective problems were fundamentally different. The principle

and purpose of the freedom rides whereby black and white Americans endeavor to combat racial discrimination have little in common with the heroic struggle of the Angolan people against the iniquity of Portuguese colonialism.[56]

That is, indigenous peoples and colonized groups do not always share the same colonial experiences, nor do they always agree on the way forward. There is more than one decolonial project. Eve Tuck and K. W. Yang are primarily focused on settler colonialism in the United States, on the repatriation of indigenous land and life.[57] María Lugones and Chandra Mohanty are primarily focused on the coloniality of gender and the prospects for a decolonial feminism.[58] Sylvia Wynter is primarily focused on the mechanisms employed to colonize the racialized dark-skinned peoples of Africa, the West Indies, and the United States, all the while seeking creative new (decolonial) articulations of "the human."[59] Each, from their own positionality, makes a tenable case for decolonization, but I believe that it would be a mistake to reduce each of these nuanced decolonial projects to one overarching project. Following Lugones, I would suggest a nonmodern, rather than a premodern, way forward—decolonization left open ended, allowing disparate decolonial groups to creatively reimagine their own social, cosmological, ecological, economic, and spiritual relations, their own ways of being nonmodern.[60] Fanon writes:

> We believe the conscious, organized struggle undertaken by a colonized people in order to restore national sovereignty constitutes the greatest cultural manifestation that exists. . . . The development and internal progression of the actual struggle expand the number of directions in which culture can go and hint at new possibilities. The liberation struggle does not restore to national culture its former values and configurations. This struggle, which aims at a fundamental redistribution of relations between men, cannot leave intact either the form or substance of the people's culture. After the struggle is over, there is not only the demise of colonialism, but also the demise of the colonized. . . . This new humanity, for itself and for others, inevitably defines a new humanism.[61]

Decolonial philosophy, so conceived, is not a *return* but motion toward new forms of humanity, toward nascent cultures. As Wynter eloquently writes: "The maps of spring always have to be redrawn again, in undared forms."[62]

My second worry has to do with the way people often talk about culture and cultural products in decolonial discourse. It is quite easy to interpret the call to decolonize as a call to reject colonizers and anything that is theirs—*their* language, *their* conceptual frameworks, *their* political and economic institutions, *their* values and norms, *their* cultural practices. In public decolonial discourse, one is often confronted with calls to decolonize one's education, one's diet, one's culture, etc.[63] In this, it is far too easy to be Manichaean: black or white, good or evil, ours or theirs.[64] The consumption of beef, pork, and fast food becomes a white Anglo-American thing, a colonial imposition. The consumption of *maíz* (corn), squash, yuca, insects, and backyard horticulture becomes an indigenous/pre-Columbian thing.[65] This creates a distorted depiction of the diversity, the mixtures, the cultural exchanges that have transpired over centuries.[66] As Alain Locke suggests, all modern cultural products bear the mark of some other cultural influence. All modern cultural products are composite. They are amalgams, products of intercultural exchange and cultural reciprocity.[67] It is problematic to see cultural products as things proprietarily owned by one racial or ethnic group, for this sets up a situation where an (imperial) racial or ethnic group can lay claim to all of the achievements of modern civilization: art, science, medicine, and so on. On such a view, certain foods are Anglo colonial foods; certain pastimes, like golf or square dancing, are white colonial cultural practices. This would seem to suggest that colonized people should divest from colonial cultural goods and practices. But would we expect the descendants of colonized peoples in the United States to abandon English, Melville, penicillin, blue jeans, basketball, or peanut butter? Would we expect them to seek out their "authentic" African or pre-Columbian cultures and languages?[68] This would seem wrongheaded to me. I would argue that cultural goods are not proprietarily owned by any racial or ethnic group.[69] And, secondly, I would argue that we can decouple the scientific attitude (and rationality) from the acquisitive ends for which they are directed in our contemporary milieu.[70]

Let us take Mohandas Gandhi, for example. In *Hind Swaraj*, Gandhi denounces the sick, diseased (British) culture imposed on the Indian people. The Indian was compelled to accept Western garb—sport coat and slacks—and Western education as the mark of a proper gentleman. British colonizers constructed railroads, industrialized modes of production, and implemented modern high-yield agricultural practices, each a mark of civilization. Through colonialism, Indian people were compelled to think of their (Indian) civilization as crude and embryonic. They were brought to believe that India only really entered into true civilization through colonial "development." Gandhi qua decolonial figure calls for the wholesale rejection of English textiles, railroads, (Western) medicine, compulsory education, and lawyers.[71] In place of western European civilization, Gandhi evokes a purportedly unmatched Indian civilization, extolling Indian swadeshi (self-reliance), khadi (handwoven cloth), Ayurvedic medicine, religious education, and a Varna/caste-based division of labor. What we get is a Hindu nationalist perspective of India, glaringly hostile to the Western scientific attitude, modern medicine, and compulsory education.[72] Here, again, I would only suggest that if we did not see cultural products as things proprietarily owned by one racial or ethnic group, and if we did not approach decolonization in a Manichaean fashion, we would not need to make such stark tradeoffs. Perhaps our modes of knowledge creation, our approaches to systematic study of the cosmos, and the ways in which we educate the young and heal the sick could be detached from the teleological systems designed to exploit "the underdeveloped" and amass wealth for modern imperialists.

My third and final worry, concerns the cultural propensity to neglect the material/economic/ecological aspects of decolonial philosophy. It irks me when decolonial philosophy limits itself to benign academic gestures, to "a freeing of the mind."[73] Something seems amiss when the decolonial work ends with a psychological account, an assertion of bad faith, an unpacking of particular ideas or myths that subordinate, or an account of the logic that sustains modern colonialism. Do not get me wrong, substantial conceptual and psychological barriers will need to be surmounted. New decolonial cultures will need to be conceived and articulated. But I want to emphasize the need to confront and ameliorate the material/economic/ecological realities of colonized populations. Decolonial philosophy seems like mere window dressing if it fails to address the plundering, ecological degradation, climate injustice, and the wretchedness that is often inflicted on colonized populations. Decolonial philosophy seems superficial if it fails to contribute (in some way) to the destruction of the teleological systems that turn nature, women, and other subordinated populations into passive objects or raw materials to be exploited and manipulated.

Césaire, in *Discourse on Colonialism*, offers a striking condemnation of Western bourgeois society. He warns that we cannot only worry about the titans of industry, bankers, and politicians. In his words, we must worry about "all of the tools of capitalism, all of them, openly and secretly, supporters of plundering colonialism, all of them responsible, all hateful, all slave-traders, all henceforth answerable for the violence of revolutionary action."[74] (Maybe we, too, are complicit?) Césaire's charge extends to US domination and to American empire:

> Do you not see the tremendous factory hysterically spitting out its cinders in the heart of our forests or deep in the bush, the factory for the production of lackeys; do you not see the prodigious mechanization, the mechanization of man; the gigantic rape of everything intimate, undamaged, undefiled that, despoiled as we are, our human spirit has still managed to preserve; the machine, yes, have you never seen it, the machine for crushing, for grinding, for degrading peoples?[75]

Decolonial philosophy must address questions of capitalist exploitation. The material conditions must be addressed. Perhaps this means that those of us in American philosophy have to critically reassess our (acquisitive) American culture and our capitalist exploitative tendencies.[76]

Notes

1. See, for example, Sumantra Maitra, "Subversion in the Garb of Social Justice," *National Review*, April 9, 2018, https://www.nationalreview.com/2018/04/subversion-in-the-garb-of-social-justice/; Scotty Hendricks, "PC Philosophy, or Why Some University Students Just Kant Even," *Big Think*, January 17, 2017, https://bigthink.com/scotty-hendricks/pc-philosophy-or-why-some-students-just-kant-even-learn-about-non-western-thinkers; and Ryan Nefdt, "Decolonizing Philosophy," *Africa is a Country*, June 30, 2017, https://africasacountry.com/2017/06/decolonizing-philosophy.

2. See, for example, Maura Judkis, "'This Is Not a Trend': Native American Chefs Resist the 'Columbusing' of Indigenous Foods," *Washington Post*, November 22, 2017, https://www.washingtonpost.com/lifestyle/food/this-is-not-a-trend-native-american-chefs-resist-the-columbusing-of-indigenous-foods/2017/11/21/a9ca5be6-c8ba-11e7-b0cf-7689a9f2d84e_story.html?utm_term=.808f436df385; Luz Calvo and Catriona Rueda Esquibel, *Decolonize Your Diet: Plant-Based Mexican-American Recipes for Health and Healing* (Vancouver: Arsenal Pulp, 2015); Sandeep Bakshi, Suhraiya Jivraj, and Silvia Posocco, eds., *Decolonizing Sexualities: Transnational Perspectives, Critical Interventions* (Oxford: Counterpress 2016); Maria Lugones,

"Heterosexualism and the Colonial / Modern Gender System," *Hypatia* 22, no. 1 (2007): 186–209; and Kyle Powys Whyte, "Indigenous Climate Change Studies: Indigenizing Futures, Decolonizing the Anthropocene," *English Language Notes* 55, nos. 1–2 (2017): 153–162.

  3. I am grateful for the critical comments and suggestions I received on earlier drafts of this paper from Anna Cook (University of the Fraser Valley), Leonard Harris (Purdue University), Phillip McReynolds (UNC-Charlotte), and Corey McCall (Elmira College).

  4. Maria Lugones, "Toward a Decolonial Feminism," *Hypatia* 25 no. 4 (2010): 742–759, 750.

  5. See Sylvia Wynter, "Unsettling the Coloniality of Being/Power/Truth/Freedom: Towards the Human, After Man, Its Overrepresentation—An Argument," *New Centennial Review* 3 no. 3 (2003): 257–337, 318; Sylvia Wynter, "The Pope Must Have Been Drunk, the King of Castile a Madman: Culture as Actuality, and the Caribbean Rethinking Modernity," in *The Reordering of Culture: Latin America, The Caribbean and Canada in the Hood*, ed. Alvina Reprecht and Cecilia Taiana (Ottawa: Carleton University Press, 1995): 17–41, 29; Leonard Harris, "Autonomy Under Duress," *African-American Perspectives on Biomedical Ethics*, ed. Harley Flack and Edmund Pellegrino (Washington, DC: Georgetown University Press, 1992): 133–149, 144; and Lugones, "Toward a Decolonial Feminism," 745. Foucault writes: "By *episteme*, we mean, in fact, the total set of relations that unite, at a given period, the discursive practices that give rise to epistemological figures, sciences, and possibly formalized systems; the way in which, in each of these discursive formations, the transitions to epistemologization, scientificity, and formalization are situated and operate. . . . The episteme is not a form of knowledge (*connaissance*) or type of rationality which, crossing the boundaries of the most varied sciences, manifests the sovereign unity of a subject, a spirit, or a period; it is the totality of relations that can be discovered, for a given period, between the sciences when one analyses them at the level of discursive regularities." See Michel Foucault, *The Archaeology of Knowledge and the Discourse on Language*, trans. A. M. Sheridan Smith (New York: Vintage, 2010), 191.

  6. By 1441, Portuguese ships had rounded Cape Bojador and established trade with the Kingdom of Jolof (in present-day Senegal). In 1441, Antão Gonçalves returned to Lisbon with the first (recorded) cargo of West African slaves and gold. See W. E. B. Du Bois, "The Rape of Africa," in *The World and Africa* and *Color and Democracy* (New York: Oxford University Press, 2007), 29, 28–51; and Sylvia Wynter, "1492: A New World View," in *Race, Discourse, and the Origin of the Americas*, ed. Vera Lawrence Hyatt and Rex Nettleford (Washington, DC: Smithsonian Institution Press, 1995): 9, 5–57. *Nota bene*, the European slave trade began decades prior to Columbus's expedition of 1492. Some scholars argue that the slave trade was an integral and ever-present piece of the colonial triadic

model: Man-Indio-Zanj/Slave; or Colonist-Native-Negro. See Du Bois, "The Rape of Africa," 28; Wynter, "1492: A New World View," 9; and Kristie Dotson, "On the Way to Decolonization in a Settler Colony: Re-introducing Black Feminist Identity Politics," *AlterNative* 14, no. 3 (2018): 194, 190–199.

7. Here, *pace* the sneers of my Dutch and French colleagues, I consider England a part of Europe.

8. See Du Bois, "The Rape of Africa" and Wynter, "1492: A New World View."

9. See Columbus, Christopher. 1893. "Spanish Letter to Luis De Sant Angel, 1493." In *The Columbus Memorial*, ed. George Young (Philadelphia: Jordan Bros), 37–49; See Wynter, "1492: A New World View."

10. Ferdinand, King of Aragon, "Letter to the Taino/Arawak Indians, 1493," in *American Philosophies*, ed. Leonard Harris, Scott Pratt, and Anne Waters (Malden, MA: Blackwell, 2002): 9–10.

11. Wynter, "The Pope," 19.

12. See Bartolomé Las Casas, *An Account, Much Abbreviated, of the Destruction of the West Indies*, ed. Franklin W. Knight (Indianapolis: Hackett, 2003).

13. John Locke, *Second Treatise of Government*, ed. C. B. Macpherson (Indianapolis: Hackett, 1980), 18. See John Smith, *Advertisements for the Unexperienced Planters of New-England, or Any Where; or, the Path-way to Erect a Plantation*, in *Travels and Works of Captain John Smith, 1580–1631*, ed. Edward Arber (Edinburgh, UK: John Grant, 1910), 934.

14. Locke, *Second Treatise*, 20.

15. Locke, 21.

16. Locke, 23–28.

17. Locke, 29.

18. Wynter, "Is 'Development,'" 300. I use the term "modern," as it is often used in decolonial literature, to loosely capture those colonial projects that arise out of Europe during the fifteenth century and evolve over the next four centuries.

19. Aimé Césaire, *Discourse on Colonialism*, trans. Joan Pinkham (New York: Monthly Review, 2000), 42–43.

20. See Las Casas, *An Account*, 7, Eve Tuck and K. Wayne Yang, "Decolonization Is Not a Metaphor," *Decolonization: Indigeneity, Education & Society* 1, no. 1 (2012): 6, 1–40; Kyle Powys Whyte, "Indigeneity and U.S. Settler Colonialism," in *Oxford Handbook of Philosophy and Race*, ed. Naomi Zack (New York: Oxford University Press, 2017), 79–80, 91–101; Leanne Betasamsake Simpson, *As We Have Always Done* (Minneapolis: University of Minnesota Press, 2017), 15; Anna Cook, "Intra-American Philosophy in Practice: Indigenous Voice, Felt Knowledge, and Settler Denial," *Pluralist* 12, no. 1 (2017): 74–84, 79–80; and Dotson, "On the Way," 192–193. There are at least two types of colonialism: external colonialism and settler colonialism. In external colonialism, goods/wealth are extracted from the colony for the home country; the colonizer remains a foreigner (see Fanon,

The Wretched, 5). In settler colonialism, the colonizers come to stay/settle. They come to civilize and populate the colonized lands, which often entails the genocide or erasure of the indigenous population. See Tuck and Yang, "Decolonization," 4–6; Whyte, "Indigeneity," 96; and Dotson, "On the Way," 191.

21. Césaire, *Discourse*, 32–33.
22. Lugones, "Toward a Decolonial Feminism," 742.
23. Fanon, *The Wretched*, 4.
24. Phenotype-based racial categories were not introduced until the eighteenth century. See Lee A. McBride III, "Racial Imperialism and Food Traditions," in *The Oxford Handbook of Food Ethics*, ed. Anne Barnhill, Mark Budolfson, and Tyler Doggett (New York: Oxford University Press, 2018), 333–344, 334; Immanuel Kant, "Of the Different Human Races," in *The Idea of Race*, ed. Robert Bernasconi and Tommy Lott (Indianapolis: Hackett, 2000), 8–22, 17–20; and Thomas Jefferson, *Notes on the State of Virginia*, ed. William Peden (Chapel Hill: University of North Carolina Press, 1982), 139–143.
25. See Wynter, "The Pope Must Have Been Drunk," 24 and 29; Wynter, "Unsettling," 260; and Lugones, "Toward a Decolonial Feminism," 743.
26. Fanon, *The Wretched*, 7.
27. Lugones, "Toward a Decolonial Feminism," 743.
28. Lugones, 743.
29. See Fanon, *The Wretched*, 7; Césaire, *Discourse,* 33; and Du Bois, "The Rape of Africa," 33–34.
30. Lugones, "Toward a Decolonial Feminism," 744.
31. Fanon, *The Wretched*, 6.
32. Césaire, *Discourse*, 33.
33. Fanon, *The Wretched*, 6.
34. Fanon, 7.
35. See Wynter, "Is 'Development,'" 305; and Fanon, *The Wretched*, 149.
36. Michel Foucault, *The Essential Foucault*, ed. Paul Rabinow and Nikolas Rose (New York: New Press, 2003), 264.
37. Lugones, "Toward a Decolonial Feminism," 745.
38. See Lugones, "Toward a Decolonial Feminism," 745; Whyte, "Indigeneity," 96–97; Tuck and Yang, "Decolonization," 6; and Mohandas Gandhi, *The Penguin Gandhi Reader*, ed. Rudrangshu Mukherjee (New York: Penguin, 1996), 59, 62.
39. Titles of canonical books from the (European) Enlightenment: (i) *Novum Organum Scientiarum* (Sir Francis Bacon, *The New Organon* [1620]); (ii) *Discours de la méthode pour bien conduire sa raison, et chercher la vérité dans les sciences* (Rene Descartes, *Discourse on the Method of Rightly Conducting One's Reason and of Seeking Truth in the Sciences* [1637]); (iii) *Scienza Nuova* (or, *Principi di Scienza Nuova d'intorno alla Comune Natura delle Nazioni*) (Giambattista Vico, *The New Science* [1725]).

40. Wynter, "Is 'Development,'" 307; see Foucault, *The Essential*, 132.

41. Vandana Shiva, "Reductionist Science as Epistemological Violence," in *Science, Hegemony, and Violence*, ed. Ashis Nandy (New Delhi: Oxford University Press, 1988), 232–256, 235.

42. John Smith, *Advertisements for the Unexperienced Planters of New-England, Or Any Where; Or, The Path-way to Erect a Plantation*, included in *Travels and Works of Captain John Smith, 1580–1631*, New Edition, ed. Edward Arber (Edinburgh: John Grant, 1910), 935.

43. Vandana Shiva, *Staying Alive: Women, Ecology and Development* (Brooklyn, NY: South End, 2010), 2; see Wynter, "Is 'Development,'" 302.

44. Shiva, *Staying Alive*, 6.

45. Wynter, "Is 'Development,'" 302.

46. See Ashis Nandy, "Counter-Statement on Humanistic Temper," *Mainstream*, October 10, 1981, 16–18; and Kyle Powys Whyte, "Is it Colonial Déjà Vu? Indigenous Peoples and Climate Injustice," in *Humanities for the Environment: Integrating Knowledges, Forging New Constellations of Practice*, ed. J. Adamson, M. Davis and H. Huang (New York: Earthscan/Routledge, 2017), 88–104.

47. Foucault, *The Essential*, 94.

48. Fanon, *The Wretched*, 2.

49. See Fanon, 178; Wynter, "The Pope Must Have Been Drunk," 33–34; and Chandra Talpade Mohanty, *Feminism Without Borders* (Durham, NC: Duke University Press, 2003), 8.

50. Mohanty, *Feminism Without*, 7; Fanon, *The Wretched*, 2.

51. See, for example, Elizabeth Millán Brusslan, "Philosophy Born of Colonial Struggle: One Theme or the Whole Story of the Latin American Philosophical Tradition?," *APA Newsletter on Hispanic/Latino Issues in Philosophy* 15, no. 1 (2015): 13–14; Gregory F. Pappas, "Limitations and Dangers of Decolonial Philosophies: Lessons from Zapatista Luis Villoro," *Radical Philosophy Review* 20, no. 2 (2017): 265–295; and Mariana Ortega, "Decolonial Woes and Practices of Un-knowing," *Journal of Speculative Philosophy* 31 no. 3 (2017): 504–516 for pointed criticisms of particular decolonial philosophers.

52. Césaire, *Discourse*, 44 and Fanon, *The Wretched*, 178.

53. Césaire, *Discourse*, 44–45.

54. See Dale Turner, "What is American Indian Philosophy? Toward a Critical Indigenous Philosophy," in *Philosophy in Multiple Voices*, ed. George Yancy (New York: Rowman & Littlefield, 2007), 197–214, 201; Whyte, "Indigeneity," 95; and Lugones, "Toward a Decolonial Feminism," 753.

55. See Turner, "What is American," 199; and Dotson, "On the Way," 196.

56. Fanon, *The Wretched*, 154; see Patricia Hill Collins, *Black Feminist Thought* (New York: Routledge 2009), 246.

57. Tuck and Yang, "Decolonization," 1–5.

58. Lugones, "Toward a Decolonial Feminism," 747; Mohanty, *Feminism Without*.
59. Wynter, "The Pope Must Have Been Drunk," 30; Wynter, "Unsettling," 329.
60. Lugones, "Toward a Decolonial Feminism," 742–743.
61. Fanon, *The Wretched*, 178.
62. Wynter, "The Pope Must Have Been Drunk," 30. See Aimé Césaire, *Notebook of A Return to the Native Land*, trans. Clayton Eshleman and Annette Smith (Middletown, CT: Wesleyan University Press, 2001), 34.
63. See, for example, Maitra, "Subversion"; Hendricks, "PC Philosophy"; Nefdt, "Decolonizing Philosophy"; Judkis, "This is Not a Trend"; and Calvo and Esquibel, *Decolonize Your Diet*.
64. Fanon, *The Wretched*, 6, 14, 43. Of course, Fanon states that "the colonial world is a Manichaean world" (see Fanon, 6). It is a world designed by the colonizers to treat the colonized differently through compartmentalization. He also states that "During the insurrectional stage every colonist reasons on the basis of simple arithmetic. . . . 'It's them or us' is not a paradox since colonialism, as we have seen, is precisely the organization of a Manichaean world, of a compartmentalized world" (see Fanon, 14). But this does not preclude the possibility of a future decolonial culture freed of this type of Manichaean baggage.
65. Jeffrey Pilcher, *Planet Taco: A Global History of Mexican Food* (New York: Oxford University Press, 2012), 27. See Judkis, "This is Not a Trend"; and Calvo and Esquibel, *Decolonize Your Diet*.
66. McBride, "Racial Imperialism," 339.
67. See Alain Locke, *The Philosophy of Alain Locke*, ed. Leonard Harris (Philadelphia: Temple University Press, 1989) 73, 203; Alain Locke, *The Works of Alain Locke*, ed. Charles Molesworth (New York: Oxford University Press, 2012), 241; Alain Locke, *African American Contributions to The Americas' Cultures: A Critical Edition of Lectures by Alain Locke*, ed. Jacoby Adeshei Carter (New York: Palgrave, 2016), 12–16; and Jacoby Adeshei Carter, "Like Rum in the Punch," in *African American Contributions to The Americas' Cultures: A Critical Edition of Lectures by Alain Locke*, ed. Jacoby Adeshei Carter (New York: Palgrave, 2016), 107–174, 123.
68. Furthermore, what would this mean for long-standing diasporic cultures?
69. McBride, "Racial Imperialism," 338.
70. See Lee McBride, "Leftist Democratic Politics," in *Jahrbuch Praktische Philosophie in globaler Perspektive* [Yearbook of practical philosophy in a global perspective], ed. Michael Reder, Dominik Finkelde, Alexander Filipovic, and Johannes Wallacher (Freiburg, Germany: Verlag Karl Alber, 2017), 74–92, 78–79; and John Dewey, *Liberalism and Social Action: The Later Works, Vol. 11: 1935–1937*, ed. Jo Ann Boydston (Carbondale: Southern Illinois University Press, 1987), 297.
71. Gandhi, *The Penguin Gandhi Reader*, 23.

72. See Nandy, "Counter-Statement" and Shiva, "Reductionist Science." Gandhi implies that the heart of Indian civilization is Hindu, despite the existence of vast populations of Muslim, Buddhist, Jain, and Christian people in India. This speaks to my first worry regarding the reversion back to an oversimplified and perhaps romantic notion of the native culture prior to colonial contact.

73. Tuck and Yang, "Decolonization," 19.

74. Césaire, *Discourse,* 54–55.

75. Césaire, 77.

76. See Steve Biko, *I Write What I Like* (Johannesburg: Picador Africa, 2004), 106–107; and McBride, "Leftist Democratic Politics," 77.

CHAPTER TWO

Without Land, Decolonizing American Philosophy Is Impossible

Kyle Whyte and Shelbi Nahwilet Meissner

The way, and the only way, to check and to stop this evil, is for all the Redmen to unite in claiming a common and equal right to the land, as it was at first and should be yet; for it never was divided, but belongs to all for the use of each.

—Tecumseh, 1810[1]

The expropriation of the accumulated knowledge of Native peoples is one legacy of colonization. Decolonization will require the repatriation and the rematriation of that knowledge by Native peoples themselves.

—Lee Maracle, 1996[2]

Decolonization requires the repatriation of Indigenous land and life.

—Eve Tuck and K. Wayne Yang, 2012[3]

Recently, there have been several calls for papers, special issues of journals, and conferences themed around the "decolonization" of academic philosophy. In the instances we have in mind, the places of academic philosophy generally being referred to are Anglophone philosophy departments in the United States. In these and other contexts, the word "decolonize" can be employed in ways that are at times confusing when *land* is not at the heart of event planning and philosophizing. Decolonization, as we have inherited the concept, refers to diverse, land-based political projects and the land-centric philosophies guiding them. By "inherit," we mean that we come to these traditions of decolonial practice and theory from at least two sources: our own peoples and the Indigenous intellectual traditions of North America.

First, our own Indigenous peoples, Potawatomi and Luiseño/Cupeño, have living histories of resisting US and European colonialism, fighting for land, and having to reconstitute our societies repeatedly in response to forced relocation, assimilative education, land dispossession, bodily violence, and environmental pollution.[4] These histories frame our peoples' contemporary struggles. They involve generations of philosophical discourse about and practice-based experiences in land-centered action. Decolonial practice and philosophizing are already occurring—and have for some time—through the numerous Indigenous traditions that flow from and through these histories and on toward the future. Land cannot be extricated from these decolonial traditions.

Second, Indigenous persons throughout Turtle Island[5] have philosophized about the land as part of their efforts to critique colonialism and offer land-based conceptions of and strategies for decolonization. Going back to early accounts of Indigenous anticolonial resistance movements, Indigenous peoples' actions and the records of some of their words articulate the close connection between land and colonial oppression and land and decolonization. So, it should not be surprising that more contemporary scholars of decolonization, including Lee Maracle, Leanne Simpson, K. Wayne Yang, Megan Bang, Eve Tuck, Sandy Grande, among many others, have also emphasized land in their work on decolonization. In this body of work, as was the case historically, the struggle for collective self-determination and the rematriation of lands is tied to Indigenous efforts to protect our futurities. By *futurities*, we generally mean the continuance of land-based relationships and responsibilities for the sake of the coming generations.

What does the connection between land and decolonization mean for philosophy in "America"? Regardless of what is meant by "American philosophy," we feel there is the same answer to this question. We can take "American philosophy" to refer to any contexts of higher education on "American soils" where various traditions of philosophy are taught and researched, whether these philosophies stem from Europe or anywhere else in the world.[6] More pertinent to the audience for this chapter, we can also take "American philosophy" to refer to an academic field in which the subject matter is taught at institutions of higher education in the United States and abroad, published in journals such as the *Transactions of the Charles S. Peirce Society*, and discussed at academic conferences like the Society for the Advancement of American Philosophy (SAAP). The subject matter, including course readings and publications, largely favor the predominance and perspectives of US white men, such as John Dewey. Of course, important scholars have attempted to reform the diversity of the canon, such as Scott Pratt, Charlene Siegfried, Denise James, Danielle Lake, and Leonard Harris, among others. They have expanded greatly the number of philosophers who are read and discussed, which has generated new philosophical knowledge that would have been impossible to establish prior to their efforts.

In this chapter we will focus exclusively on how *decolonizing* the ways that philosophy is practiced in much of Anglophone higher education is about *land*. By "decolonizing," we mean both anticolonial critique and decolonial action. In fields such as Indigenous studies, there is much precision on the different meanings and conceptions of *anticolonialism*, *decolonizing*, and *decolonial*.[7] Here, we will remain agnostic in our definitions for the sake of our purpose in this chapter. What we do want to emphasize, however, is that while justice-oriented efforts to revise canons and histories and amend teaching styles are liberatory in critical respects, *decolonizing* a field is a different endeavor given how the concept of decolonizing is so closely tied to land in the traditions we have inherited and practice. We acknowledge there are other traditions that may or may not dovetail with ours. While we lack the space here, we want to note emphatically that Indigenous conversations about land-based decolonization and rematriation are in critical dialogue with people of color in the Americas about coalitional potentials and futurities, including major conversations with African diasporic peoples.[8]

In this essay, we will first note some ideas about how land is understood by Indigenous persons. Next, we offer a brief slice of some of the Indigenous traditions that center land in both the critique of colonialism and the pursuit of decolonization and Indigenous futurity. Indeed, decolonization refers to Indigenous resistance practices and the philosophies guiding them, which date back to the arrival of European colonizers. Next, we will emphasize the necessary interrogation of the land-based practices perpetuated by American philosophy. Finally, we will gesture at steps that would be necessary in decolonizing American philosophy. However, we ultimately believe that decolonizing American philosophy is impossible.

A Note about Land

While this chapter will remain at a general level, we wanted to begin with some ideas about how land is understood in English by Indigenous persons and in fields such as Indigenous studies. Land rarely refers to mere spaces where people exercise political sovereignty, historic markers, or environments providing ecosystem services. Rather, the traditions we are familiar with seek ways to articulate land as *relationships*. There are entire philosophical universes focused on articulating concepts of different relationships that constitute land. These concepts are invoked in a diverse range of intellectual, educational, and political discourse concerning Indigenous culture and self-determination.

In Anishinaabe languages, there is not necessarily a word for *land* that directly corresponds to English. Words such as *gidakiiminaan* may approximate land, environment, or earth. A number of Indigenous leaders, activists, and knowledge keepers such as Sophia Rabliauskas infuse their work with philosophies operating at the nexus of language and land. Rabliauskas has taken action to protect a large boreal region called *Pimachiowin Aki* (the land that gives life). They have made great efforts to offer a philosophy of the land. For example, the organization Rabliauskas is part of, called Pimachiowin Aki, defines *ji-ganawendamang gidakiiminaan* (keeping land) as a concept

> [consisting] of the beliefs, values, knowledge, and practices that guide Anishinaabeg in their interaction with *aki* (the land and all its life) and with each other in ways that are respectful and express a reverence for all creation. The cultural tradition is given tangible manifestation in harvesting sites, habitation and processing sites, traplines, travel routes, named places, ceremonial sites, and sacred places such as pictographs associated with powerful spirit beings. These attributes are dispersed widely across a large landscape and concentrated along waterways, which are an essential source of livelihood resources and a means of transportation. Anishinaabe customary governance

and oral traditions ensure continuity of the cultural tradition across generations.[9]

Such philosophies of *gidakiiminaan* are used across many discourses and always include complex interrelationships and the responsibilities ("respectful," "reverence") connecting humans and nonhumans.

In a recent discussion about Indigenous scientific traditions and how they relate to climate science today, Melanie Goodchild describes *gidakiiminaan* as "everything in creation—the plants, the animals, the water, sun, moon, stars, all the beings, and us. We're included in that. We're not separate from that and it's our sacred responsibility to be a part of that. So we're always in relationship with the rest of creation. That's in our language."[10] Christine Sy writes that "Anishinaabe language theorist Helen Roy Fuhst, translating the word *aki*, contends that land is everything physical—the earth and universe that we live in—and that this physicality is animated with constant motion and movement." Sy goes on to state that "seeing relationships as animated through persons, inclusivity, reciprocity, and mutual reciprocity must shape then how humans carry out their relationship with land." Citing James Dumont, Sy describes four principles of relationships: "First, all beings are persons (e.g., human, tree), and therefore all relationships are personal. Second, all relationships are inclusive. Third, all relationships are familial (i.e. kinship, relatives). And fourth, relationship is reciprocal and mutually reciprocal, meaning that relationships are maneuvered through a back and forth between two or more persons, and each person in a relationship has the ability to enact their volition."[11] For Goodchild and Sy, land is bound up with philosophies and practices of intergenerational relationships and responsibilities.

Across traditions beyond Anishinaabe peoples, there are many more articulations of land that are no less complex and precise. In Salish traditions, Jeanette Armstrong writes that

> language was given to us by the land we live within. . . . All my elders say that it is land that holds all knowledge of life and death and is a constant teacher. It is said in Okanagan that the land constantly speaks. It is constantly communicating. Not to learn its language is to die. We survived and thrived by listening intently to its teachings—to its language—and then inventing human words to retell its stories to our succeeding generations. It is the land that speaks *N'silxchn* through the

generations of our ancestors to us. It is *N'silxchn* [Okanagan language], the old land/mother spirit of the Okanagan people, which surrounds me in its primal wordless state. It is this *N'silxchn* which embraces me and permeates my experience of the Okanagan land and is a constant voice within me that yearns for human speech. I am claimed and owned by this land, this Okanagan. Voices that move within as my experience of existence do not awaken as words. Instead they move within as the colors, patterns, and movements of a beautiful, kind Okanagan landscape. They are the Grandmother voices which speak. . . . The English term *grandmother* as a human experience is closest in meaning to the term *Tmixw* in Okanagan, meaning something like loving-ancestor-land-spirit.[12]

For Armstrong, land is about relationships and responsibilities (e.g., "listening") that connect humans and nonhumans across generations.

Traditions such as those involving *gidakiiminaan, aki,* and *n'silxchn* can be understood as warning against approaches to decolonization that would separate land from conditions that somehow seem to be distinct from land, including healing, cultural integrity, sexual health, political consciousness, gender justice, and economic independence. There is incredible precision in Indigenous philosophical traditions when discussing different concepts and practices of land-based theorizing, which can be found in literatures that center Indigenous feminisms, two-spirit activism, rematriation/repatriation, survivance, specific Indigenous linguistic expressions of "the land," and beyond. For these reasons, debates in other traditions of philosophy about whether land is a necessary or sufficient condition for decolonization can be rather disconnected from Indigenous philosophy, since they run the risk of isolating the meaning of land in ways that detach complex, futurity-seeking relationships and responsibilities from an understanding of land.

In fact, literatures in Indigenous feminisms, two-spirit activism, rematriation/repatriation, and survivance have precisely critiqued scholars who argued for the centrality of land as a sufficient condition. Lee Maracle, for example, argues that "Native women have been asked to back-burner their issues as though the rematriation of our governing structures were somehow separate and secondary to nation-building."[13] This and similar critiques are not based on the insufficiency of land. Rather, the problem is that categorizing land as a sufficient or necessary condition for decolonization must assume a rather limited definition of land, such as "territory control," "access to ecosystem services," "political sovereignty," or an insular form of independence. Such definitions can presuppose or perpetuate the conditions for the pervasiveness of other forms of oppression, such as patriarchy and cultural supremacy.

In work such as that of Rabliauskas, Sy, Goodchild, or Armstrong, further elaboration on their conceptions of land would yield rather detailed philosophies of relationships and responsibilities *of the land* that seek to resist different oppressions and engender healing. Note that although this chapter will not focus on articulating the details of Indigenous conceptions of land, we do hope to have conveyed something of the sheer size and nuance of this conversation in Indigenous philosophy. We hope readers will take seriously the implications for the positions offered here.

Indigenous Decolonizing Traditions

We want to begin this section by mentioning straightforwardly that diverse communities of Indigenous persons today are simply continuing ongoing philosophical and theoretical traditions. This continuance occurs across activism, research, cultural maintenance and reclamation, governance, ceremony, and numerous other activities and practices. The communities vary between localized, place-based groups, in which members have close kinship relationships and detailed protocols for participation, to more open and public conversations involving Indigenous persons of diverse heritages, such as contexts of ongoing engagements on environmental justice issues (e.g., resistance to the Dakota Access Pipeline). These communities, in different ways, are rooted in the intergenerational interpretation and intellectual exchange of ancient and more recent philosophies. They involve constructive dialogue about arguments and concepts, debate across different intellectual positions, performances and artistic expressions, consensus-building processes, and critical conversations about power and privilege. Regardless of what happens in academic philosophy in Anglophone philosophy departments, the communities we are describing just now—and their land-based practices—have and will always persist in North America. One can be a member of one or more of these communities without ever having been aware of or made oneself known to "American" philosophy.

One of the areas that many Indigenous philosophical communities have converged upon is the critique of colonialism and the investigation of what—if possible—constitutes decolonial action. This section will give a brief survey of some of the histories and expressed philosophies that strongly ground anticolonial critique and decolonial action in the land. We will not be able to elaborate on each example (especially in terms of how land itself is specifically defined) or provide an exhaustive treatment of any one community or intellectual tradition. Here, we mainly want to express that the topic of decolonization is not new, whether in the sense of people who used that exact word or people who were working on the same project as expressed in their actions, without necessarily using the English term "decolonization." The topic of decolonization did not begin in European or European diasporic academies. Moreover, we emphasize—again—that references to *land* (in what follows) offer substantially more complex concepts of relationships and responsibilities than we will be able to cover in this chapter. We hope our note in the previous section provided some preliminary background that would help those reading this section to grasp what is ultimately meant by Indigenous persons when they connect decolonization to land and critique colonial oppression as land dispossession.

The philosophies of Indigenous peoples of Turtle Island and across the Americas have traditions of anticolonial critique and decolonial action. Across Turtle Island and the Americas, Indigenous peoples have resisted colonial oppression in defense of their homelands for hundreds of years. The Inca Rebellion (1534), the Tupak Amaru movements (1572, 1779), the Yucatan Maya resistance movements (1517–1534), the Pequot War (1636), Lenape resistance in Kieft's War (1643), the Great Revolts of the Maya (1546, 1761), the Pueblo Revolt (in coalition with Apaches) (1680), and Pontiac's War (1763), were responses to European land theft, whether through dispossession or tributes, imprisonment or murder, or cultural and religious assimilation (which often included burning and other destruction of religious places). Records, stories, and traditions of memory making about these actions are hard to disentangle from the efforts at restoration, regeneration, and rematriation of Indigenous lands today. We will next consider some of the authors' own traditions, in brief.

In what is now called "California," Indigenous decolonizing traditions were enacted in the era of Spanish missionization and continue throughout the forced establishment of the United States. In response to rape, land theft, and enslavement, Kumeyaay revolutionaries rose up against Spanish soldiers and missionaries, burning Mission Basilica San Diego de Alcalá to the ground in 1775.[14] Richard Carrico describes the uprising as a calculated attempt by the Kumeyaay to rematriate their stolen people and cultural items in defense of sacred land.[15] In 1785, Tongva medicine woman Toypurina led an armed revolt at the Mission Gabriel to protect her ancestral land from Spanish colonization.[16] Rooted in Tongva land-based cosmologies, Toypurina's spiritual and political leadership is linked to her role as a medicine woman, to her commitments to the futurity of her people, and to the Tongva creation story.[17] The Tongva, who fought alongside Toypurina and were later captured by the Spanish, were subjected to public whippings by Spanish missionaries for deigning to follow the leadership of an Indigenous woman.[18]

In 1852 Antonio Garra Kaval led the Cupeño Uprising in which several united California Indian tribes took up arms against the newly established US government to wrest back control of their sacred lands, known as Kúpa, in Southern California. Cupeño epistemology links Garra's leadership at Kúpa to his political and spiritual responsibilities to land through clan, nation, and kinship. In 1902, when the Cupeño were told they were to be forcibly relocated from their sacred home at Kúpa (now called "Warner Springs"), the leader of the Cupeño Blacktooth clan stated the following:

> You see that graveyard out there? There are our fathers and our grandfathers. You see that Eagle-nest mountain and that Rabbithole mountain? When God made them, He gave us this place. We have always been here. . . . These Hot Springs always Indian. We cannot live anywhere else. We were born here and our fathers are buried here. . . . If you will not buy this place [for us to continue to live here] we will go into the mountains like quail, and die there, the old people and the women and children . . . If we cannot live here we want to go into those mountains and die. We do not want any other home.[19]

California Indian decolonizing initiatives are ancient, continuous, and deeply connected to land. Not only were the aforementioned decolonizing acts undertaken with the intent to protect Indigenous homelands from encroaching colonizers, leaders like Toypurina, Kaval, and Blacktooth were following original instructions imparted to them through ancient kinship and governance structures that come from the land.

Diverse movements of the Indigenous peoples of the Great Lakes and Northeast in the 1700s and 1800s, during the transatlantic fur trade period and establishment of the United States, are another case of anticolonial critique and decolonial action. In the *Message from the Western Indians to the Commissioners of the United States* in 1793, the authors wrote, "You have talked to us about concessions. It appears strange that you expect any from us, who have only been defending our just rights against your invasions. We want peace. Restore to us our country, and we shall be enemies no longer."[20] Often, in these writings, words like "country" and "restoration" refer to particular land-based ways of life. Shawnee leader Tecumseh, who was an architect of anticolonial political alliance building and confederation, argued the following:

> Will we let ourselves be destroyed in our turn without a struggle, give up our homes, our country bequeathed to us by the Great Spirit, the graves of our dead, and everything that is dear and sacred to us? I know you will cry with me, "Never! Never!"[21]

Tecumseh described land in terms of "home," "country," and "sacred," and demonstrates how it is composed of ancestral and spiritual relationships.

Scholars, such as Susan Sleeper-Smith, have sought to recover kinship-based traditions and philosophies for protecting land during the transatlantic fur trade period. In the early nineteenth century, Madeline Bertrand sought to counter US pressure to remove Potawatomi peoples from their lands in what is now Michigan, Indiana, and parts of Illinois. Though exercising her Catholicism in ways that reflected Potawatomi culture, Bertrand strengthened kinship connections, deeply rooted in particular lands, to mobilize and fortify resistance to US intentions to dispossess Indigenous peoples of their homelands in the Great Lakes. Bertrand, among other Indigenous women whose lives are recovered by Sleeper-Smith and other scholars, exemplifies how bonds of kinship based on trust, consent, and accountability were never disconnected from the meaning of land and connection to the land.[22]

The treaty-making processes in the Great Lakes and Northeast were contexts in which decolonial ideas were also issued. Aimée Craft has analyzed the newspaper accounts of the 1871 negotiations of the first treaty, which involved Anishinaabe, Cree, and Canadian representatives. Craft writes that "Chief Ayeeta-pe-pe-tung spoke to the Queen's negotiators about his 'ownership' and his view that rather than owning it, he was *made of the land*."[23] D. Ezra Miller has researched how in the treaty of October 23, 1826, with the Miami Tribe, one Potawatomi leader, Awbanawben, told the following to US settlers in a speech:

> You said we could not stay here. We would perish. But what will perish [?] But what will destroy us [?] It is yourselves destroying us. . . . You trampled on our soil, and drove it away. Before you came, the game was plenty, but you drove it away. . . . You point to a country for us in the west, where there is game . . . but the Great Spirit has made and put men there who have a right to that game and it is not ours.[24]

David Martinez's work on Native American intellectual traditions recovers a number of examples of writers in the nineteenth century in the Great Lakes and Northeast region who were centered in the land. For example, Martinez quotes an 1835 speech of William Apess (Pequot):

> Look at the treaties made by Congress, all broken. Look at the deep rooted plans laid, when a territory becomes a state, that after so many years the laws shall be extended over the Indians that live within their boundaries. Yeah, every charter that has been given was given with the view of driving the Indians out of the states . . . and this is the course that has been pursued for nearly two hundred years . . . [Talking about the U.S. president] the Indians they cannot live among civilized people, and we want your lands and must have them and will have them. As if he had said to them, "We want your land for our use to speculate upon; it aids us in paying off our national debt and supporting us in Congress to drive you off."[25]

In these treaties and speeches, we see the articulation of land-based decolonizing philosophies and practices. Colonialism is directly identified as involving land theft and dispossession. Indigenous treaty makers and speakers sought to do what they could to protect land for the sake of the well-being of the coming generations.

Land and Decolonization Today

Contemporary scholar-activists from Indigenous studies, philosophy, and other academic disciplines have also articulated "decolonization" as fundamentally land based. The history of decolonial philosophies in Turtle Island and nearby regions has been centered on colonialism as a form of land dispossession. Decolonization, in turn, requires Indigenous peoples to resume meaningful relationships and responsibilities to the land. Many Indigenous theorists have been adamant about this: Vine Deloria Jr., in *God is Red*, wrote that "American Indians hold their lands—places—as having the highest possible meaning and all their statements are made with this reference point in mind."[26] Winona LaDuke's 1994 article "Traditional Ecological Knowledge and Environmental Futures" understands decolonization, especially the struggle against extractive industries, as practices of land-based protections of Indigenous futures.[27]

Scholars of Anishinaabe traditions over the last fifty years, including LaDuke, Gerald Vizenor, Deborah McGregor, Grace Dhillon, and Larry Gross have argued for the ways in which decolonization of knowledge, culture, and self-determination are tied to land-based conceptions of indigenous futurity.[28] For McGregor, for example, she writes that "we often find ourselves in the position of reacting to the colonizers, and we spend too much precious time and energy deconstructing their intents, labels, and activities. Maybe we need to spend more time being proactive in our communities."[29] McGregor goes on to share that "I believe it is a welcome and exciting prospect that we can learn indigenous knowledge from our children and those yet to be born. There is hope, and that must count for something. It is true that indigenous knowledge comes from our ancestors, but it will also come from our future."[30]

Lee Maracle's work on decolonization in the 1980s and 1990s connected rematriation and land. She writes, "The expropriation of the accumulated knowledge of Native peoples is one legacy of colonization. Decolonization will require the repatriation and the rematriation of that knowledge by Native peoples themselves."[31] More recently, decolonization for Tuck and Yang is fundamentally a rematriation project in which land and life are returned to dispossessed Indigenous communities (of Turtle Island, in Tuck and Yang's example) and must be analyzed through the particularities of imposed settler conceptions of "sexuality, legality, raciality, language, religion and property."[32] As referenced earlier, it is important to note that Tuck and Yang's work is significantly tied to dialogue with African diasporic peoples on the nature of land-based coalition building. To grasp the implications of a term like "life," we encourage readers to think about the conceptions of land offered in the second section. Qwo-Li Driskill defines "decolonization" as the "ongoing, radical resistance against colonialism that includes struggles for land redress, self-determination, healing historical trauma, cultural continuance, and reconciliation" and emphasizes that although decolonization is impossible to define broadly for all communities and contexts, imagining Indigenous futures is the strongest component.[33]

Indigenous feminisms are also land-based decolonizing projects. Sexism, heterosexism, and other forms of gendered oppression cannot be disentangled from settler violence against the land. As Sarah Deer argues, sexual violence against Indigenous women has endured because it is part and parcel of the desire to seize Indigenous lands. The bodies of Indigenous women and nonbinary people, like Indigenous land, are coded as inherently rapable and exploitable by settler colonial logics. Deer notes that it is not a coincidence that there is such a high incidence of white men raping Indigenous women near the man camps around fracking sites.[34]

In an attempt to sanitize and control the land, settlers eradicated plant relatives used for basketry and entire riparian systems; they also forcibly relocated Indigenous communities to reservations where access to remaining plant life was limited. This act was an attempt at genocide, as Indigenous communities were expected to perish under these conditions. This was also an attempt at gendercide, in that it intentionally disrupted the seasonal rounds, funeral practices, and land-based gendered responsibilities of traditional Indigenous governance systems.[35] Two-spirit, nonbinary, and third-gender resistance to settlers' colonially imposed gender binary in the form of reclamation of basketry traditions, funeral traditions, and lifeways are land-based decolonial projects.

These philosophies focus on the problem of European and US dispossession of lands from Indigenous peoples. The exercise of power is tied to removing people from their lands, degrading the quality of said lands, and installing oppressive regimes of patriarchy, homophobia, death, and assimilation. In this work, and the accounts we have described so far, *land* plays a central role. Land cannot be disentangled from anticolonial critique and decolonial action. In providing a myriad of specific and general examples in this section and the previous one, we hope to convey the context in which Indigenous philosophical communities discuss, debate, and exchange information about what decolonization means. These heritages, different theories, arguments, and ideas necessarily articulate precise meanings and concepts of the land. These philosophical communities are in conversation about the very issues that Indigenous leaders, policymakers, elected officials, and others are advocating for, which are land based: rematriation, self-determination, restoration, sovereignty, reconciliation, resurgence, repatriation, and self-government.

The Settler Structure of American Philosophy

Do today's university campuses, at Anglophone institutions of higher education, reflect relationships and responsibilities in ways that are compatible with Indigenous conceptions of land? More appropriate to the topic of decolonization, our point in this section is that we have to first acknowledge that American philosophy takes place on land as American philosophy is practiced today on campuses of institutions of higher education. Yet there is little or no regard for Indigenous voices, communities, and sovereignties that spring first and foremost from that land. American philosophy occurs within journals, conferences, and lectures that take place unreflectively on campuses on occupied Indigenous land. The leaders and faculty in the institutions themselves typically preclude anything but the most superficial efforts to achieve meaningful reconciliation with Indigenous peoples. Decolonization involves directly addressing the *land-based* practices themselves of American philosophizing at institutions of higher education.

By campuses and institutions of higher education, we mean actual infrastructure. Scholars, including Anne Spice, Deborah Cowen, and Shiri Pasternak, examine the relationship between infrastructures and colonialism.[36] Cowen writes that "in colonial and settler colonial contexts, infrastructure is often the means of dispossession."[37] Spice refers to "invasive" infrastructures as "facilitating capitalist exchange, reproducing and encouraging new forms of white land ownership, and cementing settler ontologies that naturalize the existence and domination of the nation-state, colonial dispossession travels through infrastructures, as they are used to extend settlements' reach into Indigenous territories that remain unceded, unsurrendered to the Canadian state, or protected under treaty agreements with Indigenous nations. The settler state is built through a network of infrastructures, which must be normalized and maintained to assert settler jurisdiction toward nation-building projects."[38]

The actual (invasive) infrastructure of university campuses conveys a range of philosophies of education that motivate certain practices. Campuses in the United States, in their landscaping and architecture, bear no resemblance to the Indigenous lands that were forcibly taken away from Indigenous peoples. The classrooms often have chairs fixed in place, are bereft of design components that motivate learning, and centralize hierarchically the authority of the professor. The outdoor areas are landscaped according to bizarre desires to mimic various interpretations of Arcadian,

English, and other landscapes. Campus environments are not automatically places in which Indigenous learning can thrive. The best way to describe some Indigenous experiences of these campuses is as a science fiction narrative where one awakens to an age completely dominated by the desires and visions of a dominant society. The timespan of semesters or quarters, and the fact that students move from course to course often with no long-term connection across courses, imposes a fragmented and anti-relational mode of learning on students that is incommensurate with Indigenous conceptions of learning.

For example, universities like Michigan State invoke and maintain a particular settler colonial imaginary in descriptions of themselves. In the "history" section of the MSU website, there is no mention whatsoever of the Anishinaabe people or the machinations of settler colonialism required to forcibly remove them from the land now occupied by the university buildings. MSU says it was "carved out of the wilderness" and locates itself with respect to the Michigan State Capitol Building, rhetorically and conceptually erasing from the land the Anishinaabe people and the violent histories that made the university possible. MSU also proudly refers to itself as a "pioneer land grant institution," invoking imaginaries of terra nullius, discovery, and violence in its celebration of a whitewashed version of its history.[39]

American philosophy takes place, for the most part, in English, although English (like Spanish) was imposed on the people of Turtle Island. Indigenous communities throughout Turtle Island speak, formerly spoke, and/or are engaged in the reclamation of upwards of six hundred distinct languages, which comprise approximately forty language families. As is explained by countless Indigenous language activists, language is conceived of by Indigenous communities as a living entity, deeply connected to the land, the community, and to a communal, embodied sense of identity and responsibility.[40] Many speakers of Indigenous languages theorize that language comes directly from the land itself.[41]

Luiseño elders say that "atáaxum pomtéela" comes directly from the mountains and sagebrush of Southern California, while Rasmussen and Akulukjuk say that "in Nunavut, the land speaks Inuktitut. What I mean is that the land (and sea) evolved a language to communicate with (and *through*) human beings, namely an indigenous language that naturally 'grew' in that area over thousands of years of interaction between the elements and the human and plant and animal beings."[42] In Luiseño and Cupeño cosmologies, animals have their own languages, and some of our songs and prayers are in their languages. In other Indigenous cosmologies, mountains, stones, and rocks have knowledge and languages as well.[43] Indigenous languages cannot flourish when American philosophy defaults not only to languages such as English but also to Spanish and other languages that arise from colonial imposition.

American philosophy takes place within a system of higher education descended from boarding school practices. Bang and colleagues describe how standardized and taken-for-granted systems of Western education were refined through the US practices of boarding schools and foster care. In these cases, Indigenous youth were legally kidnapped from their families and forced to assimilate into dominant cultural and linguistic practices.[44] The assumption that white society is the ideal educator and the Indigenous peoples are the assumed wards continues to be promoted within the contemporary education system, according to Bang and colleagues, and is evidenced by the significant lack of Indigenous educators at the primary, secondary, and tertiary levels.[45] American philosophy is complicit in mainstream Western education's legacy of violence against Indigenous communities, and decolonizing the subdiscipline would require an acknowledgment of and an active attempt to mitigate this violence. Yet mitigation very much involves interventions starting at the level of infrastructure.

While Indigenous peoples have been philosophizing in "America" since creation, philosophy as an academic discipline has abysmally small numbers of Indigenous philosophers. Many Indigenous philosophers cite the hostility of the discipline as a reason for pursuing other academic and nonacademic positions.[46] Not only are Indigenous PhDs routinely excluded from the discipline by means of discrimination, hostility to our communities' epistemologies, and sexism, our community knowledge keepers are excluded by the Western academy via gatekeeping practices like the requirement that professors have advanced degrees (e.g., PhDs) that do not correspond to the attainment of the relevant expertise. In Indigenous communities, knowledge-sharing protocols are different than they are in the Western academy. While white men, often those perceived to be within certain adult age ranges, are typically (in our experiences) revered as the most credible producers of knowledge in Western communities, Indigenous communities often acknowledge children and elders of all genders as knowledge keepers, since they are usually closest to the spirit world in their life journeys.[47] Philosophical expertise, then, in our communities is not determined by PhDs but rather by life stage, community responsibilities, and ceremonial and cultural protocols. That Indigenous philosophical experts, our children, and our elders, are systematically excluded from the Western academy, speaks volumes about the (im)possibility of American philosophy to decolonize.

Elizabeth Cook-Lynn, reflecting on American Indian studies, writes:

> What many Native scholars of that era [mid-twentieth century] wanted and understood was that an academic discipline requires that a body of intellectual information such as the Natives of this land possess about the world be internally organized, normatively regulated, and consensually communicated. The intellectual information, the knowledge itself, found in the oral traditions of the indigenes, is grounded in language and geography. It examines age-old cultures that have been religiously opposed to exploiting nature for profit. It is said that everything originates from what is called the oral traditions of the First Nations, the oral societies of indigenous peoples on this continent, and from Mother Earth and a specific geography, and that there is tacit theory in the mythologies of origin. In turn, principles, generalized concepts, and facts result in a system of implicit ideology that if defined in the appropriate way, unifies and motivates the people from whom the knowledge originates. Thus, a major reason for the development of Native American Studies as disciplinary work was to defend indigenous nationhood in America.[48]

Cook-Lynn centers "language and geography," stating that land is central to decolonizing higher education. She argues for the importance of scholarship that "[possesses] an American Indian tribal future grounded in indigenousness and sovereignty."[49]

In circumscribing Indigenous meaning-making practices—including their infrastructural/landscape dimensions—American academic philosophy maintains the status quo of whiteness. American philosophy continues to overlook the rich and ancient Indigenous philosophical traditions that take place on this land and in relation with this land. Decolonizing American philosophy requires the interrogation of the ways in which this discipline, academia, and knowledge production (broadly speaking) take place on land and come from land. An overhaul of infrastructures, landscapes, credentialing process, and curricula (among other issues we have covered) is required for decolonizing American philosophy.

Conclusion: Without Land, No Decolonization

Where do our analyses and the traditions we draw from leave individual philosophers who work in American colleges and universities? We seek to conclude by making an ambivalent point. Vanessa de Oliveira Andreotti and colleagues discuss how "decolonization has multiple meanings, and the desires and investments that animate it are diverse, contested, and at times, at odds with one another." They warn against the "understandable impulse . . . to collapse decolonization into coherent, normative formulas with seemingly unambiguous agendas."[50] Given this complexity and the overhaul of American philosophy required, we ultimately sense that decolonizing American philosophy is impossible in practice.

In both of the authors' cases, perhaps the majority of our "work" occurs in Indigenous contexts on Indigenous lands. This can make life difficult given that we have to both fulfill and renew such responsibilities to Indigenous lands while we remain accountable to our colleagues in our jobs in philosophy and other departments in academia. Ironically, even when land-based work thrives *off-campus*, its impacts do *not* necessarily translate back toward decolonizing the academy itself. Maybe this is how it should be. While each of us has striven to improve the professional climate in our departmental life, increase opportunities for Indigenous philosophers, and produce new research in Anglophone academic venues, we would not classify any of this as decolonizing work. For this work is not land based in the sense we have sought to convey in this chapter. In fact, we ourselves even question the value of our on-campus work on a daily basis. We continually wonder whether academic work ultimately honors our ancestors and supports future generations.

At the same time, this on-campus and academic work is vital for supporting, protecting, and empowering Indigenous students, staff, faculty, administrators, and others whose lives and education are tied to colleges and universities. In a conversation between Erin Marie Konsmo and Karyn Recollet, they cite Sarah Hunt's insightful point about "rejection politics," which refers to the ideas of Indigenous peoples renouncing any engagement in settler institutions: "The lives of many Indigenous people remain bound up in state systems, both ideologically and materially, such that they cannot simply turn away from them."[51] To simply recruit more Indigenous students for philosophy programs offering courses that focus on American philosophy or making attempts to put Indigenous philosophers on par with "American" philosophers are not actually decolonizing approaches. Following Hunt, this is not to say that the aforementioned actions are *not* absolutely necessary steps toward cocreating a more just discipline. Here we are not actually criticizing these approaches in terms of their significance for peoples' lives and for the establishment of certain types of ethical conduct and certain types of justice. But decolonization, as it requires a connection to land (as we have understood it here), suggests an entirely different trajectory of action than those just discussed. Indigenous philosophizing, as we have shown, comes from Indigenous lands, and the cosmologies are kinship networks that are part of its very definition, as discussed earlier. Importantly, land is a critical concept for understanding the structures and cultures of colonial power.

We are not alone in these sentiments. We feel our sentiments are shared when we review how decolonization has been taken up by scholars working in relation to other academic fields. In a 2018 study, Adam Gaudry and Danielle Lorenz articulate three different categories for *indigenizing* higher education in Canada, where only the third is referred to as decolonizing. The first, *Indigenous inclusion*, "is a policy that aims to increase the number of Indigenous students, faculty, and staff in the Canadian academy."[52] The second, *reconciliation indigenization*, "is a vision that locates indigenization on common ground between Indigenous and Canadian ideals, creating a new, broader consensus on debates such as what counts as knowledge, how should Indigenous knowledges and European-derived knowledges be reconciled, and what types of relationships academic institutions should have with Indigenous communities."[53]

The third and only category Gaudry and Lorenz offer that can be seen as "decolonizing" is *decolonial indigenization*. This refers to "[envisioning] the wholesale overhaul of the academy to fundamentally reorient knowledge production based on balancing power relations between Indigenous peoples and Canadians, transforming the academy into something dynamic and new."[54] The key examples of decolonial indigenization that Gaudry and Lorenz give are land based. One model of the "treaty-based" approach is that there should be two or more separate universities, one of which is an Indigenous institution. They write, "However, in keeping with treaty principles, the Indigenous side of any such 'dual university' would still need to be administratively autonomous and be able to protect the integrity of Indigenous knowledge and community participation."[55] On the resurgence model, they cite Jennifer Matsunaga, who understands that

"Indigenous resurgence . . . reasserts the connection between land-centred decolonization rather than decolonizing settler's minds and institutions."[56] The resurgence model is community based, and involves

> on-the-land and community-based research and learning. Intellectual resurgence, above all, recognizes that immense amounts of complex Indigenous knowledge resides in communities, and it is these communities who are best able to govern access to that knowledge and how it is transmitted. Decolonial indigenization involves constructing research programs that rebuild capacity for Indigenous intellectual institutions to determine their own intellectual priorities and establishing local institutions to govern research projects in order to move beyond research collaboration with outsiders to community-led research projects.[57]

For Gaudry and Lorenz, "Resurgent research paradigms can build capacity in communities, supporting communities in rebuilding traditional knowledges and traditional institutions."[58]

Following Gaudry and Lorenz, decolonization refers to land-based practices that either require independent institutions or involve empowering the intellectual and research institutions that are already present in Indigenous peoples themselves. Here decolonization is a political project that requires the rematriation of land and life to Indigenous communities and usurping the colonial nation-state. If we apply *decolonization* to ordinary campus life in Anglophone philosophy departments, this is likely outside the scope of American philosophy as a field, as well as outside the scope of a conference theme or special journal issue.

The stakes here of mischaracterizing the goals of decolonization are enormous for Indigenous peoples and communities. The importing, co-opting, and "metaphoricization"[59] of terms like "decolonize" hamper the political and cultural goals of Indigenous communities who, as we have shown, have been engaged in land-based resistance for the restoration of our lifeways, governance structures, and languages since settlers first arrived to strip them from us. Gaudry and Lorenz cite the work of Rauna Kuokkanen. In one of Kuokkanen's essays, they argue that "it is the academy that is responsible for 'doing its homework' and addressing its ignorance so it can give an 'unconditional welcome' not only to indigenous people but also to their epistemes, without insisting on translation."[60] In this regard, for American philosophy to decolonize, the subdiscipline would have to acknowledge that the academy is founded on very limited conceptions of knowledge and the world, starting with the horrific absence of *the land* in academic research, teaching, and reflections on higher education.

Notes

1. Tecumseh to Governor Harrison, August 20, 1810. Speech. Indian Historical Society. William Henry Harrison Papers and Documents, 1794–1864.

2. Lee Maracle, *I Am Woman: A Native Perspective on Sociology and Feminism* (Vancouver: Press Gang, 1996), 92.

3. Eve Tuck and K. Wayne Yang, "Decolonization Is Not a Metaphor," *Decolonization: Indigeneity, Education & Society* 1, no. 1 (2012): 1–40.

4. The authors have decided to capitalize the word Indigenous given the word's meaning in this essay.

5. We use "Turtle Island" to reflect certain uses in inter-Indigenous discourse, which belong to some cultures. We do not use the term to replace the problematically totalizing concept of North America with another problematically totalizing concept.

6. Bryan W. Van Norden, *Taking Back Philosophy: A Multicultural Manifesto* (New York: Columbia University Press, 2017).

7. Devon Abbott Mihesuah, *Indigenous American Women: Decolonization, Empowerment, Activism* (Lincoln: University of Nebraska Press, 2003), 20.

8. Kristie Dotson, "On the Way to Decolonization in a Settler Colony: Re-introducing Black Feminist Identity Politics," *AlterNative: An International Journal of Indigenous Peoples* 14, no. 3 (2018): 190–199.

9. Quote from Executive Summary of Pimachiowin Aki as a World Heritage Project, UNESCO, https://whc.unesco.org/en/documents/160693 (accessed 8-20-20).

10. Melanie Goodchild, "Beyond Prediction," YouTube video (University of Waterloo, 2018), accessed February 13, 2019, https://www.youtube.com/watch?v=U81i0Mrzhr0.

11. Waaseyaa'sin Christine Sy, "Relationship with Land in Anishinaabeg Womxn's Historical Research," in *Reshaping Women's History*, ed. Julie Gallagher and Barbara Winslow (Urbana-Champaign: University of Illinois Press, 2018): 222–236.

12. Jeanette Armstrong, "Land Speaking," in *Speaking for the Generations: Native Writers on Writing*, ed. Simon Ortiz (Tucson: University of Arizona Press, 1998): 175–194.

13. Lee Maracle, "Decolonizing Native Women," in *Daughters of Mother Earth: The Wisdom of Native American Women*, ed. Barbara Alice Mann (New York: Praeger, 2006), 29–51.

14. Richard L. Carrico, "Sociopolitical Aspects of the 1775 Revolt at Mission San Diego De Alcala," *Journal of San Diego History* 43, no. 3 (1997): 777–780.

15. Carrico, "Sociopolitical Aspects."

16. Charles Sepulveda, "Sacred Waters: Theorizing Kuuyam as Decolonial Possibility," *Decolonization: Indigeneity, Education & Society* 7, no. 1 (2018): 40–58; Antonia I. Castañeda, "Malinche, Calfia y Toypurina," in *Feminism, Nation and Myth: La Malinche*, ed. Rolando Romero and Amanda Nolacea Harris (Houston, TX: Arte Público, 2005): 82–97.

17. Sepulveda, "Sacred Waters."

18. Castañeda, "Malinche," 82–97.

19. Cecilio Blacktooth, "In the Name of the Law: The Cupeño Removal of 1903," trans. Celsa Apapas and Phil Brigandi, *Journal of San Diego History* 64, no. 1 (2018): 1–60, 26.

20. Message from the Western Indians to the Commissioners of the United States, 1793, accessed August 24, 2020, http://nationalhumanitiescenter.org/pds/livingrev/expansion/text6/negotiations.pdf

21. Quoted in "Eastern Indians Wars," The Price of Freedom: Americans at War (website), accessed August 24, 2020, https://amhistory.si.edu/militaryhistory/printable/section.asp?id=3#:~:text=Will%20we%20let%20ourselves%20be,cry%20with%20me%2C%20%E2%80%9CNever!

22. Susan Sleeper-Smith, *Indian Women and French Men: Rethinking Cultural Encounter in the Western Great Lakes* (Boston: University of Massachusetts Press, 2001); and Susan Sleeper-Smith, "Women, Kin, and Catholicism: New Perspectives on the Fur Trade," *Ethnohistory* 47, no. 2 (2000): 423–452.

23. Aimée Craft, "Living Treaties, Breathing Research," *Canadian Journal of Women and the Law* 26, no. 1 (2014): 1–22.

24. D. Ezra Miller, "'But It Is Nothing Except Woods:' Anabaptists, Ambitions, and a Northern Indiana Settlerscape, 1830–1841," in *Rooted and Grounded: Essays on Land and Christian Discipleship*, ed. Ryan D. Harker and Janeen Bertsche Johnson (Eugene, OR: Pickwick, 2016): 208–217.

25. David Martinez, ed., "An Inquiry into the Education and Religious Instruction of the Marshpee Indians," in *The American Indian Intellectual Tradition: An Anthology of Writings from 1772 to 1972* (Ithaca, NY: Cornell University Press, 2011): 55–79.

26. Vine Deloria, *God Is Red* (New York: Putnam, 1973), 62–63.

27. Winona LaDuke, "Traditional Ecological Knowledge and Environmental Futures," *Colorado Journal of International Environmental Law and Politics* 5 no. 127 (1994): 127–148.

28. Lawrence W. Gross, *Anishinaabe Ways of Knowing and Being* (New York: Routledge, 2016); Grace L. Dillon, *Walking the Clouds: An Anthology of Indigenous Science Fiction* (Tucson: University of Arizona Press, 2012); and Ger-

ald R. Vizenor, *Manifest Manners: Narratives on Post-Indian Survivance* (Lincoln: University of Nebraska Press, 1999).

29. Deborah McGregor, "Coming Full Circle: Indigenous Knowledge, Environment, and Our Future," *American Indian Quarterly* 28, nos. 3–4 (2004): 385–410.

30. McGregor, "Coming Full Circle," 404–405.

31. Maracle, *I Am Woman*, 92.

32. Tuck and Yang, "Decolonization Is Not a Metaphor," 21.

33. Qwo-Li Driskill, "Doubleweaving Two-Spirit Critiques: Building Alliances between Native and Queer Studies," *GLQ: A Journal of Lesbian and Gay Studies* 16, nos. 1–2 (2010): 69–92, 69.

34. Sarah Deer, *The Beginning and End of Rape* (Minneapolis: University of Minnesota Press, 2015), xxi.

35. Deborah A. Miranda, "Extermination of the Joyas: Gendercide in Spanish California," *GLQ: A Journal of Lesbian and Gay Studies* 16, nos. 1–2 (2010): 253–284; and Sepulveda, "Sacred Waters."

36. Anne Spice, "Fighting Invasive Infrastructures: Indigenous Relations against Pipelines," *Environment and Society* 9, no. 1 (2018): 40–56. Spice cites, in this passage, the work of Shiri Pasternak. See Shiri Pasternak, "Jurisdiction and Settler Colonialism: Where Laws Meet," *Canadian Journal of Law and Society* 29, no. 2 (2014): 145–161.

37. Deborah Cowen, "Infrastructures of Empire and Resistance," Verso Books (blog) January 25, 2017, https://www.versobooks.com/blogs/3067-infrastructures-of-empire-and-resistance.

38. Spice, "Fighting Invasive Infrastructures," 45.

39. "The Nation's Pioneer Land-Grant University," accessed October 22, 2017 at https://msu.edu/morrill-celebration/history.html and on file with author; "Morrill Act Sesquicentennial: Celebrating the Enduring Power of the Land-Grant Vision of Higher Education," accessed October 22, 2017, https://msu.edu/morrill-celebration/ and on file with authors.

40. Wesley Y. Leonard, "When Is an 'Extinct Language' Not Extinct? Miama, A Formerly Sleeping Language," *Sustaining Linguistic Diversity: Endangered and Minority Languages and Language Varieties*, ed. Kendall A. King, et al. (Washington, DC: Georgetown University Press, 2008): 23–33; Derek Rasmussen and Tommy Akulukjuk, "My Father Was Told to Talk to the Environment First Before Anything Else: Arctic Environmental Education in the Language of the Land," in *Fields of Green: Restorying Culture, Environment, and Education*, ed. Marcia McKenzie, et al. (Cresskill, NJ: Hampton, 2009): 285–298; Wesley Y. Leonard, "Producing Language Reclamation by Decolonising 'Language,'" in *Language Documentation and Description*, ed. Wesley Y Leonard and Haley De Korne, vol. 14 (London: EL Publishing, 2017) 15–36; Patricia A. Shaw, "Language and Identity, Language and the Land. BC Studies," *British Columbian Quarterly* 131

(2001): 39–55; Shaylih Muehlmann, "'Spread Your Ass Cheeks': and Other Things That Should Not Be Said in Indigenous Languages," *American Ethnologist* 35, no. 1 (2008) 34–48; Barbra A. Meek, *We Are Our Language: An Ethnography of Language Revitalization in a Northern Athabaskan Community* (Tucson: University of Arizona Press, 2010); and Eva M. Jewell, "Social Exposure and Perceptions of Language Importance in Canada's Urban Indigenous Peoples," *Aboriginal Policy Studies* 5, no. 2 (2016): 99–113.

41. Rasmussen and Akulukjuk, "My Father Was Told"; Cutcha Risling Baldy, "Why We Gather: Traditional Gathering in Native Northwest California and the Future of Bio-cultural Sovereignty," *Ecological Processes* 2, no. 17 (2013): 1–10.

42. Rasmussen and Akulukjuk, "My Father Was Told," 279.

43. Vine Deloria, *Custer Died for Your Sins* (Norman: University of Oklahoma Press, 1988); Gregory Cajete, *Native Science* (Santa Fe, NM: Clear Light, 2000).

44. Megan Bang, et al., "Muskrat Theories, Tobacco in the Streets, and Living Chicago as Indigenous Land," *Environmental Education Research* 20, no. 1 (2014): 37–55.

45. Marie Battiste, "Introduction," *Reclaiming Indigenous Voice and Vision* (Vancouver: University of British Columbia Press, 2011): 192–196; Marie Battiste, "Maintaining Aboriginal Identity, Language, and Culture in Modern Society," *Reclaiming Indigenous Voice and Vision* (Vancouver: University of British Columbia Press, 2011): 196–208; Teresa L. McCarty, et al., "Hear Our Languages, Hear Our Voices: Storywork as Theory and Praxis in Indigenous-Language Reclamation," *Daedalus: Journal of the American Academy of Arts and Sciences* 147, no. 2 (2018): 160–172.

46. V. F. Cordova, "Letter from Co-Editors," *APA Newsletter on American Indians in Philosophy* 1, no. 1 (Fall 2001), 2, https://cdn.ymaws.com/www.apaonline.org/resource/collection/13B1F8E6-0142-45FD-A626-9C4271DC6F62/v01n1AmericanIndians.pdf.

47. Kim Anderson, *Life Stages of Native Women: Memory, Teachings, and Story Medicine* (Winnipeg: University of Manitoba Press, 2011).

48. Elizabeth Cook-Lynn, "Who Stole Native American Studies?," *Wicazo Sa Review* 12, no. 1 (1997): 9–28.

49. Cook-Lynn, "Who Stole," 16.

50. Vanessa de Oliveira Andreotti, et al., "Mapping Interpretations of Decolonization in the Context of Higher Education," *Decolonization: Indigeneity, Education & Society* 4, no. 1 (2015): 22.

51. Erin Marie Konsmo (Métis) and Karyn Recollet, "Afterword: Meeting the Land(s) Where They Are At: A Conversation between Erin Marie Konsmo (Métis) and Karyn Recollet (Urban Cree)," in *Indigenous and Decolonizing Studies in Education*, ed. Eve Tuck, K. Wayne Yang, and Linda Tuhiwai Smith (New York: Routledge, 2018): 238–251, 246; see S. Hunt, "*Red Skin, White Masks*: Rejecting

the Colonial Politics of Recognition" (panel discussion at Simon Fraser University, British Columbia, October, 2014).

52. Adam Gaudry and Danielle Lorenz, "Indigenization as Inclusion, Reconciliation, and Decolonization: Navigating the Different Visions for Indigenizing the Canadian Academy AlterNative," *Alternative* 14, no. 3 (2018): 218–227.

53. Gaudry and Lorenz, "Indigenization as Inclusion," 218–227.

54. Gaudry and Lorenz, 218–227.

55. Gaudry and Lorenz, 224.

56. J. Matsunaga, "Two Faces of Transitional Justice: Theorizing the Incommensurability of Transitional Justice and Decolonization in Canada," *Decolonization: Indigeneity, Education & Society* 5 (2016): 33, also cited in Gaudry and Lorenz, 224.

57. Gaudry and Lorenz, 224–225.

58. Gaudry and Lorenz, 225.

59. See Tuck and Yang, "Decolonization Is Not a Metaphor"; and Andreotti et al., "Mapping Interpretations."

60. Rauna Kuokkanen, "What Is Hospitality in the Academy? Epistemic Ignorance and the (Im)Possible Gift," *Review of Education, Pedagogy, and Cultural Studies* 30, no. 1 (2008): 60–82.

CHAPTER THREE

Decolonizing the West

JOHN E. DRABINSKI

> Would America be America without her Negro people?
>
> —W. E. B. Du Bois, *Souls of Black Folk*

In the reflections that follow, I want to make a straightforward claim: "the West" cannot be understood in terms of white, European racial civilization or cultural-historical space. This is of course the conventional resonance of the term: when we say, "the West," we typically mean white Europe and its settler colony in North America. I argue in this chapter that such resonance conceals the racial violence that lies not only *inside* but that is also *constitutive of* the idea of the West. In part, this is borrowed from Antonio Benítez-Rojo in his book *The Repeating Island*, which claims that every culture is fundamentally syncretic. But I want to say more here to underscore both how "the West" or "the Western tradition" is constructed as a site of racial oblivion and how habitual association of the West and things Western with a kind of racial-civilizational purity reifies the very terms under critique. And so, I wonder, in particular, if a certain deconstructive approach wouldn't prove more productive, identifying internal contradictions inside racial discourse in order to dismantle "the West"? In such a moment, deconstruction becomes a form of decolonization.[1] Édouard Glissant was right when he wrote that the West is a project, not a place. What then do we mean by "the West"? What does it mean when we think about the racial-historical composition of this putative "place," emphasizing the entanglement of "the West" with blackness as both a politically constructed category and a culturally complex space that simultaneously draws close to and pushes away from the white West? That is, what is "the West" if we conceive the name outside of fantasies of a total colonial gaze?

My way into this question entails a bit of bricolage, but intentionally so. What may at times seem like a series of impressionistic readings or evocations is undertaken deliberately with the objective of a more definitive portrait of what it means, in the context of the black Americas, to deconstruct the colonial terms of thinking the West as "the West" without racial qualifiers. The question of colonialism *inside* the West is largely undertheorized while also being at the heart of so many discussions of the black liberation struggle. And so it is important to be deliberate in how we approach the question of colonialism and decolonization when thinking about the significance of the black Americas and, in particular, the foundations of African American intellectual history, culture, and political life. It is a nation within a nation, for sure, and therein lie the terms of colonial characterization. But this is also a nation formed by (as well as constitutive of) the colonial force of everyday, institutional racism, and therein lie the terms of deconstructing the West as "the West." Theorizing this "as well as" in what follows requires a re-theorization of the West in a decolonial register and thus a movement to reentangle things "Western" with the violence that produced them while also attending to the resistance, cultural production, and counternarratives outside of, but in relation to, that same violence: the Americas between whiteness and blackness, perhaps.

Place and Project

The fantasy projected by the colonial gaze is manifold, and in the context of the United States it is dedicated to maintaining a robust sense of white innocence. That innocence, to which nearly every social, cultural, and political institution is dedicated, conceals the founding violence and catastrophe that the gaze reenacts in each moment. We live the wounds of that violence. It is elemental to thought itself. Colonialism was a total project. It left nothing untouched, from clothing and cuisine to philosophy, religion, and language, to the institutional structures that make sense of everyday life and beyond. Indeed, much of what in recent years has come to be called "Afropessimism" is a response to the totalizing work of this project and its seemingly endless shadow. Frantz Fanon, for example, argues convincingly in *Black Skin, White Masks* that colonialism's project of antiblackness renders expressions of black life abject as an a priori; the condition for the possibility of blackness—the ontology that is already sociogeny—is the condition for the impossibility of black thriving. In the context of the United States, we see the same in so much of Richard Wright's fiction, which turns time and again to the equivalence of black visibility with death. Pessimism as racial fatalism as race realism. Colonialism as abjection of blackness.

But colonialism was also a total project that internalized its own contradiction and its own counterproductions and forms of resistance. Colonialism was therefore a project whose closed system is the stuff of myth rather than concrete, material, and historical experience. The work of thinkers of black cultural production—and we do not see anything like this in Fanon's and other Afropessimist work—hesitates on these very grounds, seeing vernacular cultural forms hidden in the seams of life under everyday racial violence. Life itself is a kind of resistance. To live *as* black and to create out of blackness, rather than in response to white oppression, is simultaneously resistance and the creation of an alternative world. To be sure, colonialism and its companion project of antiblackness in the United States is dedicated to the elimination of its other, to neutralize the capacity of its other to make meaning outside of systems of abjection. This is colonialism's and antiblack racism's highest aspiration. And yet, the "other" not only survives this eliminationist impulse but also makes a world and then worlds. How do we reckon with this double movement *inside* the colonial world?

Worldmaking in the interstices of an antiblack world is certainly a sense of resistance but also something much more banal. This strikes me as crucial. Life goes on, even in the worst conditions imaginable, whether on the plantation or in the abject spaces of poverty, exclusion, and extrajudicial violence. The wreckage of the Americas—genocide, the Middle Passage, the plantation, colonialism, and twists and turns in the history of racial segregation and degradation—produces melancholia, for sure, and that is part of colonialism's legacy. But the wreckage also produces (and was sustained by) porous systems of exchange and creation. What does it mean to not just listen to and hear those voices but to also register them inside the system that makes the wreckage?

To that end, Paul Gilroy's paradigm-shifting work *The Black Atlantic* continues to pay plenty of dividends over a quarter century after its publication. Written in order to complicate, if not outright displace, the fixation on the United States in studies of black cultural production, Gilroy's book sets out a series of key claims that, in their own way, speak to the wider problem of decolonization. It is a book that decolonizes in two gestures. First, Gilroy's work establishes a sense of modernity in the black Atlantic world that exceeds (and therefore is not reducible to) European modernity and its white inheritors in the United States. This shift in perspective, aligning our gaze with cultural production as both resistance and world-making, remarks and remakes our sense of the colonial and postcolonial eras in a south Atlantic context, moving away from the one-way traffic of colonial power and its alienation. Gilroy's grasp and articulation of the capacity of black worlds to transform sites of relation—contact with European traditions, intellectual production in both mixed or rotten English and colonial languages, and so on—shifts so much of how we think about historical experiences of race and racism. Decentering the colonizer is a simple economy, yet one of the most pressing and, in the end, hardest-won struggles in decolonial work. Second, and related, *The Black Atlantic* anchors what Gilroy terms *countermodernity* in alternative foundations of thought—namely sound and its expressive power. This anchor links his work with trends in the Francophone and Anglophone Caribbean, modes of thought in work by Kamau Brathwaite and Édouard Glissant that, for example, underscore expressive culture's transcendence of the Manichean structure of colonial life. Something *other* happens in black cultural spaces, something other than what colonialism had made of the world.[2] This second decolonial gesture fulfills the promises of the first; the capacity to produce is not just a sign of survival but also, further and decisively, a sign of founding conceptions of being and knowing in a subaltern class. This founding, it is important to note, is an event without relations of dependency defining the politics of cultural production: decentering the colonial in a second moment.

I say all of this by way of extended introduction in order to underscore the key movement in any work of decolonization: contesting, then overturning, the idea of center. Part of what is both so nefarious and so fecund about racial colonialism—its past and its obstinate hold on the present and future of the imagination—is its ability to dictate the terms of its own contestation and then succession. To wit: I take one of the insights of Achille Mbembe's notion of necropolitics to be just that: the world as we know it, a world forged in the machinery of colonial atrocity, offers only the capacity to legislate death as a path to liberation. Necropolitics is an ontology of the colonial project. But the pessimism of the necropolitical must also reckon with the facts of what Gilroy calls the *countermodern*, the fact that social death produces a necropolitical order *and* produces traditions of protest, resistance, love, community, and simply a world and worlds. The center is rendered unstable at the very moment in which subaltern worlds become worlds of cultural production rather than reactivity.

What I am arguing here begins at the crossroads of necropolitics and countermodernity. Colonial worldmaking is necropolitics. There can only be death and those who legislate the terms of our finitude. Colonial worldmaking also produces its *tout autre*, an other who is not subject *to*, in the sense of subjection as subjugation, the white gaze and is instead the subject *of* its own activity. Countermodernity is both produced by and unthinkable within colonial logic. That is colonialism's paradox, its enigma, and its force of self-interruption. But my deeper claim entails a third moment: identification of a *différance* at the center of the colonial creation of "the West." Put simply, the creation of "the West," as an imperial project, projected across the Atlantic as a point of identification (white European migrants) and distinction (abjection of indigenous and Africa-descended peoples), builds its unassimilable other into the very idea of the West. Neither dialectical negation nor dialectical remainder, the abject functions as a deconstructive supplement after which we can no longer deploy "the West" as a legitimate, racially specific term.

What, then, is the West under this deconstructive work and its alteration of the white racial regime? This is no simple question but rather an initial characterization: the West is a production of white racial modernity while simultaneously being the site of the Afropostmodern. Such simultaneity renders "the West" as an unstable yet diverse and hemispheric category. Imagining a "West" without a center—a decolonized West—is complicated, but here I want to outline the terms of its meaning. I begin with a short reflection of the meaning of the colonial in the context of African American history and life and then shift to the function of sound in thinking about countermovement to (perhaps against) white racial modernity. In the space cleared by these reflections, we will be well positioned to respond to our guiding question: what is a decolonized West?

Limits and Possibilities in the Decolony

Is it correct or even possible to characterize African Americans as a colonized people?

This is rightly a fraught question. In its global practice, the colonial relation historically consisted of distance, occupation, and administration from abroad, a relation that generates the rhetoric and figure of "the metropole" as a critical concept. The metropole functions in anti- and postcolonial discourse as a way of characterizing the pervasiveness of "the center" in constructing and maintaining the colonial system. Colonialism as a system names a peculiar mix of conquest, control, and separation, from the racial economy of the plantation to the transatlantic geography of its politics. Whatever few white Europeans lived in the colony were vastly outnumbered, in nearly every case, by the population of those enslaved, indentured, or governed through occupation. It was profit from a distance, labor at a distance, from metropole to colony: a centuries-long system of exploitation at every level. Even settler colonies in, for example, southern Africa operated according to the logic of the metropole-colony relation, which was as much psychological and ontological as political and economic. That is, while the colonial relation was perhaps first and foremost about relations of exploitation and maximizing extraction, the efficiency and totalizing force of colonialism—part and parcel of extractive relations—required transformation of the colonized themselves. Metropolitan governance is no easy exercise of power. It requires the colonial relation to be a total project, leaving nothing untouched in either the political or psychological spheres of life. Colonialism's power and capacity to cast a long historical shadow draws from both of these aspects. This leaves at the very moment of independence a set of institutions incompatible with local and regional cultural histories, as well as psychological, epistemological, and ontological forms of alienation that introduce such complications to processes of decolonization that even the term "decolonize" seems a utopian dream. This is what it means to have practiced a total project of violence and alienation and then to have left in a historical instant. The rhetoric of estrangement from origins and place that pervades so much anticolonial and postcolonial discourse comes from this kind of alienation.

This was of course *not* the experience of emancipation from slavery in the United States. I have in mind here, by contrast, Martinique and Guadeloupe, where questions of independence or departmentalization dominated anticolonial struggle, dividing thinkers such as Aimé Césaire and Édouard Glissant. Across the Caribbean and Africa, independence initiated the pressing question of how to reconstruct institutional life—political representation, economic systems, education, and so on—after the colonizing power left. When the colonizing power leaves under the standard structure of both settler colonialism in places like Zimbabwe or South Africa, and administration from abroad in Guinea and Ghana, the colonized are thrust to the center of the nation as the constitutive power of the state. A certain theoretical approach is dictated by these terms. Here we can think of Fanon's sweeping, profound reflections on the masses and the lumpen proletariat and those on Algeria and the Global South more broadly in *The Wretched of the Earth* and similarly themed essays. We can see how those reflections theorize the demands for a new form of life in the postcolony. Such reflections are directed toward *the new* yet are also formed by the particular kinds of violence constitutive of the past. Those questions, issues, and consequent theorizations are neither available nor demanded when the Civil War in the United States comes to an end in 1865 and the Emancipation Proclamation becomes practice rather than a rallying cry in the midst of war. To put it bluntly, when the enslaved are emancipated at the end of the war, they remain in community—however involuntary, and to whatever forms of extreme terror, violence, and exploitation—with the former enslavers. White and black Americans live side by side in the immediate wake of emancipation. To my mind, Booker T. Washington's opening chapter of *Up from Slavery* gives one of the most compelling descriptions, a modest and mundane account through and through, of this moment of elation that was also accompanied by utter confusion about what a future based on a mixed community past and present might mean. How can life be imagined in this shared space? The unfolding of American history after Reconstruction is a story of catastrophic terror (the Klan), violence (the everydayness of extrajudicial killing), and exploitation (sharecropping, segregation, and its post–civil rights era cognates), plain and simple. It is not a story shared by others in the postcolony. The whites do not go home. They share the space of home and refashion all the old violences in a desperate, largely successful, clinging to racial power.

So, in what ways, if any, does it make sense to think of colonialism as a feature of African American life? Thinkers from the Black Panther and Black Power era often claimed colonial status. Those claims proceed, in part, by evoking the title and spirit of W. E. B. Du Bois's 1934 essay "A Negro Nation Within a Nation," which recasts motifs and arguments dating back to nineteenth-century African American thought, in particular Martin Delany and his development of arguments for what were then called "colonization" plans. Du Bois and others note that despite the *physical* or *geographical* proximity of black and white Americans, the economic, social, political, and cultural differences are so stark and striking that we *ought to be* or *are justified in* thinking of African American life as administered from abroad. Formally, then, there is an interesting argument for characterizing African Americans as a colonized people. But as the tradition evolves and new forms of analysis emerge, importantly, in the era of anticolonial struggle and decolonization, even that agreement is split by a structural disagreement: are African Americans colonized because of an economic system of exploitation and extraction (in the view of Black Panther Huey Newton) or because of a wider, longer sense of forced estrangement from African origins and Africanness (as Kwame Ture and Charles Hamilton saw it)?

This dispute, such as it was, is largely centered on a debate about the ultimate sources of antiblack exploitation and oppression and, therefore, sites of emphasis for thinking about black liberation. In that sense, the conflict was one over economic relations, which allowed Newton to imagine connections across the Global South, and cultural politics, which allowed Ture to conceive new modalities of being black through transatlantic connections. Newton's work on solidarity and radical intervention across race and gender lines, especially in his later essays collected in *To Die for the People*, reflects his collapse of any easy distinction between how capitalism extracts labor and resources from the Global South and how white people oppress black people in the United States and abroad. But Ture, especially in the coauthored *Black Power*, shifted that sense of coloniality away from questions of capitalism and the Global South toward the specificity of antiblackness domestically and in the Atlantic world more broadly. At the same time, Newton and Ture, when seen in the context of "a nation within a nation," are dealing with the same problem: how do we think about black liberation when black people are not enfranchised as part of ongoing, de facto political struggle and are instead governed from the outside in nearly every phase of life? "Colonial subjects," Ture and Hamilton write in *Black Power*, "have their political decisions made for them by the colonial masters, and those decisions are handed down directly or through a process of 'indirect rule.' Politically, decisions which affect black lives have always been made by white people."[3] So, the nation within a nation is colonial for precisely that reason: whatever the proximity to whites, black communities and places are administered from afar. The communities separated by the proverbial train tracks may as well be an ocean apart. That leads to conditions of political exploitation, affirming Newton's articulation of the colonial condition and forms of cultural abjection and alienation, which was a key concern in Stokely Carmichael's turn away from the integrationist struggle of Martin Luther King Jr.'s movement and toward visions of black power and radical independence.

If the language of colonialism adheres to the situation of antiblackness in the United States, then what does resistance and decolonization look like? And, more pointedly, what does it mean to theorize decolonization inside the geographic *West*?

Sounds of Worldmaking

Let me return to where I began. In *The Black Atlantic*, Gilroy's primary concern is with the routes and roots of aesthetic formation in the Atlantic world. What is groundbreaking about the work is how it prompts us to think about diasporic exchange outside the confines of racial nationalism or any nationalism whatsoever, something that later collections like *Between Camps* and *Darker Than Blue* continue with increasing sophistication. In place of racial nationalism, Gilroy articulates a sense of fluid, excessive points of contact that produce new forms of thinking about blackness and identity. And in so doing, Gilroy argues for the central role of the aesthetic in buttressing strategies of resistance and for the resiliency of cultural formation under regimes of abjection and exploitation. Gilroy advocates for thinking about blackness outside the center-margin distinction that dominates so much racial discourse.

The aesthetic, then, when registered in a wider philosophical sensibility, is more than the transmission of feeling and the creation of standards or foundation pieces of the good, the beautiful, and the sublime. Under conditions of racial abjection, the aesthetic becomes increasingly central to and urgent for matters of identity formation and contact between ethno-racial groups having at least family resemblance, if not a shared history. This is Gilroy's claim. But like so many profound interventions in fraught issues, this claim promises more than *The Black Atlantic* itself can deliver. I am thinking here of Gilroy's reflections on what he calls the *slave sublime*, a sense of sound that gives a certain sense of unity to diasporic cultural production by drawing on a shared painful past and rendering it aurally. Expressive culture has its particular power in these sorts of moments. Real intellectual work is done, whether in memory, representation, in or setting out contrary, subversive forms of knowing and being: sound as epistemology and ontology, then, not just aesthetics.

For me, this is a key shift in Gilroy's work and opens *The Black Atlantic* to a variety of new senses of significance. If we return to the place from which Gilroy wanted to gain some distance, the United States, the function of sound in structuring ways of knowing and being has its own history. That history, I argue, forms the key concept of worldmaking, which, as we shall see, does real decolonizing work by deconstructing the West as a project and reclaiming its differentiation and disassembling character as a place.

What is sound? And what does it do to memory, history, knowing, and being?

We can recall here a passage from Frederick Douglass's *Narrative of the Life of Frederick Douglass*, in which he remembers a moment traversing a field and hearing enslaved workers in the distance singing what he described as "the prayer and complaint of souls boiling over with the bitterest anguish." This moment in *Narrative* is not one among others, nor is it an occasional remark. Rather, it is the moment in which Douglass gives content to the meaning of the experience of slavery. For that experience, there are no adequate words; this is something that quietly dominates the opening chapters of *Narrative* and is only interrupted when Douglass recalls the function of sound in articulating that experience. Writing the experience of slavery, then, is both being at a loss for words and fixated on the sound of a pain without redemption. He writes:

> They told a tale of woe which was then altogether beyond my feeble comprehension; they were tones loud, long, and deep; they breathed the prayer and complaint of souls boiling over with the bitterest anguish. Every tone was a testimony against slavery, and a prayer to God for deliverance from chains. The hearing of those wild notes always depressed my spirit, and filled me with ineffable sadness. I have frequently found myself in tears while hearing them. The mere recurrence to those songs, even now, afflicts me; and while I am writing these lines, and expression of feeling has already found its way down my cheek. To those songs I trace my first glimmering conception of the dehumanizing character of slavery.[4]

The sound of singing carries with it such deep pain that it remains, for him, unthinkable or unrepresentable while also communicating something of slavery's essence—from the perspective of the enslaved. The song is moving. Douglass is drawn to the sound. He is also crushed by its meaning, precisely because it brings such intense clarity to his own condition. In beauty, also in terror. The sublime. It is important to note, too, that the sound of these "wild notes" is what allows Douglass to generate a *conception* of slavery and its dehumanizing character, full of the intensity—*glimmering*—of insight commanded by the traumatic experience itself. Sound *thinks*, carries concepts within it, and in that sense fills the space opened by the failure of words to bear the meaning of enslavement.

What for Douglass remains the shock of thinking inside sound, and then its capacity to carry something essential about slavery's dehumanizing effects and affects, for later African American thinkers becomes the foundation of the African American intellectual tradition. Pain in sound is testimony and witness but also meaning and enunciation that *creates*. The transformative text on these issues comes a half century later as the final chapter of Du Bois's *Souls of Black Folk*, which documents the movement of the spirituals from the songs of slavery to the sound that links that past to forms of life in the present and then the future. Du Bois is characteristically careful in his formulation of the meaning of the spirituals. Their performance, the *enactment* of sound and its effect on the singer and listener, grounds the aesthetic dimensions of African American life and reflects certain ways of knowing and being that mark that life with distinctiveness. That distinctiveness and its repetition inside the identity group "African American" is precisely why Du Bois can so directly link the spirituals to the idea of *tradition*.

"Tradition" is a curious concept. It lives from a common origin while also producing variation, dispute, conflict, and progress. The spirituals, which are the systemization and iterability of what Douglass reports from plantation life, are simultaneously fecund and grounding. Alain Locke develops this suggestive notion in Du Bois when he writes in "The Negro Spirituals" that

> the Spirituals are really the most characteristic product of the race genius as yet in America. But the very elements which make them uniquely expressive of the Negro make them at the same time deeply representative of the soil that produced

them. Thus, as unique spiritual products of American life, they become nationally as well as racially characteristic.[5]

The turn to the national in Locke's opening remarks to "The Negro Spirituals" proves a potent claim and insight in his work, but for present purposes it is worth sitting with the notion of race genius and expressive life in the African American tradition. Race genius, marking the specificity of cultural production, generates *spiritual products*. Spiritual products express the inner life of *a people*, and indeed this is what both Du Bois and Locke see as so important about the Negro spirituals: they ground identity. Identity is grounded—and this is crucial—not in opposition to another group, in this case a dominant group that subjugates as a matter of its own identity, but in relation to/between the members of the group itself. This was exactly how James Baldwin defined the African American tradition: as an expressive culture generated by "the relation Negroes bear to one another."[6] That bearing of relation, generative of the spirituals and what comes after, produces a particular cultural tradition and an identity that cannot be reduced to opposition and reactivity or to atavism and its nostalgia for origins. It is instead a way of being and knowing rooted in place, drawing from a shared history and memory of living in the geographic site we can call *the West*.

The legacy of Du Bois's and Locke's exploration of the spirituals as a philosophical event underpins the later development of what Ralph Ellison and Albert Murray (among others) articulate as the blues aesthetic. Du Bois and Locke, building from Douglass's witnessing of the song in the field, mark the sound of culture as a foundational event, the founding of *a people*. That is what tradition means in this context, simultaneously linking and delinking race and culture—a project begun in Du Bois's famous (or infamous, in some contexts) 1897 essay "The Conservation of Races," in which he argued for racial essentialism (appealing to blood and "the great races of the world") alongside an appeal to the need for cultural production and the formation of authentic personhood among African Americans. When Du Bois and then Locke turn to the spirituals as a cultural foundation, they are all-in with the notion of culture as a site of identity formation. Ellison and Murray allow that idea to blossom, drawing from the explosion of jazz (Louis Armstrong and Duke Ellington, in particular) in the American imagination and a revisionist assessment of the blues that turns the blues sound into an aesthetic and metaphysical event. Reality itself is changed by the sound of black suffering—namely, the reality of and for African Americans. That change—a metaphysical intervention and eruption—is an expression of resistance in the form of performance, pleasure, and community making. Aesthetics is metaphysics, ontology, and a certain kind of politics. "When the Negro musician or dancer swings the blues," Murray writes, "he is fulfilling the same fundamental existential requirement that determines the mission of the poet, the priest, and the medicine man."[7]

Murray has it right. If the blues secularizes and popularizes the sound of African American suffering, which is not suffering writ large but only and always a specific history and memory of pain, then it is in some sense an entire world unto itself. Or, more precisely, it grounds an articulation of a world of relations between black people, sound exchanged in the world of *a people*, and so speaks to modes of being, knowing, and creating outside the white gaze and its capacity to dominate and subjugate through reification of "the center." Poet, priest, and medicine man: a whole world is there in sound. And in sound, a different kind of relation to place and its history. A decolonizing of the West percolates in this mixture of the aesthetic, epistemology, and ontology. The Being of beings against the Being of the colony.

Deprojecting the West

If Glissant is right that the West is not a place but a project, then the question of decolonizing the West as a concept is addressed to dismantling it as a projection. What does it mean to deproject what functions as racial ideology?

The projection of the ideology of the West as a fundamentally white geography turns on two items: the invisibility of black people/traditions and the imagination of total subjugation at the hands of white people. That is, if the West is identified with whiteness and white people, then those subjugated as the very condition of the founding of the Atlantic world's extension of "Westernness"—the United States as a Western nation, culture, and political formation—must remain mute or external to the project and the reality it makes.[8] But of course, that is simply not true. If we take a step beyond Gilroy's notion of the countermodern—his conception of black cultural production in late modernity, which is dependent in some sense on white modernity for its meaning—and shift toward the African American tradition as worldmaking *between black people for black people*, then a very different portrait of our geography of reason is drawn. In this geography of reason, thinking is generated *inside* the white West as both a reactive force (countermodernity) and as the generation of a new and distinct people. The spirituals express a mode of being in *this* place but also outside it. For this place, the West in its projection of a white fantasy cannot contain what the spirituals say and know. The spirituals speak to something essential about the West; they are its reckoning with having lived from racial violence for centuries, beginning in slavery and then living into its long, enduring aftermath. Neither remainder nor sublation, the spirituals extend the West into the pain of memory and history. For the white West, this means entanglement with the pain it produced and a future that must think from inside that complex site: whiteness and its geographic space. Thinking the white West, then, is to be drawn in each turn back to not just *participation* in disastrous violence but also to a life *rooted* in said violence. This shift also embeds the African American tradition inside the West as a supplement that dismantles the imagined coherence of the West as a white and only white tradition. Du Bois and Locke, then Ellison, Murray, and others, show us how the pain rendered in the sound of the spirituals becomes an aesthetic, an epistemology, and an ontology of black life in the United States, as well as perhaps in the Americas more broadly.[9] In that moment of making a world, pain is transformed from melancholia to mourning, at the very least, and then to something vastly more in grounding a tradition that is not reactive but fecund.

If decolonization means decentering the colonial measure of whiteness, then reckoning with the African American tradition as a (if not *the*) West, enacts decolonizing work as a matter of simple principle. And if we think back to Du Bois's title—"A Negro Nation Within a Nation"—we can see how the key deconstructive move is borne by the word *within*. Inside the nation, a Western nation in every register and history, there is another nation: a world alongside and a world outside. But also there is a world *within*, which is a double movement that folds into the nation in the same moment that it withdraws from it. The spirituals are just this. The nation is unthinkable without the production of the pain to which the spirituals are testimony. Entanglement. Immanence. The nation within a nation is thereby marked by distance, sharing space that is simultaneously not space. Dismantling. Spacing. In a zigzag, the center shifts, and new models of thinking emerge from "the West" as a conflicted, fraught space and *not* a single, supremacist racial project and projection. The West as a geography of reason is rhizomatic. It is made of the stuff of double consciousness, never a single consciousness. No root. Just roots and routes.

In all, then, the issue of what constitutes *American* philosophy as Western philosophy, and indeed philosophy of the Americas as such, is deeply entangled in questions of empire and empire's effort to bridge the Atlantic world. This is where racialization is so utterly crucial, both in the mounting of the project of the West and the in the dismantling of the same. The mounting of the project is clear: what we mean both colloquially and analytically by "the West" is the life and tradition of white people. This survives migration. I am struck often by how professional philosophy appeals to "non-Western traditions" as a catch-all for nonwhite traditions, whether those traditions are inside or outside the reach of white European imperial history. But Glissant's argument is compelling and reveals such appeals as a reproduction—wittingly or unwittingly—of the racial ideology of whiteness. Whiteness remains, in that gesture, a center. But it's not. The West is conflicted space entangled with centuries of racial violence. People were made in the machinery of that violence. Worlds were created in that machinery. The West is a project that made white people, yes, and that is a history of intense political and epistemological violence. Everything is distorted in that frame.

If we rethink the West in this fashion, as comprising contrary hegemonies and not just orders of subjugation, then I think we can hear Gilroy's conception of countermodernity in a slightly different register. Countermodernity in *The Black Atlantic* has both a broad and a narrow function, both of which articulate the meaning of modernity in two sites: European self-formation, imperial through and through, and the black Atlantic exchange of ideas. Two modernities emerge on this account in a tense relationship but also as independent formations. But if I am right in the reflections above, it is not enough to say that there is both white modernity and black modernity? We have to reentangle white modernity in its violence *and* understand black cultural production as both generated by and transcendent of that same violence. In such embedding *between* and *inside*, the West emerges as a site to be thought of in fragments. Fragments bear violence; something was broken deliberately, and worlds were made in that violence and in the aftermath of shattered traditions. Fragments are bound together to make new things, seamed by the fecundity of survival and the obstinate character of human communities living under the most unimaginable conditions. The geographic space called "the West" and the imagination attached to that space must account for this breaking apart and the diversity of communities, traditions, and conceptual languages produced in its wake. There is no center here. There is only proliferation of differences. Different traditions. Entangled traditions.

Notes

1. Derrida makes this exact identification between deconstruction and decolonial work. See Jacques Derrida, *Who's Afraid of Philosophy: Right to Philosophy I*, trans. Jan Plug (Stanford, CA: Stanford University Press, 2002), 105.

2. It is worth noting here how this shift is both an advance on Frantz Fanon's legacy, which in *Black Skin, White Masks* and related essays was deeply committed to an ontological pessimism about blackness and black cultural expression, and a transformation of the postcolonial moment away from the sole question of national independence toward questions of cultural production as resistance, worldmaking, and subaltern meaning formation. For thinkers such as Peter Hallward in *Absolutely Postcolonial* and Chris Bongie in *Friends and Enemies*, this is a troubling turn and neutralizes earlier anticolonial politics. But, for me, it is fundamentally a deepening of politics. Colonialism was so deeply committed to structures of shame and abjection in the colonies around questions of language and expression—a sense of abjection to which Fanon was still tied when he wrote about pidgin, Creole, and the blues as subjugated voices—that rethinking those questions on local, rather than metropolitan, terms is plenty political as an act. In fact, it goes straight to the heart of how colonialism sought to subject its subject. So, liberatory struggle *ought* to unroot oppression at this root, alongside more common or basic questions of national independence.

3. Kwame Ture and Charles Hamilton, *Black Power: The Politics of Liberation* (New York: Vintage, 1992), 6–7.

4. Frederick Douglass, *Narrative of the Life of Frederick Douglass* (Mineola, NY: Dover, 1995), 8–9.

5. Alain Locke, "The Negro Spirituals," in *The Works of Alain Locke*, ed. Gary Molesworth (Oxford: Oxford University Press, 2012): 105–112.

6. James Baldwin, "Many Thousands Gone," in *The Price of the Ticket* (New York: St. Martin's Press, 1985), 72.

7. Albert Murray, *The Omni-Americans: Black Experience and American Culture* (New York: Da Capo, 1970), 58.

8. It is worth noting here, as a way of marking the very real limits of my claims, that this characterization does not take account of indigeneity. For me, that is a vastly different question; African American claims to place and home, which is the key item in the present reflections, are staked on stolen land. Reckoning with *that* form of violence, a violence that preconditions another violence—and what it means for thinking through the whole of the violence constitutive of

the West—broadens the meaning and experience of colonialism. Indigenous communities and nations bear genocide and settler colonialism as a condition of their being in modernity. That is a different story and too long to tell alongside this one about African Americans. But it is also a story that is entangled with Westernness and Western memory and history.

9. I argue for the continuity between orality in the Afro-Caribbean tradition and the spirituals in the African American tradition in John E. Drabinski, "Orality and the Slave Sublime," in *The Caribbean Oral Tradition: Literature, Performance, and Practice*, ed. Hanétha Vété-Congolo (New York: Palgrave, 2016): 109–127.

PART TWO

DECOLONIZING THE AMERICAN CANON

CHAPTER FOUR

Enlightened Readers

Thomas Jefferson, Immanuel Kant, Jorge Juan, and Antonio de Ulloa

Eduardo Mendieta

We Are What We Read

The eighteenth century was not simply the age of criticism, as Immanuel Kant referred to his own time in his magisterial *Critique of Pure Reason*.[1] It was also the age of the rediscovery of the Americas, and thus, of the emergence of a new conception of nature.[2] At the pinnacle of this new conception of nature is Alexander von Humboldt.[3] But Humboldt himself was inspired by some precursors, among them Condamine, Juan, and Ulloa, to name those who will play a key role in the argument developed in this chapter. Between the so-called discovery of the New World, its subsequent conquest, and its opening in the second half of the eighteenth century, South America for the most part remained closed off to other European nations and powers other than Spain and Portugal. With the papal bull *Inter Caetera* issued by Pope Alexander VI in May 1493, and the treatise of Tordesilla of June 7, 1494, which divided the discovered lands along a meridian 370 leagues west of the Cape Verde Islands (located off the Western coast of Africa), the Americas were essentially granted for conquest and control to both Spain and Portugal.[4] This modus operandi partly ended in 1735, when a special joint scientific mission between Spain and France brought a group of "naturalists" to South America to measure the earth and to prove or disprove Sir Isaac Newton's hypothesis that the earth is not a sphere but a spheroid that bulges at the equator. Charles-Marie de La Condamine, an exemplar of what was called the "Renaissance man," led the scientific expedition; but he was also a scientist *avant la lettre*. He was a mathematician, geographer, astronomer, and all-around naturalist. In this expedition, he also had other scientists, but noteworthy among his company were Jorge Juan and Antonio de Ulloa, two Spaniards who were military men but also scientists. From this scientific expedition there emerged what could be referred to as a veritable literature—one that was to impact how Europeans and Americans came to understand the "New Continent" as well as nature itself. This literature, a synergy of travelogue, scientific journal, adventure memoir, ethnography, and experimental notebooks, called forth a unique and hitherto unknown reader—a reader that I will call the Enlightened Reader. This is a reader who was just as interested in nature, and the means of getting to know it, as in the persona of the scientist who made such knowledge available and of nature and culture as "legible" to the perspicacious reader.[5] Legibility is a quality of texts but also of culture. Therefore, this new reader read prodigiously, irreverently, and with neither censures nor forbidden lists. This Enlightened Reader, furthermore, is one who in the motto of the Royal Academy (*Nullius in verba* [take no one's word for it]) only took knowledge on the authority of scientific evidence. It can be argued that this literature prepared the ground for the readership that would make Diderot and D'Alembert's *Encyclopédie* (Encyclopedia, or systematic dictionary of the sciences, arts, and crafts [1751–1772]), one of the most successful and distinctive publications of the Enlightenment.[6]

Several factors converged during the eighteenth century in creating the so-called Enlightened Reader. First, we have the development of scientific academies or royal societies that contributed to the scientific collaboration among the different European nations. Second, there emerged a distinct genre of scientific writing that combined travelogue, scientific reporting, experimental journal writing, natural philosophy speculation, and ethnographic-anthropological reportage that exemplified the writing of the figure we would later call the "scientist"—the experimenter, explorer, and scientific investigator. Third, the emergent academies of science were instrumental in providing the scientific vetting and imprimatur of the reports, books, and travelogues produced by the different scientific enterprises that these academies financed or promoted.[7] A network emerged that facilitated and accelerated the dissemination of scientific information. As Robert Darnton noted, it could be claimed "that the modes of communication have replaced the modes of production as the driving force of the modern world," to which he added, "I would argue that every age was an age of information, each in its own way, and that communication systems have always shaped events."[8] In the mid-eighteenth century the communication system consisted mainly of the scientific travelogue and the scientific expedition journal.[9] This was the system par excellence that shaped the consciousness of the age. We know that Immanuel Kant's favorite literary form as a reader was travelogue, and among some of the travelogues he read are those of Jorge Juan and Antonio de Ulloa, members of the La Condamine expedition, as we will see. If "we are what we read," as Robert Manguel has claimed, then the scientific literature of the eighteenth century constituted a certain kind of critical reader, whose primary orientation was a comparative and evaluative one.[10] A new kind of reader began to be nourished by this emergent and unique literature. Furthermore, inasmuch as these texts circulated across national boundaries and continents, they constituted a transnational readership that began to share what Mary Louise Pratt has called in her magnificent *Imperial Eyes*, a "planetary consciousness": this is a view of the world, of the planet, as constituting a unified, organic whole.[11] Arguably, no one exemplified this spirit and attitude better than Thomas Jefferson, who in addition to being one of the Founding Fathers of the United States, was also a figure of the Enlightenment. Exemplifying Darnton's claim about systems of communication, Jefferson was not only a bibliophile but could also be thought of as the first librarian of the republic. This in fact can be taken literally, as his voluminous personal library became the core of what today is the largest library in the world: namely, the United States Library of Congress, which is the largest in terms of shelf space and number of volumes.

What is distinctive about the eighteenth century is that although the scientific media available to an emergent enlightened readership was circumscribed, these materials were read avidly and voraciously, precisely because of their paucity. In this chapter we will discuss how Jefferson and Kant, two titans of the transatlantic Enlightenment, were reading the same books. Yet they were also coming to different conclusions from their reading. The aim here will be to explore this divergence: what propelled and motivated these two Enlightenment figures to arrive at such divergent views on the reading they were doing—reading that was crucial to the age? If we are to "decolonize" the Western philosophical canon, we have to be attentive not only to the invidious ways in which the colonized "other" is constituted by the canon but also by the ways in which that constitution is predicated on both deliberate and inadvertent misreadings. As "decolonial" readers, that is, as readers who must be attentive to the ways in which we coexist within a "colonial present"—a present reverberating with the ripples of coloniality—we have to learn and relearn how to read the Western philosophical canon as a series of omissions, silences, appropriations, and expropriations. Part of this task, then, is being attentive to what the architects of the canon read, did not read, and misread, whether deliberately or unconsciously.

Glossing on Walt Whitman's enthusiastic poetic response to Margaret Fuller's view that while books cannot replace human experience, they are nonetheless a "medium for viewing all humanity, a core around which all knowledge, all experience, all science, all the ideal as well as the practical in our nature could gather."[12] Alberto Manguel writes the following, which may stand as the epigraph for this chapter:

> For Whitman, text, author, reader and world mirrored each other in the act of reading, an act whose meaning he expanded until it served to define every vital human activity, as well as the universe in which it all took place. In this conjunction, the reader reflects the writer (he and I are one), the world echoes a book (God's book, Nature's book), the book is of flesh and blood (the writer's own flesh and own blood, which through a literary transubstantiation become mine), the world is a book deciphered (the writer's poems become my reading of the world).[13]

At the core of Manguel's reading of Whitman is the metaphor of the Enlightened Reader. This reader is one who always exercises the utmost generosity not only toward what they read but also toward the writers they read, as well as toward what they read about and in the content of the text that mirrors author, reader, and world.

I will proceed by offering a succinct sketch of Thomas Jefferson as a figure of the Enlightenment who made deliberate efforts to cultivate the art of an expansive and cosmopolitan reading practice, one that was decisive when referring to the rights of all humans. I will also reflect on his paradoxical views on slavery. Then I will turn to a discussion of Jorge

Juan and Antonio de Ulloa's fascinating two-volume *Voyage to South America*.[14] Ulloa was also the author of a two-volume work titled *Noticias Secretas de America*, which also played an important role in the eighteenth century. While Juan and Ulloa appear to be only minor figures in the bibliography of the Enlightenment, it is clear that both exemplified the Enlightened Reader. They read past the literature of the Conquest, seeing American nature and culture with new eyes. Most importantly, Jefferson quotes Juan and Ulloa in his important *Notes on the State of Virginia*, noting explicitly that despite all he had "read" about South America, he had learned the most from Ulloa. However, here I will focus on the passage that both Jefferson and Kant read and cited, regretfully having to forgo further analysis of their rich writings and readings. Finally, I will turn to Kant's missing library and his readings, or misreadings, as I will argue.

Jefferson: The Father and Librarian of the New Republic

In the epilogue to his award-winning 1960 book, *The Jefferson Image in the American Mind*, Merrill D. Peterson wrote: "Jefferson is an old, old subject, but the quest for the *historical* Jefferson, under the formal discipline of scholarly inquiry, is young."[15] This sentence cannot but evoke a contrast with religious and biblical figures, where a distinction is made between the holy or kerygmatic and the historical or factual. There is in fact something kerygmatic about Jefferson. Jefferson was almost the sole writer of the American Declaration of Independence. He was also secretary of state, a two-term president (1801 to 1805; 1805 to 1809), and initiated the Louisiana Purchase (unconstitutionally in 1803), which doubled the territory of the United States. He also commissioned the Lewis and Clark expedition (1804 to 1806), which essentially led to discovery of the American West. Jefferson had an incredible impact on the United States. At the heart of the kerygmatic Jefferson is what Gary Wills, in his critical, balanced, and insightful *Inventing America: Jefferson's Declaration of Independence*, referred to as Jefferson's articulation of the grammar of US *political liturgy*.[16] Most Jefferson scholars contend that this grammar is framed around three key philosophemes: liberty, reason, and science (in its practical form of experimentalism). Or as Adrienne Koch and William Peden put it: "Not politics, but the image of moral freedom and peace which had animated democracy for the Greeks, Republicanism for the Romans, the Eternal City for the Middle Ages, Scientific Utopia for the tyrant-ridden Renaissance, and modern representative democracy for eighteen-century America and France—this was still, as it had always been, his cherished ideal."[17]

Indeed, Jefferson distinguishes himself among presidents for his Enlightenment outlook and for his level of education. In the words of one of his biographers, Jefferson "became America's most learned president, its best-read leader, one of its most distinguished men of science."[18] From journals that he left, essays, and the voluminous correspondence he conducted (in the Jefferson papers there are nearly nineteen thousand letters) and to which we now have access, we can surmise that Jefferson was extremely well read.[19] He knew Greek and Latin, languages he was so comfortable with that in his old age he would read the classics in their original.[20] But he also spoke and read French, Italian, and Spanish. The kerygma of Jefferson is that he was a consummate statesman who pursued power for the sake of democratic self-rule and eschewed dogmatism (whether religious or metaphysical) in the name of experimentalism, fallibilism, and democratic meliorism. To borrow from the title of Peterson's epilogue to his book, Jefferson continues to project a long shadow, one that seems to be growing longer as know-nothing populism feverishly corrodes the public mind. Since 1960, when Peterson announced that *historical* research into Jefferson was still in its infancy, we have seen an explosion of masterful works on him. Take for instance, Dumas Malone's masterful six-volume *Jefferson and His Time*, which began in 1948 with the last volume published in 1981. In 1975 Malone was awarded the Pulitzer Prize for history for the fifth volume in the series.[21] There is Gary Wills's previously mentioned close reading of Jefferson's drafting of the declaration of independence; Noble E. Cunningham Jr.'s *In Pursuit of Reason: The Life of Thomas Jefferson*;[22] the recent biography by Jon Meacham, *Thomas Jefferson: The Art of Power*, also a winner of the Pulitzer Prize;[23] or the even more recent book by John B. Boles, *Jefferson: Architect of American Liberty*, with its liturgical subtitle.[24] We may be closer to the historical Jefferson, but the kerygmatic Jefferson continues to grow in power as well.[25]

Jefferson was not only a polyglot but also a bibliophile—and a consummate one at that. Already as a young man he had begun gathering his library, which he tended "like a garden."[26] His first collection, acquired when he was twenty-seven, was already a sizable library. Unfortunately, this was lost during a fire that destroyed Shadwell, Jefferson's youthful country home. The estimated value of that library was £200; still, the library was "doubtless a creditable one," for a young lawyer.[27] From his commonplace notebooks of the time, which did survive, we can surmise that the library, in addition to law books, also contained many of the Greek and Roman classics. These commonplace notebooks contained many extracts from such classics.[28] By the time he turned forty, according to his own self-reporting, his library had grown to 2,640 volumes. When he lived in Paris, representing the United States, he would wander the Quai, hunting for volumes among the secondhand bookstalls, "hand-picking" volumes, and "gathering the treasures of classical learning, of humanism and the Renaissance, of the advanced, and rational European age in which he was so active."[29] He would also buy books for colleagues such as James Madison.[30] Or he would display his extensive knowledge of books by the kind of recommendations he would make to close friends or family members, such as we find in a letter from August 19, 1785, to his favorite nephew Peter Carr. In this letter, for instance, Jefferson advises Peter to read Goldsmith's history of Greece, which will give him a "digested view of the field." Then he proceeds to make some author recommendations: "Take up ancient history in the detail, reading the following books, in the following order: Herodotus, Thucydides, Xenophontis Hellenica, Xenophontis Anabasis, Arrian, Quintus Curtius, Diodorus Siculus, Justin. This shall form the first stage of your historical reading, and is all I mention to you now."[31]

By the time he retired, as we know, Jefferson had amassed perhaps the largest and most specialized library of any person on the North American continent. When the British burned the young Library of Congress in 1814, Jefferson offered his own library to Congress, at a price to be decided by Congress itself but with the stipulation that the library should be taken in its entirety.[32] An independent bookseller tabulated for Congress Jefferson's library at 6,487 volumes, valued at $23,950. From the official congressional record, we can gather that the acquisition of Jefferson's library turned into a political battle, notwithstanding external appraisals that trying to put a price on such a library was "absurd and impossible," or that such a library "for its selection, rarity and intrinsic value, is beyond all price."[33] Thus, in addition to having played a key role in the creation of the Library of Congress in 1802, he paved the way for its second incarnation when he sold his own library to Congress after its destruction by the British in 1814.[34] When the last of the wagons transporting his library from Monticello to Washington were about to depart, Jefferson relayed to Samuel Harrison Smith, editor of the *National Intelligencer*, that his library "is the choicest collection of books in the United States, and I hope it will not be without some general effect on the literature of our country."[35] It was the choicest, in particular, because it contained the largest collection of Americana of any library in the country. Francis C. Gray, a literary gentleman recommended to Jefferson by John Adams, deemed Jefferson's collection of books on North and South America as undoubtedly "the finest in the world."[36] Indeed, Jefferson had made a point of gathering as many books as possible relating to the Americas.

This brings us to the specific books that serve as a bridge, or pivot, between Jefferson and Kant, and that is Jorge Juan and Antonio de Ulloa's *A Voyage to South America* and Antonio de Ulloa's *Noticias Americanas: Entretenimiento Físico-Histórico sobre La América Meridional y al Septentrional Oriental*.[37] The first is a book that appeared in Spanish in 1748 but was quickly translated into English in 1760 and 1765, with a third edition in 1772. While we cannot confirm that this book was in Jefferson's library, it was likely published both in its Spanish original and in the English translation, since it was printed by the printer of the Royal Academy and had its imprimatur. This book was based on information gathered during the La Condamine scientific voyage that had become famous by the second half of the eighteenth century. The second book appeared in Spanish in 1772.[38] And we know that Jefferson was familiar with the book because he quotes it twice in his *Notes on the State of Virginia* and refers to it in his correspondence with James Madison from September 1, 1785, in which he specifically writes, "Don Ulloa, in the original, is not to be found."[39]

Jefferson refers to Ulloa in two places in his *Notes on the State of Virginia*. The first is in Query V, which concerns geological aspects of Virginia, and it is found in a long footnote at the very end of the query. The second reference is in Query VI, which begins as an assessment of the geography of Virginia and Northern America but turns to a consideration of the peoples that populated these regions before the arrival of the European "men." The citation comes at the end of the following paragraph:

> From these sources I am able to say, in contradiction to this representation, [the sources are his own experience with Native Americans and what he has read; and the representation refers to the negative representations of them in the literature] that he is neither more defective in ardor, nor more impotent with this female, than the white reduced to the same diet and exercise: that he is brave, when an enterprise depends on bravery; education with him making the point of honor

consist in the destruction of an enemy by stratagem, and the preservation of his own person free from injury; or perhaps this is nature; while it is education which teaches us to honor force more than finesses: that he will defend himself against an host of enemies, always chusing [sic] to be killed, rather than + surrender, though it be to the whites, who he knows will treat him well.⁴⁰

Here, "+" indicates a footnote. The footnote is quite long, as it includes a citation from Ulloa in the original Spanish, as well as a long commentary on the passage and a circumlocution that leads to an important insight. I will offer my translation of the Spanish passage, which admittedly is a stilted, convoluted, and what we would these days call a "baroque" Spanish. It should be noted that the text was composed in the second half of the eighteenth century. This is another way of saying that Jefferson's command of Spanish was quite proficient and that he was comfortable reading such demanding Spanish texts. The cited passage reads:

Indians are not fearsome because of their courage, as they are for their treachery and the cunning that they use in order to commit it. Vanquishers by surprise, they are inhuman to the extreme, without knowing either mercy or compassion, and this they do in cold blood, taking pleasure in the carnage. When defeated, they are the most cowardly and pusillanimous that can be witnessed: in the first case they take complacency in shedding the blood of the unlucky that they have surprised; and in the second, they pretend to be innocent, they humiliate themselves to the extreme of self-contempt, and excuse their inconsiderate compulsion and with pleading and entreaties give sure proof of pusillanimity. All of these are properties that agree with cowardice and treachery, which is their proper character: or what is referred to in the histories of the conquest on their great acts is in a figurative sense, or the character of these peoples is not now as it was then; but what is without doubt is that the nations of the northern subsist in the same liberty that they have always had, without having been subjected by any foreign Prince, and that they live according to their own regime and the customs of their whole life, without there having been cause for their character to change. In this is seen the same that takes place in the nations of Peru, and the whole of southern America, subjugated, which they never have been.[41]

The note begins with Jefferson acknowledging his intellectual gratitude and debt to Ulloa for being the main source of his knowledge about South America, while also expressing his surprise at finding the sort of claims in the passage he then quotes and that I have just translated. The surprise stems from the seeming negative character of the claims made by Ulloa. They are also surprising in light of what we find in other passages in Ulloa's work, such as those we may find in *A Voyage to South America*, which abounds in passages filled with greater sympathy and comparative analysis of South American indigenous populations. Jefferson proceeds to note that had Ulloa been familiar with North American Native Americans, he would have come to different conclusions. In fact, had Ulloa had the opportunity to consult with Frenchmen, Englishmen, and Americans familiar with North American Native Americans, he would have found that none of them ever begged for their lives when facing subjugation by an enemy and, in fact, would have heard the contrary: namely that they court death at "every possible insult and provocation." This then leads Jefferson to conclude that had Ulloa been aware of such opinions and knowledge, he would have reversed his logic. Jefferson writes that Ulloa would have come to the following conclusion:

> Since the present Indian of North America is brave, and authors tell us, that the ancestors of South America were brave also; it must follow, that the cowardice of their descendants is the effect of subjugation and ill treatment [42]

Then, Jefferson uses Ulloa's own words to strengthen his claim that he, Ulloa, would have arrived at this conclusion:

> For he observes, ib. §. 27: "Los obrages los aniquilan por la inhumanidad con que se les trata" (the forced labors annihilate them because of the inhumanity with which they are treated).[43]

The footnote is in accord with the overall tenor of the text that it means to support and illuminate, which is a complicated encomium mixed with some prejudices particular to the times. Jefferson had incredible admiration and respect for the Indian peoples of the Americas, but he also felt they had to submit to the march of the white "men." Thus, he advocated that they be relegated to other lands (what later would become reservations), making room for the rolling locomotive of European civilization. His evaluation of Native American Indians, most notably, was in stark contrast to his evaluation of black people. He thought the former could be assimilated to "white" civilization, whereas people of color could not. As John B. Boles put it in his *Jefferson: Architect of American Liberty*, "Jefferson believed that Indians, unlike blacks, could become competent citizens, especially after interbreeding with whites—a practice he supported. Blinded by his assumptions about the superiority of European ways, Jefferson did not foresee Indian recalcitrance or the harm his approach would do to their culture."[44]

Even when Jefferson is praising Native Americans, he is still derogating them, just as he does black people, whom he thinks are by nature inferior.[45] Still, Jefferson thought that both are nevertheless inferior to whites and cannot be fully assimilated to European ways. There is a distinct element that nonetheless unites and mitigates Jefferson's racist and prejudicial views both by the standards of his time and ours: his views on slavery and any kind of dispossession and exploitation that demeans and dehumanizes a people. Query XVIII of *Notes on the State of Virginia* must be read as one of the most intense immanent critiques of the devastating and corrosive effects of slavery on both "master" and "slave." As Jefferson writes (and it merits extensive quoting):

> There must doubtless be an unhappy influence on the manners of our people produced by the existence of slavery among us. The whole commerce between master and slave is a perpetual exercise of the most boisterous passions, the most unremitting despotism on the one part, and degrading submissions on the other. The children see this, and learn to imitate it; for man is an imitative animal.[46]

Slavery destroys the humanity of both master and slave. But furthermore

> can the liberties of a nation be thought secure when we have removed their only firm basis, a conviction in the minds of the people that these liberties are of the gift of God? That they are not to be violated but with his wrath? Indeed I tremble

for my country when I reflect that God is just: that his justice cannot sleep for ever: that considering numbers, nature and natural means only, a revolution of the wheel of fortune, an exchange of situation, is among possible events.[47]

Slavery corrodes the character of a people supposedly committed to belief in the inalienable and God-given freedom of every human being. It also undermines the very foundation of the republic that unites them under that belief. Under a just God, the granter and giver of human freedom, a condition anathema to that order, is logically fated to be abolished. Jefferson, in 1781, when he wrote the *Notes*, turns into the prophet of the American abolition of slavery:

> The spirit of the master is abating, that of the slave rising from the dust, his condition mollifying, the way I hope preparing, under the auspices of heaven, for a total emancipation, and that this is disposed, in the order of events, to be with the consent of masters, rather than by their extirpation.[48]

Emancipation can come either through reason, through the bullet, or via the guillotine, as Jefferson would witness some years later in Paris. Jefferson witnessed the French Revolution and was a not-so-distant participant. Evidently, Jefferson wanted emancipation through reason rather than through carnage. Jefferson biographer Noble E. Cunningham put it eloquently and incisively when he wrote: "To the twentieth-century mind Jefferson's view on race stand in contrast to the liberal stance that he took on most of the major issues of the day; yet his repeated condemnation of the institution of slavery and his insistent arguments that steps must be taken to bring it to an end placed him in advance of most—but far from all-eighteenth-century persons."[49] What Cunningham calls Jefferson's "liberal stance" is in fact a visceral, existential, even ontological abhorrence of any kind of exploitation and subjugation of any human, both of which informed his reading and advocacy of the abolition of slavery. In this, Jefferson was ahead of Kant, as is the argument being developed here.

The contrast between Jefferson's and Kant's views on race and slavery, however, is not meant to be an unequivocal and unquestioned encomium of Jefferson's view on both. I am neither writing a hagiography of Jefferson, nor attempting to lessen "the paradox that the author of the Declaration of Independence was one of the largest slaveholders of his time."[50] While Jefferson was a critic of slavery, and had in fact called for its abolition in Virginia, he also was a slave owner and a politician that was in practice a realist and accommodationist who thus did not push for his antislavery views and their implementation. Nonetheless, the question of Jefferson's relationship to both race and slavery must be approached from two perspectives: the personal and the historical. From the personal perspective, we know that Jefferson was a slave owner who benefited greatly from the "peculiar institution" and who in many ways was no different from other slave owners. In the historical record, in fact, we have an advertisement in the *Virginia Gazette*, from September 14, 1769, by Jefferson seeking help in the recovery of his runaway mulatto slave Sandy.[51]

As Joyce Appleby put it: "In the abstract, slavery scratched at his conscience, but in practice, Jefferson accepted the institution pretty much as he found it, going along with the norms of his fellow planters. He treated his slaves as possessions, offering their labor to his sons-in-law as gestures of generosity. He personally got rid of slaves whom he considered insubordinate, and he sold slaves when he was short of money."[52] Furthermore, Jefferson's determination to become a wealthy and successful planter, which was required if he was to build and maintain Monticello, meant "regrettably, that Thomas Jefferson was doomed to be a slaveholder—for slave labor was the sine qua non of this enterprise."[53] Still, throughout his life, he maintained a deeply ambivalent relationship to slavery. From a historical perspective, we have to focus on what Peterson called the "Jefferson Image" or what I refer to as the kerygmatic Jefferson; that is, the Jefferson who played a significant role in the abolitionist movement and eventually in the struggle against racial prejudice. It is telling how abolitionists appealed to Jefferson, who was seen primarily as the "heroic voice of imperishable freedoms" to such an extent that for a time Jefferson's name was chained to the cause of abolition: "Abolitionism was Jeffersonianism!"[54] Still, Jefferson, like other "iconic" figures in American history such as George Washington, James Madison, and John Marshall, was also a slaveholder. To this extent, Jefferson shared with other Founding Fathers the moral flaw of both subscribing and benefiting from an institution that went against their avowed belief in human equality. Still, precisely because of his antithetical beliefs about human freedom and equality, we should be impelled to ponder how "anyone born in the bosom of a misogynist, slaveholding aristocracy could have dreamed of a society of equals."[55]

The Science of Liberty: Juan and Ulloa's Reporting on the Conditions of the Spanish Colonies

For most of the sixteenth and seventeenth centuries the American continent had been coastally explored, surveyed, and mapped. Europeans, however, were busy conquering the Amerindian peoples (i.e., American Native Americans), who lived in the great indigenous urban centers: what is today central Mexico, Peru, and Ecuador—the areas where the Incas ruled. By the time the Europeans arrived, the Mayan Empire had for all intents and purposes disappeared. It was during the eighteenth century that the continent began to be explored. The expedition of La Condamine is surely the most famous, if only because it spawned its own literature. The scientific expedition was made up of the following individuals: M. Pierre Bouguer, astronomer; M. Louis Godin, mathematician (who brought along his cousin, Jean Godin de Odonais); Captain Verguin of the French Royal Navy; M. de Morainville, a draftsman; Joseph de Jussieu, botanist; Dr. Jean Senièrgues, physician; M. Hugot, watchmaker and general technician and tool maker; M. Mabillon; M. Couplet, nephew of a member of the Academy; and the proper subjects of this section, Jorge Juan and Antonio de Ulloa.[56] Both were captains in the Spanish Navy but also mathematicians, mapmakers, ethnographers, jack-of-all-trade scientists, and, as we will discover, secret agents of the Spanish king. As ethnographers and anthropologists but also as mathematicians-turned-naturalists, both Juan and Ulloa became perspicacious, voracious, and generous readers of a lifeworld that up to that point had been presented to them in the invidious, prejudicial, and derogatory literature of the Spanish Conquest. They were writers of the Enlightenment, as well as readers that came to exemplify the Enlightened Reader they were helping to create and nurture.

Juan and Ulloa joined the scientific expedition in Cartagena, as the French and Spaniards sailed to the Americas from different ports. From Cartagena the entire expedition traveled to Panama, which country they crossed by both river and land, then made their way to Quito, which granted them the most accessible and closest point of entry to the equator. At the equator they could carry out the measurements and observations necessary to establish the truth of Newton's postulation that the earth is not a perfect sphere but more like a squashed orange: flat at the poles with a bulging midsection at the equator. The expedition left in 1735, and many of its members either died of tropical diseases, were killed in dramatic fashion, stayed and integrated themselves into Ecuadorian society, or survived to return a decade later after an undeniably harrowing experience. La Condamine became doubly famous not only because he was the leader of the expedition but also because he took the least comfortable and less well-known path in returning to Europe, namely by way of the Amazon River, which he mapped extremely accurately, providing Europeans with the best survey of the world's most formidable river. In fact, reading Victor Wolfgang von Hagen's account of the decade-long voyage reads like an Edgar Rice Burroughs narrative or an installment of Henry Walton "Indiana" Jones, Jr. adventures.

Juan and Ulloa, who incidentally were twenty-two and nineteen, respectively, at the beginning of the expedition, contributed to the scientific aspects of the amazing trek while also keeping extremely detailed diaries and notes they were able to judiciously use when they returned to Spain in 1746. Ulloa's return to Spain was as full of mishaps and adventures. At one point, due to the conflict between France and England during those years, Ulloa's ship was captured by the English. He was held prisoner, but once it was discovered that he was an officer and a scientist in the Spanish Navy, he was introduced to a member of the Royal Society and soon became a member himself. He was freed and allowed to return to Spain, which he did in 1746, where he met up with his colleague Jorge Juan.[57] The two men then combined their journals, notes, and maps to produce the two-volume *Voyage to South America*, which in addition to containing several maps also contains many illustrations and sketches of different dwellings, cities, villages, and dresses of criollos and mestizos. They also produced another two-volume work, this one tellingly titled *Noticias Secretas de América* (Secret news from America), which was originally a report to the Crown of the management and life of the South American colonies.[58]

Ulloa, after other royal appointments, returned to America in 1758, now as the governor and superintendent of the mercury mines at Huancavélica, Peru. Despite his efforts to modernize the enterprise and to root out some of its corruption, he failed and was removed from his post in 1763, leaving behind a report on his governance of the mines that dates from November 4, 1758 to May 1763.[59] His stay and experience in Peru undoubtedly informed his *Noticias Américanas*, from 1772, which mainly focused on South America. This is the work that Jefferson quotes in his *Notes on the State of Virginia*.

Returning to *A Voyage to South America*, Juan and Ulloa produced something hitherto unknown and no longer seen or produced. Von Hagen's description of their book is very apt:

> So already the Spanish contingent was dipping behind the façade of colonial Spain and finding that the magnificent exterior hid many lamentable and sordid bits of social masonry. All that they observed, all that they heard and dug out, these young men of Spain put into their truly encyclopedic notebooks. History, geography, natural history, the case of society, rituals, customs, all that was very quaint or very ridiculous, diseases, pharmacopoeia, industries, systems of construction, methods of planting, the manner of coastal seamanship . . . nothing escaped the intelligent curiosity of these young Spaniards. *It was the most complete picture that Spain ever had of its colonies.*[60]

This truly encyclopedic work indeed provided the most complete picture of the Spanish colonies the world had ever seen.[61] The work was not only comprehensive but also filled with acute and sometimes sympathetic observations of the local populations. One such observation is the following, important because it is what Kant seems to be referring to when he mentions Ulloa by name in his *Physical Geography*. The quote is from the third edition, which modernizes the spelling. The quote is lengthy so we have a better idea of what Kant was reading and how he may have been interpreting these passages:

> Both sexes are observed to be possessed of a great deal of wit and penetration, and also of a genius proper to excel in all kinds of mechanical arts. This is particularly conspicuous in those who apply themselves to literature, and who, at a tender age, showed a judgment and perspicuity, which, in other climates, is attained only a long series of years and the greatest application. This happy disposition and perspicuity continues till they are between twenty and thirty years of age, after which they generally decline as fast as they rose, and frequently, before they arrive at that age, when they should begin to reap the advantage of their studies, a natural indolence checks their farther progress, and they forsake the sciences, leaving the surprising effects of their capacity imperfect.

What seems like an ethnographic observation in the text in fact turns into a kind of mass psychological assessment. But Juan and Ulloa continue, providing their own sympathetic assessment of the putative stunted growth of the otherwise evident talent and "genius" of the locals:

> The principal cause of the short duration of such promising beginnings, and of the indolent turn so often seen in these bright geniuses, is doubtless the want of proper objects for exercising their faculties, and the small hopes of being preferred to any post answerable to the pains they have taken. For as there is this country neither army nor navy, and the civil employments very few, it is not at all surprising that the despair of making their fortunes, by this method, should damp their ardor for excelling in the sciences, and plunge them into idleness, the sure forerunner of vice, where they lose the use of their reason, and stifle those good principles which fired them when young and under proper subjection.

These observations may strike the modern reader as rather obvious, but for the eighteenth-century observer, quick to reach for conceptions of the innate character of peoples, it would have seemed rather generous. It should not be forgotten that these were observations based on the impressions of two rather young scientists working for the Crown as naval officers. Then they conclude the assessment of the "genius" of the Americans, with the following comparison:

> The genius of the Americans being more forward than that of the Europeans, many have been willing to believe that it also sooner decays; and that at sixty years, or before, they have outlived that solid judgment and penetration, so general among us at that time of life; and it has been said that their genius decays, whilst that of the Europeans is hastening to its maturity and perfection. But this is a vulgar prejudice, confuted by numberless instances, and particularly by the celebrated father Fr. Benito Feyjoo, Téatro critico, vol. iv, essay 6. All who have travelled with any attention through these countries, have observed in the native of every age a permanent capacity, and uniform brightness of intellects; if they were not of that wretched number, who disorder both their minds and bodies

by their vices. And indeed one often sees here persons of eminent prudence and extensive talents, both in the speculative and practical sciences, and who retain them, in all their vigor, to a very advance age.[62]

Here is an exemplary case of hermeneutical generosity as well as cultural intelligence. Juan and Ulloa refused the racist clichés of their time and instead aimed to provide a balanced and fair assessment of the cultural practices and character of the peoples they were meeting for the first time. What is noteworthy is that both had likely been fed the prejudicial literature produced by the conquistadores. The question should not only be about how we should read these passages today. The question, instead, should be the following: how did eighteenth-century readers read these passages, which brazenly challenged the assumed intellectual superiority of Europeans and sought to place "Americans" on the same footing as them? Looking at Kant's reading of these passages may provide us with one possible answer.

Kant's (Un)critical Reading

Like Socrates, Kant is well known for never having left his native city: Athens, for the former, and Königsberg, for the latter. Socrates did leave Athens briefly but only under the imperative of fighting for his city during the Peloponnesian Wars; Kant only left Königsberg when he was beginning as a teacher and worked as a private tutor for the royalty. Kant scholar Paul Guyer opens his indispensable book *Kant* with the wonderful and brief biographical sketch that begins by listing the eventful lives of most early modern European philosophers only to claim that Kant's was so uneventful that the only "drama in Kant's life was intellectual, so the story of his life must be told through his works."[63] Kant's life in fact can be (and for the most part has been) written as the succession and notoriety of his works (i.e., Kant's life was the sum of his great philosophical texts). For a long time we relied on the brief biographical details provided in Ernst Cassirer's *Kant's Life and Thought* and Karl Jaspers's *Kant*, which was part of the first volume of his *The Great Philosophers*.[64] It was only until relatively recently that a true biography of Kant could be found, namely Manfred Kuehn's *Kant: A Biography*.[65]

As if imploding from within the dogma of having to write Kant's life as the succession and sum of his books, Willi Goetschel wrote a magisterial study of Kant's evolving, revolutionizing writing style. Kant's paradigm-shifting three *Critiques* were not written as if guided by divine inspiration but through an attentiveness to style that sought to match the content of the works. The *Critiques* revolutionized both philosophical thinking and how philosophical texts would come to be written. Goetschel carefully analyzes each period in Kant's long writing life, demonstrating the shifts, as well as the inspiration and reasoning behind the shifts, in the evolution of his thinking and writing. Goetschel's book is titled *Constituting Critique: Kant's Writing as Critical Praxis*.[66] As I think about the readership that emerged in Kant's century, I also wonder whether one could write a book similar to Goetschel's but one focused on Kant's reading practice. This would require researching Kant's archives in much the same way Jefferson's biographers researched his: by being attentive to Jefferson's reading and how it left traces in his correspondence and published texts. Let us imagine, à la Borges, that there is such a book: *The Book as Freedom: Kant's Reading as a Critical Praxis*. The following are notes that went into the drafting of this book.[67]

In contrast to Jefferson, who received from his father a substantial inheritance and a privileged education, Kant came from humble origins. In the language of modern US universities, he was a "first generation" university student. Kant began his teaching career as a private tutor in 1748 and continued until 1754. On September 27, 1755, he defended his second dissertation, "New Exposition of the First Principles of Metaphysical Knowledge," thus earning his *venia legendi*, which allowed him to lecture at the university. He was a lecturer from 1755 until 1770, when he was appointed professor of logic and metaphysics at the University of Königsberg. As a lecturer Kant had a grueling schedule, lecturing over forty hours a week; during this period, his income depended on student tuition and the general popularity of his courses.[68] Thus, he taught classes that had a broad appeal, such as his courses on physical geography and, later, his anthropology course. Kant came to understand his lecturing as a form of civic duty, as to him these courses were about providing Königsbergers with *Weltkenntnisse*, or knowledge of the world: what we would nowadays call a "cosmopolitan" education. Until his appointment as professor, however, Kant was always attempting to supplement his income and trying to live within his means. This may partly explain why in 1766, due to a fire in his old neighborhood, he decided to move into the house owned by Johann Jakob Kanter. Kanter also happened to run a bookstore on the first floor of his house, which had apartments and rooms large enough to serve as classrooms or lecture halls. Kanter also published the *Königsbergische Gelehrten und Politischen Zeitungen*, which visitors to his bookstore could read for free.[69] Kanter's house was described as the "old City Hall" and was located in the center of Königsberg, close to the *Stadtgericht*, or city courthouse.[70] One of the advantages of living in Kanter's large house is that Kant had access to the latest publications and importations of books from abroad, which he could read without having to buy them. It was in Kanter's bookstore that Kant was likely introduced to the latest publications from either the English or French academies of science, as well as the latest publications by Hume, Rousseau, and other luminaries of the then ongoing European Enlightenment.

It was during his years as a lecturer that Kant also worked in the city's public library, the *Schloßbibliotek*, which also served as the university library. He held this position for four years until 1770, notwithstanding how unappealing and physically uncomfortable the job was, as in the winter months the library was unheated. His duties there included ordering books to maintain the library's collection, and, given Kant's views about *Weltkenntnisse*, the popularity of his courses on geography and anthropology, and the explosion of travel literature during this time, Kant would have ordered some of the same volumes that would have interested Jefferson. Travel literature was singled out by Kant as one of the best sources of knowledge about human beings, second only to travel itself.[71]

All of the above is mentioned to establish why Kant left a what was a relatively small library. In 1922 Arthur Warda published a book that used a variety of sources to reconstruct the contents of Kant's library at the time of his death.[72] What Warda's findings show is the relative absence of travel literature and that in fact Juan and Ulloa's writings were not among the books in Kant's library. Yet, a reading of Kant's lecture on anthropology and his lectures on physical geography reveal that he had done extensive reading across a variety of disciplines. The lectures in anthropology, in particular, reveal Kant to have been a very well-read lecturer and philosopher.[73] Another source that confirms Kant's voracious reading habits is his correspondence, in which he sometimes discusses the books he was reading.[74] Using these sources, we can now compile a comprehensive list of Kant's lectures. For our purposes, we can establish that Kant had read, or at least perused, Juan and Ulloa, as he quotes one of their books discussed in this chapter: *Physical Geography*.[75] Here is the quote:

> Don Ulloa notes that in Cartagena in America and the surrounding regions the people become very clever very early, but their reason does not continue to grow at the same rate thereafter. The inhabitants of the hottest zone are exceptionally indolent. In some cases, this laziness is tempered to an extent by the government and by force. If an Indian sees a European walking somewhere, he supposes that he has to attend to something; when he comes back, the Indian presumes that the man has accomplished what he set out to do; but if he sees him go a third time then he thinks that the European has lost his reason, whereas in fact he has merely gone for a walk, which no Indian does, or is able to conceive of doing. The Indians are very cautious, and both these qualities [viz. indolence and caution] are also characteristic of the inhabitants of the far north. Their mental laziness is probably brought about by brandy, tobacco, opium, and other strong things. [Belief in] magic derives from timidity; and from magic comes superstition, similarly jealousy. Timidity made Indians behave like slaves in the days when they had kings, and caused them to respect them as idols, just as their indolence cause them to choose to go hungry in the forests rather than work according to the commands of their lords.[76]

Kant's reference here is rather peculiar when compared to the full passage, which I quoted above from the English translation that was already available in the 1870s. From what we read in Juan and Ulloa's discussion of Cartagena, the intention is not to demean the indigenous peoples of the area but rather to provide an insight into why their diligence and genius apparently diminished so soon. Both authors do discuss the use of tobacco, rum, and spirits but not opium; and they do not discuss slavery or superstition in the chapter in question. Kant seems to be running several different sources into his commentary or perhaps attributing to Ulloa his own prejudices, which he repeated throughout his lectures on anthropology.

Conclusion: On the Generosity of the Reader

In this chapter I have triangulated North America, South America, and Prussia by way of two pivotal Enlightenment figures brought together by a text or texts. These texts were crucial in the dissemination of scientific knowledge—they were not mythologies or demonologies about the Americas. These texts and their offshoots, furthermore, inaugurated a new type of literature that called for the education of a new kind of reader—the Enlightened Reader. This type of literature has been—perhaps pejoratively—called "travel literature." But as I have indicated, it was much more than this: it was a truly scientific literature in the sense that it reported on discoveries, discussed experiments, delineated the process of making scientific tools, articulated findings, and showed correlations of data. This literature also reported on peoples, geography, climate, fauna, flora, fluvial mappings—all with descriptions of customs, cuisine, racial mixings, and the character and ethea of the American peoples. These texts were a cornucopia of hitherto unknown facts and practices from a continent and peoples that Europe was most certainly eager to know about. These texts, in short, appeared like encyclopedias of the future; they were envoys, eager to be known and to educate, from a continent beckoning the Old World to its lands promising exotic treasures, landscapes, and peoples. At the same time, texts like those by Juan and Ulloa were reports on the status of the European "experiment" in the Americas. By the mid-1700s, a century and a half had passed since the first Europeans had landed in the Americas. Texts about the Americas from the travels of the eighteenth century were in a way a report card on the European "experiment" in the Americas. The conquest, subjugation, and extermination, both deliberate and inadvertent, of Amerindians, the Middle Passage from Africa and subsequent development of an economy and culture based on slavery and the subordination of nonwhites, most importantly, presented a challenge to Enlightenment figures and the political project of emancipation that was underwritten by the mind that dared to think for itself—*sapere aude*! For this mind, liberty, equality, and fraternity went hand in hand. I have sought to illustrate this challenge by focusing on Jefferson and Kant, both of whom confronted slavery and the subordination of the Amerindian but with different responses. Jefferson's ultimate attitude to any form of subordination and derogation was rejection. By contrast, Kant, notwithstanding theoretical declarations in the same vein, seemed inured to the consequences that slavery would have (and had already had) on the character of a people. By rereading these two figures through studying the texts they read and how they read them, I have aimed to illustrate how we can engage in practices of decolonizing the canon and reading in non-Eurocentric ways that make us children of the Enlightenment and, most importantly, Enlightened Readers.

Notes

1. I want to thank Corey McCall for his enlightened reading of my text and for some excellent suggestions for improvement. I also want to thank Grant Silva and Shaila Washwami for the invitation to present a version of this text as a keynote to a graduate student conference at Marquette University in 2019.

2. The claim can be found in a footnote to the preface of the first edition of the *Critique*: "Our age is, in especial degree, the age of criticism [*Kritik*] and to criticism everything must submit. Religion through its sanctity, and lawgiving through its majesty, may seek to exempt themselves from it. But they then awaken just suspicion and cannot claim the sincere respect that reason accords only to that which has been able to sustain the test of free and open examination." See Immanuel Kant, *Critique of Pure Reason*, trans. Norman Kemp Smith (New York: St. Martin's Press, 1929), 9.

3. See Andrea Wulff, *The Invention of Nature: Alexander von Humboldt's New World* (New York: Alfred A. Knopf, 2016).

4. See J. R. Hale, *Renaissance Exploration* (New York: W. W. Norton, 1968), 64–65.

5. See Hans Blumenberg, *Die Lesbarkeit der Welt* (Frankfurt am Main: Suhrkamp, 1986). See also Clifford Geertz, *Works and Lives: The Anthropologist as Author* (Stanford, CA: Stanford University Press, 1988), see chap. 2.

6. See Robert Darnton, *The Business of Enlightenment: Publishing History of the Encyclopédie 1775–1800* (Cambridge, MA: Belknap, 1979).

7. See Roger Hahn, *The Anatomy of a Scientific Institution: The Paris Academy of Sciences, 1666–1803* (Berkeley: University of California Press, 1971).

8. Robert Darnton, *George Washington's False Teeth: An Unconventional Guide to the Eighteenth Century* (New York and London: W. W. Norton, 2003), 25.

9. For an excellent overview of the importance of scientific expeditions and their impact in Europe, see Rob Iliffe, "Science and the Voyages of Discovery," in *The Cambridge History of Science, Volume 4: The Eighteenth-Century Science*, ed. Roy Porter (Cambridge: Cambridge University Press, 2003): 618–645.

10. Alberto Manguel, *A History of Reading* (New York: Viking, 1996), 173.

11. Mary Louise Pratt, *Imperial Eyes: Travel Writing and Transculturation*, 2nd ed. (New York and London: Routledge, 2008).

12. Manguel, *A History of Reading*, 167.

13. Manguel, 168.

14. George Juan and Antonio de Ulloa, *A Voyage to South America Describing at Large, The Spanish Cities, Towns, Provinces, &c. on That Extensive Continent, Undertaken by Command of the King of Spain*, trans. John Adams, 3rd ed. (London: Lockyer Davis, Printer of the Royal Society, 1772).

15. Merrill D. Peterson, *The Jefferson Image in the American Mind* (Charlottesville: Thomas Jefferson Memorial Foundation and University Press of Virginia, 1998), 456. Italics added for emphasis.

16. Gary Wills, *Inventing America: Jefferson's Declaration of Independence* (New York: Vintage, 2018), vi.

17. Thomas Jefferson, *The Life and Selected Writings of Thomas Jefferson*, ed. Adrienne Koch and William Peden (New York: Modern Library, 2004), xli.

18. Willard Sterne Randall, *Thomas Jefferson: A Life* (New York: Harper Perennial, 1994), 14.

19. See the Monticello Foundation's website: https://www.monticello.org/site/research-and-collections/number-letters-jefferson-wrote.

20. Jon Meacham, *Thomas Jefferson: The Art of Power* (New York: Random House, 2012), xxii. See also Dumas Malone, *The Sage of Monticello* (Boston: Little, Brown, 1981), 185–199.

21. Dumas Malone, *Jefferson and His Time*, 6 vols. (Boston: Little, Brown, 1981).

22. Noble E. Cunningham Jr., *In Pursuit of Reason: The Life of Thomas Jefferson* (Baton Rouge: Louisiana State University Press, 1987).

23. Meacham, *Thomas Jefferson*.

24. John B. Boles, *Jefferson: Architect of American Liberty* (New York: Basic Books, 2017).

25. For an insightful appraisal of the recent scholarship on Jefferson I recommend Merrill D. Peterson's introduction in Peterson, *The Jefferson Image*, v–x.

26. Jefferson, *The Life*, xxi.

27. Malone, *The Sage of Monticello*, 169.

28. Randall, *Thomas Jefferson*, 13.

29. Jefferson, *The Life*, xxv.

30. See Thomas Jefferson, *Writings* (New York: Library of America, 1984), 820–25. This letter, most appropriately entitled "Books for a Statesman" by the editors of his writings, lists books in history, geography, philosophy, as well as dictionaries and books by Pascal, Buffon, Diderot, and Voltaire, totaling 1,154 *livres* and 13 *sous*. Needless to say, the list, or the "enclosure," was formidable and ecumenical in the most positive sense possible.

31. Jefferson, *Writings*, 814–18. Quote from page 816.

32. The Library of Congress has a website dedicated to the acquisition of Jefferson's library with important original documents: https://www.loc.gov/exhibits/jefferson/jefflib.html.

33. For these quotations see Malone, *Sage of Monticello*, 177.

34. On Jefferson's role in establishing the Library of Congress in 1802, see Boles, *Jefferson*, 346–47.

35. Jefferson quoted in Malone, *Age of Monticello*, 181.

36. See Boles, *Jefferson*, 458. See also Cunningham, *In Pursuit of Reason*, 332.

37. Antonio de Ulloa, *Noticias Americanas: Entretenimiento Físico-Histórico sobre La América Meridional y al Septentrional Oriental* (Buenos Aires: Editorial Nova, 1944).

38. The Spanish edition I will refer to has a useful preface by the editor Luis Aznar, who details not only the La Condamine voyage but also provides a biographical sketch of Ulloa, as well as a history of Ulloa's publications and the history of this particular book.

39. Jefferson, *Writings*, 822.

40. Jefferson, Writings, 184–85.

41. Ulloa, *Noticias Americanas*, 252–53.

42. Jefferson, *Writings*, 185.

43. Here Jefferson is quoting a passage that occurs much later in chapter 18 of Ulloa, *Noticias Americanas*, 267, in which Ulloa in fact is talking about the inhumanity and extreme demands put on South Americans by the work imposed upon them; Jefferson, *Writings*, 185; note is at the foot of the page running from the previous page. My translation.

44. Boles, *Jefferson*, 368.

45. Jefferson, *Writings*, 270. See "Notes on the State of Virginia," Query XIV.

46. Jefferson, *Writings*, 288.

47. Jefferson, *Writings*, 289.

48. Jefferson, *Writings*, 289. See "Notes on the State of Virginia," Query XVIII.

49. Cunningham, *In Pursuit of Reason*, 62.

50. John Chester Miller, *The Wolf by the Ears: Thomas Jefferson and Slavery* (New York: Free Press, 1977), xii. This volume still remains the most comprehensive analysis of this paradox.

51. For a reproduction of the advertisement see R. B. Bernstein, *Thomas Jefferson* (New York: Oxford University Press, 2003), 144.

52. Joyce Appleby, *Thomas Jefferson* (New York: Times Books, 2003), 77.

53. E. M. Halliday, *Understanding Thomas Jefferson* (New York: Harper Collins, 2001), 142–43.

54. Peterson, *The Jefferson Image*, 457; Peterson, 172. For an analysis of the kerygmatic Jefferson in relation to abolitionism, see also Peterson's extensive discussion on pp. 171–189, which make it clear how Jefferson's ambivalent

relationship to slavery and racism did not prevent him from having a positive role in the eventual turn against the institution and its ultimate abolition. See also Dumas Malone, *Jefferson the Virginian* (Boston: Little, Brown, 1948), 264–68.

55. Appleby, *Thomas Jefferson*, 3.

56. For details on the La Condamine expedition I rely on Victor Wolfgang von Hagen's *South America Called Them: Explorations* of the Great Naturalists *La Condamine, Humboldt, Darwin, Spruce* (New York: Alfred A. Knopf, 1945), 11. This text reads more like an adventure book than a report on some of the most notable scientific expeditions of the eighteenth century. Yet, the chapter on La Condamine must surely rely on circumlocutions of several narratives published by members of his party, including La Condamine's, which are published in French but have not been translated yet. For a more sober, less colorful overview, see Pratt, *Imperial Eyes*, 16–17.

57. See Luis Aznar's introduction to Ulloa, *Noticias Americanas*.

58. Jorge Juan and Antonio de Ulloa, *Noticias Secretas de América* (Madrid: Editorial América, 1918).

59. See Aznar's introduction to Ulloa, *Noticias Americanas*, xxi.

60. Hagen, *South America Called Them*, 45–46. Italics added for emphasis.

61. See also Andrés Saumell's introduction to his edition of *Viaje a la América meridional*, in two volumes (Madrid: Historia 16, 1990). This is a Spanish edition of Juan and Ulloa's text, which Saumell claims was written solely by Ulloa, which is why Ulloa is the only one listed on the cover. Saumell's claims are based on extensive archival work, including notebooks and diaries that contain Ulloa's handwriting. Even so, Saumell's book also contains extensive and important information on the fate of the two-volume work and subsequent works.

62. Jorge Juan and Antonio de Ulloa, *A Voyage to South America*, 33–35. The passage is found in chapter 4, just in case readers have access to other editions.

63. Paul Guyer, *Kant*, 2nd ed. (London and New York: Routledge, 2014), 17.

64. Ernst Cassirer, *Kant's Life and Thought*, trans. James Haden and intro. Stephan Körner (New Haven, CT, and London: Yale University Press, 1981); Karl Jaspers, *Kant* (Orlando, FL: Harcourt Brace, 1962).

65. Manfred Kuehn, *Kant: A Biography* (Cambridge: Cambridge University Press, 2001).

66. Willi Goetschel, *Constituting Critique: Kant's Writing as Critical Praxis*, trans. Eric Schwab (Durham, NC: Duke University Press, 1994).

67. Along with Borges, I also have in mind Luciano Canfora, who has written a wonderful little book, *Libro y Libertad*, trans. Juan Manuel Salmerón (Madrid: Ediciones Siruela, 2017). A German website already exists that contains more detailed notes on Kant's reading. The website is by Elke König and most appropriately entitled "Kants Lektüre (Datenbank)" [Kant's Reading (Databank)]. It can be found here: https://www.online.uni-marburg.de/kant_old/webseitn/ka_lektu.htm.

68. Manfred Kuehn, *Kant: A Biography*, 108–9.
69. Kuehn, 159–60.
70. See the reproduction of a lithograph from 1842 in Manfred Geier, *Kants Welt. Eine Biographie* (Hamburg, Germany: Rowohlt, 2003), 122.
71. See the preface to Kant's *Anthropology from a Pragmatic Point of View* in *Anthropology, History, and Education* in *The Cambridge Edition of the Works of Immanuel Kant in Translation*, ed. Günther Zöller and Robert B. Louden, trans. Mary Gregor, et al. (Cambridge and New York: Cambridge University Press, 2007), 232.
72. Arthur Warda, *Immanuel Kants Bücher* (Berlin: Verlag von Martin Breslauer, 1922).
73. Immanuel Kant, *Lectures on Anthropology*, ed. Allen Wood and Robert Louden, trans. Robert R. Lewis, et al. (Cambridge and New York: Cambridge University Press, 2012). See also *Kant's Lectures on Anthropology*, ed. Alix Cohen (Cambridge: Cambridge University Press, 2014), which contains a series of useful critical essays.
74. Immanuel Kant, *Correspondence*, *The Cambridge Edition of the Works of Immanuel Kant in Translation*, trans. and ed. Arnulf Zweig (Cambridge and New York: Cambridge University Press, 1999).
75. For critical appraisals of Kant's physical geography see Stuart Elden and Eduardo Mendieta, eds., *Reading Kant's Geography* (Albany: State University of New York Press, 2011).
76. Immanuel Kant, *Physical Geography*, in *Natural Science* in *The Cambridge Edition of the Works of Immanuel Kant in Translation*, ed. Eric Watkins, trans. Lewis White Beck, et al. (Cambridge and New York: Cambridge University Press, 2012), 576. Bold in original.

CHAPTER FIVE

Writing Loss

On Emerson, Du Bois, and America

Corey McCall

James Baldwin begins a 1969 conversation with comedian and activist Dick Gregory at London's West Indian Student Centre by telling a story about a previous trip to London some years earlier.[1] He relates that he found himself in the British Museum where he had struck up a conversation with a guard from the British West Indies. The guard asks him where he is from, to which Baldwin replies "Harlem." This reply fails to satisfy the museum guard, who continues to press him for a more specific answer, asking about his parents ("But before that, where were you born?"). Finally, it dawns on Baldwin that what his interlocutor really wants to know is where his African ancestors had hailed from. Baldwin points out that this question is impossible for him to answer because his ancestors' "entry into America was a bill of sale." Later he relates that the name "Baldwin" was given to him as a replacement for the name he had lost, and he further implies that to be African American means having this loss inscribed upon oneself. African American history is, at least in part, the often heroic and always painful attempts by African Americans to make this loss legible by bearing witness to it and making it meaningful. Given these conditions, how does one bear the burden of one's Americanness without being crushed by it?

Furthermore, what if the idea of America and what it means to be American were constituted by loss? This is not such a far-fetched idea, although it certainly clashes with the usual triumphal story told of America as a story of progress, of brave Europeans coming to these virgin shores to claim it and make it their own in order to erect the Puritan ideal of "a Shining City on a Hill." This story of triumph usually drowns out the competing story told of America as a story of dispossession and loss. The triumphalist utopian ideal of America is one story of America; indeed, it may even be the dominant ideological tale of what America is and what it means to be American. Those who most loudly proclaim this ideal of America and this story of American identity minimize various other stories of what it means to be American: stories like Baldwin's that are constituted by dispossession and loss.

Initially this second conception of American identity, the one constituted by loss, seems to be absent from Emerson's writings. Emerson is not a writer of American loss but rather of American triumphalism. Such a view entails a white supremacist conception of American history that suppresses the dispossession of indigenous peoples and marginalizes the effects of slavery on America's identity as a republic of freedom. Indeed, James Baldwin, W. E. B. Du Bois, and other African American thinkers have defined whiteness as an attempt to evade the very question of the burden of Americanness as one defined by loss and dispossession as represented by the loss of names, cultures, families, and lands. On Baldwin's account, the substitution of a white man's name for his long-lost surname becomes a synecdoche of the loss of all these things and more.

Contrast these accounts of dispossession and loss with the dominant account of American possession and triumph according to which freedom is, in part, to be free from the burden of history and memory—or at least from the acknowledgment of history as a burden to be borne despite its often unbearable weight. No doubt Emerson's writings display his anxiety over how Americans ought to distinguish themselves from the rest of the world and thereby forge a civilization to rival what he sees as the great European ones; however, this sort of anxiety is very different from the burden and ambivalence that Baldwin has in mind when he declares, "I am an American." Both Ralph Waldo Emerson and W. E. B. Du Bois reflect upon the deaths of their firstborn sons in their work, and my essay proposes that we read these scenes of loss in terms of their very different ideas of America, what it means to be American, and how these losses in turn shape their conceptions of this identity. When we read Emerson's

"Experience" (1844) alongside Du Bois's *Souls of Black Folk* (1903), we are struck by the different approaches these two authors take in writing about loss and how they attempt to bear its burden.[2] Emerson's sense of loss isn't the same as that of du Bois and Baldwin: it's a white American sense of loss, not an African American one—and thus a disavowal of African American pain. Although both Du Bois and Emerson write their experience of loss into their work, Emerson declares that the loss of his son Waldo wasn't nearly as burdensome as he thought it would be, while Du Bois feels sadness mixed with relief at the death of his firstborn: his relief is born of the fact that his son won't have to bear the burden of American blackness—a life lived behind the veil of race. The second section of this chapter focuses on these two scenes of terrible loss before turning to the question of the necessary relationship between democracy and loss. How do their respective responses to deeply personal loss animate their writing on topics such as America, empire, self, and the world? And what happens to our conceptions of philosophy, and American philosophy in particular, when we read these two thinkers—both typically considered marginal to mainstream philosophical discourse within the United States—alongside each other on this topic of loss? I want to begin with a preliminary question, however, one that must be answered before we can proceed to these very different scenes of loss, their meaning, and their implications. The first section, on what I refer to as the "first-person political," takes up a question important both for understanding the work of Emerson and Du Bois as well as the broader questions at the center of this volume; that is, the myriad questions concerning the decolonizing of American philosophy. Accordingly, I begin with the question of the representativeness of experience and the role of leadership in the work of Emerson and Du Bois connected through their somewhat surprising shared admiration for the work of Thomas Carlyle. Whose experience matters, and whose experience is lost in the story of America? Who leads, who follows, and why? These are the basic questions at stake in this initial section.

The First-Person Political: American Genealogies, Heroic Representation, and the Question of Decolonization

Du Bois begins *Dusk of Dawn* (1940) with a consideration of what it means to write an autobiography. This is fitting, for so much of his writing stems from his own experience; however, these various autobiographical reflections admittedly exist uncomfortably with the impersonal, even objective, aims of Du Bois the social scientist.[3] Du Bois begins by worrying that his book will become "mere autobiography," presumably simply a reflection on his own personal experience without any broader implications. "But in my own experience," writes Du Bois, "autobiographies have had little lure; repeatedly they assume too much or too little: too much in dreaming that one's own life has greatly influenced the world; too little in the reticences, repressions, and distortions which come because men do not dare to be absolutely frank. My life had its significance and its only deep significance because it was part of a Problem; but that problem was, as I continue to think, the central problem of the greatest of the world's democracies and so the Problem of the future world."[4] *Dusk of Dawn* will be, then, the writing of a life through the concept of race, but it will also be the writing of a concept that takes on a life of its own.[5] Writing one's own life through the concept of race means coming to terms with one's American identity as one constituted by loss, or, as Du Bois puts it, the significance of one's life realized as a problem.

This question of the representativeness of his own experience is certainly not a new one for Du Bois in 1940; indeed, it had been one of his earliest methodological preoccupations. Robert Gooding-Williams considers this question of representativeness in a careful reading of the opening paragraphs of *Souls of Black Folk* (1903), specifically in terms of the transition from the second to the third paragraph. Du Bois famously begins *Souls* by recalling examples of the indirect questions that had often been posed to him by his fellow (white) citizens, all of which were various ways of avoiding the question they really wanted to ask: "the real question: How does it feel to be a problem?" "They approach me in a half-hesitant sort of way," writes Du Bois, "eye me curiously or compassionately, and then, instead of saying directly, How does it feel to be a problem? They say, I know an excellent colored man in my town; or, I thought at Mechanicsville; or, Do not these Southern outrages make your blood boil?"[6] Just as Du Bois cites a lack of frankness in his opening remarks on autobiography in *Dusk of Dawn*, he begins his earlier book with an observation of how people avoid directly posing the question they really want to ask. Clearly, his fellow white citizens suffer from a lack of frankness. Although he rarely answers these various questions anyhow, he begins with a direct answer, that is, with an account of his own experience of being a problem. Significantly for our purposes, Du Bois reports that he has been a problem for much of his life, "save perhaps in babyhood and in Europe."[7] His unproblematic childhood idyll is abruptly shattered when a new classmate whom he describes as "a tall girl" refuses his visiting card that students had been "merrily" exchanging until her arrival. It is in this moment that he feels his difference from his other (white) classmates for the first time.[8] How is his experience representative?

This raises the question of the representativeness of autobiography and whether one life can possibly represent the life of another individual, much less the life of a people or a race.[9] This is a question that Emerson, too, considers at various points throughout his work, and this question becomes the focus of his lectures published as *Representative Men* (1850). By what right can I speak on behalf of another? And by what authority can my voice supplant hers? Emerson sees the men in these lectures as representatives of various traits of the mind of humanity: Plato the philosopher, Swedenborg the mystic, Montaigne the skeptic, Shakespeare the poet, Napoleon the man of the world, and Goethe the writer. Emerson's Transcendentalism is indebted to German Idealism and British Romanticism, so he understands the representativeness of these great men in terms of a transcendent mind of a people. In other words, these great men represent the mind of the people. Although this may seem like a muddleheaded view, there is nothing explicitly racist about it. Yet Emerson's mentor, Thomas Carlyle, was disappointed by the essays, for they did not jibe with his demagogic sense of the heroic.

Carlyle had given his famous lectures *On Heroes, Hero Worship, and the Heroic in History* to an adoring London crowd ten years before Emerson published *Representative Men*. Ernst Cassirer captures the political significance of Carlyle's lectures, and anticipating historian Nell Irvin Painter's subsequent characterization of them, he sees how the ideas motivating these lectures were political dynamite despite Carlyle's intentions: "As Carlyle says in one of his letters 'bishops and all kinds of people had appeared; they heard something new and seemed greatly astonished and greatly pleased. They laughed and applauded.' But assuredly none of the hearers could think for a moment that the ideas expressed in these lectures contained a dangerous explosive. Nor did Carlyle himself feel this way. He was no revolutionary; he was a conservative. He wished to stabilize the social and political order and he was convinced that for such a stabilization he could recommend no better means than hero worship."[10] Despite his conservative intentions, Cassirer sees Carlyle's account of Victorian hero-worship as a pivotal stop on the way to National Socialism, though Cassirer is more circumspect than those who see Carlyle's hero-worship as a direct precursor to the *Führer* principle.[11] Carlyle sees history as a series of biographies of great men. "To him history was no system—it was a great panorama. History, he declared in his essay on biography, is the essence of innumerable biographies."[12] So we have three possibilities then: the representativeness of one as the member of a race (Du Bois), the representativeness of one as a bearer of culture (Emerson), and the representativeness of one as a leader of society (Carlyle).

Carlyle conceives of the individual hero as the representative of a people. In his book *The Right to Look*, Nicholas Mirzoeff characterizes Carlyle's project as "part of a dramatic reconfiguration of historical events into the metaphysical narratives of History that involved new technical procedures and new literary styles, derived from German Romanticism."[13] Carlyle sees history in visual terms; indeed, Mirzoeff cites one of Emerson's letters to Carlyle in which he claims "I think you see in pictures."[14] For Carlyle, history designated a field of visual simultaneity rather than a succession of discrete events: "This pictorial vision was in a sense literally History painting, that is to say, the leading genre of painting that was celebrated for its ability to sustain a narrative within a single frame and reached its highpoint as official art of the nineteenth century. In similar fashion, visuality ordered and narrated the chaotic events of modern life in intelligible, visualized forms into moving pictures."[15] The hero has the vision to order the chaotic field of simultaneous events into a coherent whole. According to Mirzoeff, "Carlyle consolidated and embodied his theory of History into the Hero, who had the vision to see History as it happened. . . . The visualized Hero was the true source of light and enlightenment, his insight stemming from a quasi-divine nobility to which it is pleasant to submit, generating its sense of the aesthetic. Indeed, visuality was named as part of the Christian Heroism of Dante."[16] Carlyle admits that the mechanism by which the hero obtains her authority over history and its subjects is mysterious, and it is that mysteriousness Max Weber will later characterize as charisma that gives Ernst Cassirer pause, leading him see Carlyle's hero as a precursor to the *Führer*.

In Emerson's texts we also find a plea for the representativeness of an individual as a member of a race. Emerson was fascinated by the Anglo-Saxon race, and he sought to show how white Americans belonged to Carlyle's allegedly master race. We tend to remember Emerson for his various declarations of cultural independence from the British (most famously in "Self-Reliance") and his impassioned defense of abolitionism, but we are less apt to recall the writer whose deep admiration for Thomas Carlyle's work led him to articulate a conception of American identity based on

Anglo-Saxon cultural values that included Anglo-Saxon racial superiority. Nell Irvin Painter points out the depths of Emerson's fascination with Thomas Carlyle and his theory of the supremacy of the Anglo-Saxon race.[17] Painter's critique rests on an incisive reading of Emerson's *English Traits*, a somewhat neglected series of lectures first published in 1856.[18] Despite his earnest plea for American self-reliance in such essays as "The American Scholar" and "Self-Reliance," by the 1850s he had become enamored of an idea of America as an integral part of a Greater Anglo-Saxony that would include both Germany and Great Britain. Surprisingly, Carlyle's virulent racism and racialism exerted a powerful influence on Du Bois as well.

Although obviously never a fan of Anglo-Saxon racial superiority, Du Bois did espouse a version of Carlyle's leadership principle in *Souls of Black Folk*, and his admiration for the black elite is something he would not overcome until the 1930s.[19] David Levering Lewis was the first to note this surprising influence in his biography of Du Bois, and it is further analyzed by Robert Gooding-Williams. Gooding-Williams flags the reference to Carlyle in the third chapter of *Souls of Black Folk*, a chapter perhaps most remembered for Du Bois's trenchant critique of Booker T. Washington. Du Bois writes of those who critique democracy and the dangers of silencing them:

> Honest and earnest criticism from those whose interests are most nearly touched, —criticism of writers by readers, of government by those governed, of leaders by those led, —this is the soul of democracy and the safeguard of modern society. If the best of American Negroes receive by outer pressure a leader whom they had not recognized before, manifestly there is a certain palpable gain. Yet there is also irreparable loss, —a loss of that peculiarly valuable education which a group receives when by search and criticism it finds and commissions its own leaders.

Du Bois distinguishes between three types of leadership: revolt, adjustment (Booker T. Washington is the key exemplar here), and self-realization, both in the demand for rights and self-formation, which is the kind of leadership Du Bois ultimately endorses.[20] I want to linger a bit longer over "this irreparable loss" that Du Bois names in the above passage. When the leader is an outsider—the most obvious candidate being a white political leader, or perhaps even a prophetic figure such as John Brown (the subject of a biography by Du Bois)—there is an undeniable gain. But there is also an irreparable loss. What are these gains and losses?

Du Bois begins the third chapter of *Souls* by commenting on a loss. "Easily the most striking thing in the history of the American Negro since 1876 is the ascendancy of Mr. Booker T. Washington. It began at the time when war memories and ideals were rapidly passing; a day of astonishing commercial development was dawning; a sense of doubt and hesitation overtook the freedmen's sons,—then it was his leading began."[21] Famously, Du Bois wants to contrast his conception of leadership with Booker T. Washington's accommodation of white Southerners who will consent to black education only on the condition that it be limited to manual labor. This compromise was unacceptable to Du Bois because it left the racist social framework intact; however, this certainly does not mean that he rejected Carlyle's conception of the hero altogether. On the contrary, his notion of the "Talented Tenth" is predicated upon Carlyle's idea of history as an artifact crafted by the heroic individual. Nevertheless, his conceptions of heroic representation differ from Emerson's in two important respects. First, even when he is at his most elitist, Du Bois believes that history can never be a teleological story, regardless of whether the teleology is Hegel's or Carlyle's, and it certainly can never be a story of racial triumphalism. Acknowledgment of loss is antithetical to a triumphal history of progress. In the third chapter of *Dusk of Dawn*, Du Bois discusses how the ideology of history as progress had become commonplace in American classrooms by 1885. Around this time the ideals of education increasingly became subject to the dictates of commerce, a resurgent trend in today's classrooms (assuming it ever left). "Invention and technique were a perpetual marvel and their accomplishment infinite in possibility; commerce was madly seeking markets all around the earth; colonies were being seized and countries integrated in Asia, Africa, South American, and the Islands."[22] Du Bois claims that he, too, would have become a booster for the commercialization of education were it not for the "race problem early thrust upon me and enveloping me."[23] His initial criticisms weren't directed at this movement itself but merely at the exclusivity of those who were permitted to participate. Du Bois always saw African American identity in global terms. Consequently, even his earliest writings sought to frame American identity in global terms, despite their glorification of heroes such as Bismarck. Despite his fascination with figures such as Carlyle and Bismarck, Du Bois's consistent efforts to understand America in global terms are evidence of his decolonial approach to philosophy, which is a consistent feature of his thought from the very beginning. His 1896 monograph, *The Suppression of the African Slave Trade to the United States 1638–1870*, focuses on various efforts by the government to suppress the English slave trade (in order to more effectively control and thereby profit from it) at the end of the seventeenth century before turning to the American context and concluding with the Civil War. Du Bois's study was one of the first to insist on the economic impact of slavery for all the nations that participated: "That the slave trade was the very life of the colonies had, by 1700, become an almost unquestioned axiom in British practical economics."[24] This early text already shows how the politics of empire is inextricably intertwined with the politics of slavery. The contrast with Emerson's efforts to expand Carlyle's account of Anglo-Saxon racial supremacy to include white Americans should be evident.

This opening section has examined how representation works in Emerson and Du Bois in order to show that both thinkers draw upon Carlyle's heroic conception of history but for very different reasons. Despite his anti-slavery stance, Emerson remains enamored of Carlyle's heroic Anglo-Saxon, and this makes it impossible for him to embrace even a nascent decolonial philosophy. Du Bois, too, is fascinated by Carlyle's hero, and this fascination is manifested in his call for the cultural elite (the "Talented Tenth") to guide African Americans as they navigate the horrors of life in a white supremacist nation. Despite his elitism, Du Bois always frames American and African American experience within a global context, and he eventually revises his earlier elitism to argue for a decolonial politics of race.[25] With these questions of political representation in mind, in the next section I turn to the specific scenes of loss found in the work of Emerson and Du Bois.

Two Scenes of Loss: How Emerson and Du Bois Represent the Experience of Grief and the Idea of America

Emerson relates the experience of his grief occasioned by the loss of his firstborn son, Waldo, in his 1850 essay "Experience." Du Bois provides a complementary account of the loss of his firstborn son, Burghardt, in his 1903 *Souls of Black Folk*. What do these losses represent, and how do they simultaneously complement one another and also provide us with very different conceptions of the idea of America? The differences are more clearly evident, so I begin with them before turning to the somewhat surprising similarities in their accounts of loss.

Conventional wisdom holds that loss leaves us bereft, but could a fundamental experience such as the death of a child leave us completely untouched? This is the question Emerson poses in "Experience." Beginning with what has become an iconic image of experience as a staircase we find ourselves in the middle of, Emerson proceeds to argue that in fact most experiences leave us untouched, for we live distracted lives caught in an interminable series of ephemeral presents stretching between past and future. If he can show that even the most extreme experiences of loss can largely pass unfelt and unremarked upon, then it follows that more mundane experiences would typically be even less remarkable. Emerson opens the essay with the question "Where do we find ourselves?" and proceeds to answer that there's a good chance we may never find ourselves at all. "We wake and find ourselves on a stair; there are stairs below us, which we seem to have ascended; there are stairs above us, many a one, which go upward out of sight."[26] Drawing on imagery from Plato's Myth of Er that concludes *The Republic*, Emerson notes that the draughts from the River Lethe that we were given were too strong, causing us to become lethargic and unfeeling. "But the genius which, according to the old belief, stands at the door by which we enter, and gives us the lethe to drink, that we may tell no tales, mixed the cup too strongly, and we cannot shake off the lethargy now at noonday."[27] As a result, Emerson asserts that we live lives that are "ghostlike," for "we glide through nature and should not know our place again."[28] The human condition is one of loss in which the tangible things we most want to grasp slip through our fingers. Indeed, this is our lot, what Emerson terms our "unhandsome condition."[29]

But this "unhandsome condition," this condition that renders everything ungraspable, seems to be a corollary of Emerson's notion of self-reliance. One of Emerson's most well-known essays, "Self-Reliance" issues a call for radical autonomy in which the individual eschews convention in favor of whim. Or at least that's how it initially seems. Indeed, Stanley Cavell reminds us that this initial reading of self-reliance in terms of autonomy is probably overhasty. Instead, he provides an account of Emerson's self-reliance as a form of "aversive thinking." Citing "Self-Reliance" as a way of interpreting Emerson's project as a work of both writing and democracy, Cavell writes:

> "The virtue in most request is conformity. Self-reliance is its aversion." I gather him there to be characterizing his writing, hence to mean that he writes in aversion to society's demand

for conformity, specifically that his writing expresses his self-consciousness, his thinking as the imperative to an incessant conversion or refiguration of society's incessant demands for his consent—his conforming itself to its doings; and at the same time to mean that his writing must accordingly be the object of aversion to society's consciousness, to what it might read in him. His imperative is registered in the outcry a few paragraphs later, "Every word they say chagrins us." Emerson is not, then, as the context might imply, expressing merely his general disappointment at some failure in the capacity of language to represent the world but also expressing, at the same time, his response to a general attitude toward words that is causing his all but complete sense of intellectual isolation.[30]

I cite Cavell's lengthy and somewhat convoluted passage because it shows that Emerson's melancholy conclusion in "Experience"—that we glide over the surfaces of the things without grasping them—is not simply a matter of knowing or not knowing the world; it has political implications as well. As Cavell notes, it is a matter of consent. Judith Shklar argues that what's at stake in the Emersonian conception of self-reliance is the process of making society's conventions one's own: instead of being defined by them, one defines them for oneself. "What, then, is self-reliance to achieve?" Shklar asks. "It is not a call to reject the usual bonds of family life but to take them as one's own discovery. Making one's own rules is a new life and, indeed, the only remaining possibility for constructing a law out of that transforming experience of nature. Nature, to be sure, might be a universal territory of exploration. Supposing that it were, then there is no reason to exclude anyone who did not turn one's back on nature."[31] As Shklar notes, Emerson's exemplar here is the Yankee farmer. "There are untutored yeomen in Vermont and in New Hampshire who were for Emerson, no less than for Jefferson before him, the embodiment of Yankee ideals."[32] Even if the situation is more complex than turning one's back on society, this conception of self-reliance remains problematic. At the very least, we can claim that Emerson's self-reliant individual finds her direct antecedents in the figures of Kant's autonomous individual and Carlyle's heroic individual. If this is true, then it would imply that Emerson's concept of self-reliance is susceptible to the same charges of racism leveled against Kant's autonomous individual and Carlyle's heroic individual.[33] Furthermore, the privilege of self-reliance assumes a political and legal framework in which one's personhood is recognized. After all, one can leave everything behind in order to become autonomous only if one has something to leave behind. If even the experience of profound loss is fungible and ultimately leaves us unmoved, then all experience is fungible. Emerson believes that our only hope lies in making experience our own, that is, in the project of attentive self-reliance. But this owning of experience through self-reliance can only be truly democratic if it acknowledges loss, something which Emerson is apparently unable to do. I return to this problem in the final section. But suffice it to say here that the problem is precisely that without the ability to feel loss, a truly democratic polity in which everyone's voice is heard and everyone's experience acknowledged remains impossible. Emerson's experience is colored through his eyes only. As Du Bois would have it, we continue to live behind the veil, despite all our democratic pretensions to the contrary.

Robert Gooding-Williams contrasts Emerson's account of self-reliance with Frederick Douglass's account of dignity won through violence. Douglass's account of his fight with the brutal slave overseer Covey is a vivid reminder of Hegel's struggle for recognition, in which violent confrontation is the condition for recognition of personhood and its attendant rights:

> In "Self-Reliance," Emerson proclaims that "the moment [a man] acts from himself, tossing the laws, the books, idolatries and customs out of the window, we pity him no more but thank and revere him." Commenting on his fight with Covey, Douglass echoes but revises Emerson when he writes that "a man, without force, is without the essential dignity of humanity. Human nature is so constituted that it cannot *honor* a helpless man, although it can *pity* him; and even this it cannot do long, if the signs of power do not arise."[34]

If one is a slave or among those whose personhood otherwise goes unrecognized by society, then one's only recourse is force: violence must be met with violence, or else the wretched man or woman will earn nothing more than pity from those in power. Gooding-Williams continues, "In rewriting Emerson, Douglass highlights a form of dependence that Emerson's great essay neglects: to wit, a slave's dependence on his master's power of arbitrary interference."[35]

Emerson's meditation on loss unfolds within this dynamic of self-reliance. "The only thing grief has taught me is how shallow it is," he reports.³⁶ Even grief "plays about the surface" and fails to capture reality as it truly is. One senses here another Kantian legacy, for even the pain of grief cannot transcend phenomena and get to the things themselves.³⁷ Emerson concludes that experience is dictated by moods, and our various moods color experience. A second image governs the essay: "Life is a train of moods like a string of beads, and, as we pass through them, they prove to be many-colored lenses which paint the world in their own hue, and each shows only what lies in its own focus. From the mountain you see the mountain. We animate what we can, and we see only what we animate. Nature and books belong to the eyes that see them."³⁸ Not even grief can touch him: "In the death of my son, now more than two years ago, I seem to have lost a beautiful estate,—no more. I cannot get it nearer to me." His final grief is that his grief leaves him untouched.³⁹ He characterizes this loss as "caducous," which the *Oxford English Dictionary* tells us is a zoological term that refers to parts of an organism that "fall off naturally when they have served their purpose."⁴⁰ The only thing, Emerson concludes, that might finally touch us is death. Douglass avers that the only thing the powerful recognize is violence and the threat of death.

Like Douglass before him, Du Bois also revises Emerson. Du Bois begins with the comingled feelings of fear and joy that dog all new parents as they gaze upon their children for the first time. "Then the fear of fatherhood mingled wildly with the joy of creation; I wondered how it looked and how it felt—what were its eyes, and how its hair curled and crumpled itself."⁴¹ But joy and fear are quickly supplanted by another mood, for Du Bois sees himself in his son:

> I held him in my arms, after we had sped far away to our Georgia home—held him, and glanced at the hot red soil of Georgia and the breathless city of a hundred hills, and felt a vague unrest. Why was his hair tinted with gold? An evil omen was golden hair in my life. Why had not the brown of his eyes crushed and killed the blue?—for brown were his father's eyes, and his father's father's. And thus in the Land of the Color-line I saw, as it fell across my baby, the shadow of the Veil.⁴²

Seeing his own features and those of his father's face in his newborn son reminds him of the tragic hardships of race that his son will have to endure as well. "I saw the shadow of the Veil as it passed over my baby, I saw the cold city towering above the blood-red land." Du Bois cannot look upon the face of his son without remembering that his tiny face is also marked for pain and suffering—that his history is a history of loss that cannot leave him untouched. Emerson writes as one who is settled and who needs to turn his back on that settlement in order to become self-reliant, while Du Bois writes as one whose life is characterized by striving. Indeed, Du Bois uses this word to characterize his response to the devastating loss of his son Burghardt. "I shirk not. I long for work. I pant for a life full of striving. I am no coward, to shrink before the awful shadow of the Veil. But hearken, O Death! Is not this my life hard enough,—is not all the world beyond these four little walls pitiless enough, but that thou must enter here,—thou, O death?"[43] Although Du Bois cannot remain untouched by this loss, there is some irony to be found in the realization that the death of young Burghardt means that his son will remain untouched by the veil: that uniquely American yet global white supremacist regime that consigns people to oblivion based solely because of the color of their skin.

Conclusion: A Politics of Loss?

We can conclude that Du Bois's response to the loss of his firstborn son opens a space for a politics of loss absent from Emerson's writings. Juliet Hooker has recently argued that the avoidance of loss defines white political imaginaries.[44] Beginning with Ida B. Wells's observation that the violence of the lynch mob was motivated at least in part by southern *"resentment that the Negro was no longer his plaything, his servant, and his source of income,"* Hooker traces the lineaments of white resentment and inability to acknowledge any losses save for their own.[45] In the early twenty-first century, white racial resentments continue to shape the white political imaginary (or at least the political imaginary of many white supporters of President Trump) at the same time as African American protests seek to dismantle the racist institutions that continue to define state power in the United States today, such as police departments, prisons, and the criminal justice system that supports them.[46]

Reading Emerson and Du Bois together on loss, Thomas Dumm reminds us that the experience of loss cannot be an end but must instead provide a beginning:

> When we turn back to the world from the place of loss, we might come to know that turning, not necessarily as redemptive,

but as resignative, as a re-signing of our contract to be with others. Thus the turn toward the world from a place of loss is the turn toward politics, toward constructing common and uncommon spaces of agonistic exchange and misunderstanding, of revelation and projection, of new coinages and destructions, partial and fragmentary, neither utopian nor dystopian, but, as Emerson would suggest, encompassing both.[47]

A politics of loss on Dumm's account would make possible the creation of new relations among individuals and groups that acknowledge loss among whites and nonwhites alike as the basis for the forging of something new, a true democracy rather than the *herrenvolk* democracy that currently obtains in the United States. In short, it would provide the basis for a remaking of our society into a truly racial democracy for the first time.

White identity resists such acknowledgment and thereby traps us in the recurrence of the same old destructive political frameworks this country was founded upon. Indeed, drawing on the work of political theorists such as Frederick Douglass, W. E. B. Du Bois, and Danielle Allen, Juliet Hooker argues that loss is the proper condition of democracy. Without the acknowledgment of loss, democracy remains either a sham or a distant dream; however, in *Herrenvolk* democracies like our own, white people are accustomed only to ruling and never sacrificing. "White dominance has resulted in a narrow political imagination that constrains the way whites understand citizenship, as asymmetrical access to institutional political power vis-à-vis racial "others." [. . .] In such an understanding of democratic politics as a zero-sum game in which gains by other groups are experienced as losses by the dominant group, white losses become magnified while black losses are rendered invisible," writes Hooker. Because the true depths of loss felt by nonwhite groups are disavowed (they occur "behind the Veil," according to Du Bois), the only losses that can be registered are those that occur to white people. Donald Trump's political success serves as a reminder that the white citizens in the United States cannot accept their loss of mastery. Hooker, in citing Du Bois's 1940 essay "The White World" from *Dusk of Dawn* in which he recounts a white friend's realization that he abided by a white code that rested on his whiteness, shows how white citizens simultaneously disavow losses that aren't perceived as their own while characterizing nonwhite citizens as outsiders that threaten their stranglehold on power.[48] Along with the awareness of this "fact" of whiteness comes the realization that whiteness is a worldview that holds "that colored folks were a threat to the world."[49] Whiteness is a code that begins with war "against the darker races carried out now and without too nice discrimination as to who were dark."[50] This code continues with exploitation, an iron law that holds that "the poor must be poor so that the Rich may be Rich," and, "finally, Empire: the white race as ruler of all the world and the world working for it, and the world piled up for the white man's use. This may seem harsh and selfish and yet, of course, it was perfectly natural."[51]

We still live in this world, one in which the purported naturalness of empire and the white presumption to rule must be lost before a truly egalitarian American society can be born. Emerson's imperviousness to the experience of loss, his self-reliance, and his glorification of Anglo-Saxon identity reinforce the foundations of this world, while Du Bois's insistence that loss is a burden that must be borne if we are to remake the world is a lesson that too many people still need to learn. Or, as Hooker writes, "If the so-called liberal democracies of the West are to become truly racially egalitarian, white citizens will need to accept the loss of political mastery. They will have to come to accept being ruled in turn."[52]

Note

1. "Dick Gregory with James Baldwin," accessed August 13, 2017, https://www.youtube.com/watch?v=yvDXdyjv674. Baldwin's recounting of this encounter is made more poignant and relevant today with news of a proposal that requires African Americans to reveal exactly where in Africa their ancestors originated. While DNA technology might eventually make this technologically possible, it raises really difficult moral and political issues related to identity. For example, might this demand be a tacit attempt by US governments to "other" African Americans and deny them equal membership in the national community? Will people be willing to answer this question? And, if not, will this lead to an under count? https://www.npr.org/2018/03/13/593272215/for-the-first-time-2020-census-will-ask-black-americans-about-their-exact-origin, accessed November 11, 2018.

2. Although these two scenes of wrenching loss have rarely been juxtaposed and analyzed, one profound exception can be found in the work of Thomas Dumm in his book *Loneliness as a Way of Life* (Cambridge, MA: Harvard University Press, 2009). I discuss Dumm's juxtaposition of Emerson and Du Bois in the final section of this essay.

3. Lorraine Daston and Peter Galison provide a historical account of the development of objectivity as an ideal of scientific research in their book *Objec-

tivity (New York: Zone, 2010). An excellent defense of Du Bois's defining role in American sociology can be found in Aldon D. Morris, *The Scholar Denied: W.E.B. Du Bois the Birth of Modern Sociology* (Oakland: University of California Press, 2015).

4. W. E. B. Du Bois, *Dusk of Dawn* in *W.E.B. Du Bois Writings*, ed. Nathan Huggins (New York: Library of America, 1986), 551.

5. Lawrie Balfour nicely summarizes Du Bois's aims in *Dusk of Dawn*: "By marrying an act of creative self-constitution to an inquiry into the constitution of the modern concept of race in this way, he offers a layered account of racial power and the possibility of freedom. Yet Du Bois is no mere example, and he trades on his readers' awareness of that fact. At 70 years of age, he is a prominent, if embattled, political figure and an established scholar and writer." See Lawrie Balfour, *Democracy's Reconstruction: Thinking Politically with W.E.B. Du Bois* (Oxford: Oxford University Press, 2011), 75–76.

6. W. E. B. Du Bois, *The Souls of Black Folk*, ed. David W. Blight and Robert Gooding-Williams (Boston: Bedford/St. Martin's, 1997), 37.

7. Du Bois, *The Souls of Black Folk*, 37.

8. Robert Gooding-Williams undertakes a close reading of the first five paragraphs of *The Souls of Black Folk* in the second chapter of *In the Shadow of Du Bois: Afro-Modern Political Thought in America* (Cambridge, MA: Harvard University Press, 2009), 70–88. In his analysis of the second paragraph of *Souls*, he argues that the Victorian practice of exchanging visiting cards was a ritual of belonging that cemented the social bond between individuals. "In [Du Bois'] view the girl's refusal is tantamount to—or, in adult society, would be tantamount—to an unwillingness to recognize him as a player in the game of card exchanges; it expresses her antipathy to acknowledging that any of the game's constitutive deontic statuses apply to him." (See Gooding-Williams, *In the Shadow*, 76.) Gooding-Williams goes on to suggest that this scene can be read as an allegory for the denial of African American membership in American society.

9. Garry Hagberg takes up this question through a reflection on the role that the concept of autobiography plays in Wittgenstein's thought. See *Describing Ourselves: Wittgenstein and Autobiographical Consciousness* (Oxford: Oxford University Press, 2011).

10. Ernst Cassirer, *The Myth of the State* (New Haven, CT: Yale University Press, 1946), 189.

11. Cassirer, *The Myth of the State*, 190–191.

12. Cassirer, 191.

13. Nicholas Mirzoeff, *The Right to Look: A Counterhistory of Visuality* (Durham, NC: Duke University Press, 2011), 138. Mirzoeff's book shows how imperial projects sought to order the visual field and highlights the various forms of resistance to this ordering of the visual.

14. Cited in Mirzoeff, *The Right to Look*, 139.

15. Mirzoeff, 139.

16. Mirzoeff, 141.

17. Nell Irvin Painter, *The History of White People* (New York: W. W. Norton, 2010). Chapters 10 to 12 focus on the racial subtext of Emerson's project and his various attempts to extend Carlyle's defense of Anglo-Saxonism to include North America.

18. Although *English Traits* has not received the attention of Emerson's other works, some exceptional work on this text has been published. For a fascinating interpretation that focuses on the role that natural history plays in *English Traits*, see David LaRocca, *Emerson's English Traits and the Natural History of Metaphor* (London: Bloomsbury, 2013).

19. Cedric J. Robinson argues that *Black Reconstruction* (1935) contains Du Bois's critique of the black elite. "One of the most revealing aspects of *Black Reconstruction* was Du Bois' assessment of the Black *petit bourgeoisie,* that element of Black society with which he had been most closely associated for most of his then 67 years." See Cedric J. Robinson, *Black Marxism: The Making of the Black Radical Tradition* (Chapel Hill: University of North Carolina Press, 2000), 205.

20. Robert Gooding-Williams, *In the Shadow of Du Bois: Afro-Modern Political Thought in America* (Cambridge, MA: Harvard University Press, 2009), 25. Both Carlyle's influence and the influence of German social thought can be found here: as Gooding-Williams notes, this is the ideal of *Bildung* developed by German Enlightenment and Romantic thinkers. Anthony Appiah analyzes the influence of German thought on Du Bois in *Lines of Descent: W.E.B. Du Bois and the Emergence of Identity* (Cambridge, MA: Harvard University Press, 2014). Appiah traces the influence of German Romantic thought, in particular Johann Gottfried Herder and Wilhelm von Humboldt, on his conception of *Bildung* and the relationship between individual and community.

21. W. E. B. Du Bois, *The Souls of Black Folk*, ed. David W. Blight and Robert Gooding-Williams (Boston: Bedford/St. Martin's 1997), 62.

22. Du Bois, *Writings*, 573.

23. Du Bois, 573.

24. Du Bois, 10–11.

25. Recently Andrew Lanham has detailed Du Bois's final years, including his work raising money for decolonial struggles in Africa and his surveillance and trial in 1951. Labeled a subversive for circulating an antinuclear petition, he was tried in federal court and financially ruined as a result. Lanham recounts how he was led to reflect on Du Bois's trial and its consequences as a result of Jeff Sessions's claim that the NAACP was an "un-American" organization during his confirmation hearings. See "When W. E. B. Du Bois Was Un-American," *Boston Review*, January 13, 2017, http://bostonreview.net/race-politics/andrew-lanham-when-w-e-b-du-bois-was-un-american.

26. Ralph Waldo Emerson, "Experience," in *Emerson: Essays and Poems*, ed. Joel Porte et al. (New York: Library of America, 1996), 471.

27. Emerson, "Experience," 471.
28. Emerson, 471.
29. Emerson, 471.
30. Stanley Cavell, "Aversive Thinking: Emersonian Representations in Emerson and Heidegger," *Conditions Handsome and Unhandsome: The Constitution of Emersonian Perfectionism* (Chicago: University of Chicago Press, 1990), 37.
31. Judith Shklar, "Emerson and the Inhibitions of Democracy," *Political Theory* 18, no. 4 (November 1990), 603.
32. Shklar, "Emerson and the Inhibitions of Democracy," 603.
33. While I've discussed the racism inherent in Carlyle's concept of the heroic individual above, Robert Bernasconi expertly traces the racism in Kant's philosophical project in several insightful pieces. See, for example, "Will the Real Kant Please Stand Up? The Challenges of Enlightenment Racism to the Study of the History of Philosophy," *Radical Philosophy* 117 (January/February 2003), 13–22.
34. Robert Gooding-Williams, *In the Shadow of Du Bois: Afro-Modern Political Thought in America* (Cambridge, MA: Harvard University Press, 2009), 177. The literature on Hegel's master-slave dialectic is vast, but a good place to start is Robert R. Williams, *Hegel's Ethics of Recognition* (Berkeley: University of California Press, 2000). Alexandre Kojéve's reading of Hegel, though idiosyncratic, is engaging and an enormous influence on twentieth-century French thought. See Alexandre Kojéve, *Introduction to the Reading of Hegel: Lectures on the Phenomenology of Spirit*, ed. Allan Bloom, trans. James H. Nichols Jr. (Ithaca, NY: Cornell University Press, 1969).
35. Kojéve, *Introduction to the Reading of Hegel*.
36. Emerson, "Experience," 472.
37. Cavell considers this Kantian heritage in Emerson's conception of experience in his earliest essays on Emerson, "Thinking of Emerson" from 1978, republished in Stanley Cavell, *Emerson's Transcendental Etudes*, ed. David Justin Hodge (Stanford, CA: Stanford University Press, 2003), 9–19.
38. Cavell, *Emerson's Transcendental Etudes*, 473.
39. Cavell, 473.
40. "Caducous," *Oxford English Dictionary*, accessed November 25, 2018, http://www.oed.com/view/Entry/25998?redirectedFrom=caducous#eid.
41. Du Bois, *Souls of Black Folk*, 159.
42. Du Bois, 160.
43. Kwame Anthony Appiah analyzes the influence of German thought on Du Bois's work, with a special focus on the Romantic roots of his conception of striving:

Consider the essay in *Souls* that Du Bois called "Of Our Spiritual Strivings" (adapted from his 1897 *Atlantic* article "Strivings of the Negro People"). The German word for striving is *streben*. In the later eighteenth century, Fichte had taken that word, which occurs often in the writings of Lutheran Pietists (who were constantly, well, striving for holiness and toward God), and made it one of the key technical ideas of his development of Kantian philosophy. Striving is Fichte's term for human action, the process in which the self-overcomes the resistance of the external world; or, as he puts it, the I acts on a resistant not-I (*nicht-Ich*). Given the intellectual world he inhabited—he conversed with Friedrich Schiller and Wilhelm von Humboldt, both of whom he knew when he had his first chair of philosophy at Jena (he later took a chair at the University of Berlin); and the works of Goethe and Herder were always near at hand—we wouldn't want to suggest the romantic taste for the idea of striving derives from him alone. But streben, like Geist, is a word that had both a wide circulation and narrower technical uses. Someone who was, like Du Bois, an heir to this intellectual history must have taken up these concepts with a sense of their philosophical weight.

(Kwame Anthony Appiah, *Lines of Descent: W.E.B. Du Bois and the Emergence of Identity* [Cambridge, MA: Harvard University Press, 2014], 54–55).

44. Juliet Hooker, "Black Protest/White Grievance: On the Problem of White Political Imaginations Not Shaped by Loss," *South Atlantic Quarterly* 116, no. 3 (July 2017): 483–504.

45. Cited by Hooker in "Black Protest/White Grievance," 483. (Hooker added the emphasis on "resentment" in the above quotation.)

46. Hooker, 483–484.

47. Dumm, *Loneliness as a Way of Life*, 166.

48. Du Bois, *Writings*, 671.

49. Du Bois, 671.

50. Du Bois, 672.

51. Du Bois, 673.

52. Hooker, "Black Protest/White Grievance," 488.

CHAPTER SIX

Latina Feminist Engagements with US Pragmatism

Interrogating Identity, Realism, and Representation

ANDREA J. PITTS

In this chapter, I focus on three Latina feminist approaches that utilize distinct strands of Anglo-American pragmatism and neopragmatism to interpret the normative dynamics of social identities. Toward this end, I examine how each author positions their view of social identities through debates about pragmatist approaches to practices of inquiry and questions of realism and representationalism. Similar to other transcultural variations of non-Anglo-American philosophical research, the three Latina feminist theorists I discuss analyze whether we can repurpose tools from US Anglo-American philosophical trajectories to address the concerns of women of color. The three approaches that I examine are Jacqueline M. Martinez's Peircean-inspired account of semiotic phenomenology; Paula M. L. Moya's conception of postpositivist realism; and Linda Martín Alcoff's critique of Rortyan antirepresentationalism.[1] Each theorist, I propose, employs arguments that effectively emphasize the historically contingent and highly contested nature of social identities while also seeking to preserve political forms of stability and a normative significance for identity. In addition, each approach responds to debates regarding whether or how to privilege first-person forms of epistemic and political authority for persons from historically marginalized groups. In this vein, the conceptual thematic of selfhood and identity within Latina feminism remains a core concern. As such, the main goals of this chapter are: (1) to examine how Latina feminist interventions within debates regarding how the epistemic and political authority of marginalized social identity categories either augment or critique existing US pragmatist and neopragmatist frameworks, and (2) how each approach thereby responds to an existing series of questions within Latina feminism through pragmatist and neopragmatist philosophical insights.

Over the past several decades, a relatively small but significant number of feminist authors have developed distinct theoretical veins of research that draw from their own experiences as Latina scholars. Many such authors have described growing up amidst mixtures of cultural, racial, and gender norms that clash with dominant Anglo-American lifeways, including the languages they speak or hear in the household, the foods they eat, and the embodied relationalities that some Latinas/os feel toward one another. A number of Latina feminist theorists also write about their experiences in academia, including about how they were able to navigate Anglo-dominant spaces, and about finding out particularly how hostile and alienating professional philosophy can be for people of color. While a great deal of the Latina theorists who have contributed to philosophical discussions of identity were trained primarily in Anglo-American and European canons in the humanities, some have been able to find resources within those traditions that create opportunities to address the existential concerns that impacted them, including racial, gendered, and cultural norms that have shaped their experiences as Latinas. However, as some theorists have noted, some extensions of such theoretical resources into their own concerns regarding issues of race, culture, and gender were, at times, met with disappointment. For example, Linda Martín Alcoff discusses her encounter in graduate school with W. V. O. Quine and her profound disappointment with his political views. In a 2012 interview with John Protevi, she states:

> I idolized Quine, yet when he came [to Brown], I discovered him to be completely inept at answering questions in public, which assured me that one could succeed in philosophy even as an introvert. I also discovered him to be the most thoughtless political reactionary one could imagine. His politics brought home for me, again, the disjuncture between philosophical

success and true philosophical wisdom. I was never again naïve enough to believe that philosophers are likely to be smarter than cab drivers, or the general voting public.[2]

Noting both her profound intellectual interest in Quine's work and her sincere dissatisfaction with his political views and interpersonal communicative skills, Alcoff's commentary points to a somewhat common experience among people of color in professional philosophy. For many scholars who seek the discipline of philosophy to unpack the complicated terms by which persistent forms of marginalization, exploitation, and violence occur, discovering that these questions are deemed irrelevant, unimportant, or obscure can be quite disheartening.

Kristie Dotson's important work in metaphilosophy expands this point. Dotson describes several patterns of exclusion within professional philosophy that tend to push diverse practitioners of philosophy out of the profession. One such pattern is exclusion via a sense of incongruence.[3] This practice involves "unequally accepting" specific justificatory norms for the profession of philosophy (including which methodologies, values, and interests are deemed philosophically acceptable or legitimate areas of study).[4] In this sense, Alcoff was surprised that Quine lacked philosophical acuity in areas of social and political philosophy, and her expectation was that these two areas of philosophical inquiry could be justifiably studied alongside epistemology. While she was confronted with a seeming incongruence in her graduate studies, fortunately for her readers, Alcoff's body of work and a number of post-Quinean feminist scholars thereafter have demonstrated that normatively laden concerns about sexism, racism, and social identities can be studied alongside classic questions within metaphysics and epistemology.[5]

Martinez also shares an interesting dimension of her graduate education that guided her to the task of studying aspects of identity as a Chicana lesbian. She notes that her training in semiotics and phenomenology led her to analyze the manner in which she was raised to abide by Anglo-dominant and heterosexual cultural norms. She writes:

> Growing up, I was taught to be white and heterosexual. Born into a typical suburban-comfortable middle-class U.S. American family in southern California, I was raised to believe that my racial and ethnic heritage was not significant to who I was or would become. I was raised to believe that male-female sexual

intimacy was the only kind of adult sexual intimacy that I could aspire to. I was raised to believe that although some people were "better off" or "worse off" than others, economic success was related entirely to education, hard work and perseverance. The fact that I was raised with these attitudes toward myself and my future is certainly related to choices that my parents made and the particular priorities they set in their own lives. But, it also has to do with a lot more than just the choices my parents made. It has to do with the specifics of a cultural time and place, the history that preceded that time and place, and the ideas about a possible future that filled that time and place. It has to do with a field of cultural norms generating a certain momentum that typifies any given time and place.[6]

Here Martinez highlights a theme that will develop in significant ways in her research. The methodological principles of "semiotic phenomenology" that Martinez develops for qualitative research in the social sciences is an attempt to engage in practices of self-understanding for her as a Chicana lesbian.[7]

In similar ways, the Latina feminist theorists examined in this chapter each have sought resources within Anglo-American canons of philosophy to extend questions regarding social identity categories that are intimately related to their lives. As I demonstrate below, US pragmatist and neopragmatist theorists like Peirce, Putnam, and Rorty have extended and challenged Latina philosophers to develop key themes within feminist theory regarding the existence of the self, articulations of structural oppressions such as racism and sexism, and possibilities for resistance. In the next section, I outline each author's engagement with US pragmatism or neopragmatism to show how this work has added or augmented discussions in the field.

Latina Feminist Engagement with US Pragmatism

First, turning to the work of Martinez, we can trace the influence of C. S. Peirce in her articulation of semiotic phenomenology. In a 2006 article, Martinez argues that Peirce's categories of "Firstness," "Secondness," and "Thirdness" provide an important model for developing a methodology to interpret the "complexities of racial, ethnic, and cross-cultural difference."[8]

Peircean semiotics carefully explores the relationship between the interpretive practices of inquirers and the practice of inquiry itself. Martinez explains:

> The researcher or scientist is always *in situ*—never outside of the context of her or his experiencing, which, of course, is never separate from the practice of "scientific intelligence" or human research of any sort. . . . The result of abandoning the typical dichotomy between "empirical" and "nonempirical" in the social scientific sense is that we now have, prior to any assertions of intelligence, knowledge or understanding, a focus on the actual conduct (thinking and experiencing) of researchers and scientists in the very formation of their practice.[9]

Martinez's emphasis here is on the processes by which scientific inquiry takes place, including how the researcher is situated within the practices of her/his/their discipline. Accordingly, she asks:

> How can semiotic phenomenology generally, and Peirce's categories specifically, take up critical issues that aim to expose the balance of power whereby the "mainstream" of Western cultures set the terms and conditions in which cultural and racialized Others are understood?[10]

Martinez expands these categories of analysis to engage how the situatedness of the researcher, as Chicana, white, heterosexual, queer, etc. plays a role in inquiry. She uses Peirce's model for communication and the action of signs to explain how Firstness, Secondness, and Thirdness relate to social scientific inquiry.[11] According to Peirce, firstness is a "quality" of the experience of immediate consciousness.[12] Secondness is the relation of difference, contrast, dependence, independence, or negation that is experienced as distinct from firstness.[13] Thirdness, then, becomes the meaning ascribed to the tendencies or predictions of Firstness and Secondness.[14] The processes of ascribing meaning to a sign arise only through the relation between Secondness and Thirdness. If a sensation remains at the level of Firstness, in which the sensation is without opposition to other signs, then it cannot become meaningful according to this framework.[15] Martinez reminds us:

> The most important point to recognize from this discussion is that almost all of our research efforts begin and remain at the

level of Thirdness, where we argue over correct interpretations and avoid examining inquiry as it occurs pragmatically in the concrete actions performed within the scientist's thinking and experiencing. This is especially true for social scientific research produced in the United States on topics concerning race and ethnicity.[16]

With respect to research, then, this means that inquiry within the social sciences that aims at "objective" replicability, which would reproduce the same results regardless of the inquirer, seems to disregard these facets of the process of inquiry that Peirce is describing.[17]

Martinez's suggestion is that we take seriously Peirce's emphasis on the process of inquiry, including the relationship between interpretation and experience to rethink our research methods with respect to race, ethnicity, and cultural difference. Namely, given the relationship between Secondness and Thirdness, inquirers will have very different orientations to the creation of meaning and the awareness of differential means to interpret experience with respect to issues of race, ethnicity, and culture. Peirce's semiotics become a springboard for examining how differing contexts and the positionality of the inquirer play a significant role in social science research.

Moreover, as Martinez argues elsewhere, Peircean semiotics also support an understanding of interpretation as an ongoing and unlimited process.[18] The relationship between the interpretant, the linguistic sign, and the object being represented is crucial. Here again, Martinez highlights the importance of understanding the role of the experience of the interpreter. The interpretant is the meaning that a person creates in response to a sign that becomes another sign itself. In this way, the meanings created for signs remain signs in other processes of meaning making. She writes the following regarding this process:

> From the perspective of semiotic phenomenology, this shift in interpretant that constitutes meaning is always specific, situated, contingent, and existential. Our goal in phenomenological research, then, is to interrogate the very circumstances in which a particular meaning is constituted to the exclusion of other possible meanings that could have been constituted. Language, and the semiotic systems of our time and place, envelop the person. Any moment of conscious awareness is never just my

own, but always reflexively interconnected to the dynamic and
ongoing semiosis in which I am inextricably bound.[19]

Accordingly, she reads the process of conducting research on identity and one's own experiences as part of a process of ongoing semiosis.

There are important normative implications of this insight. Namely, no claim can stand without connection to others. Even claims that purport to be solely about oneself or one's experiences are also implicated in other processes of inquiry. This expands our sense of accountability to others through the production of our research.[20] In this sense, Martinez's utilization of Peirce's semiotics opens space for researchers to reinterpret their own positionalities and the broader layers of meaning and influence their research might have on others. This requires a form of epistemic humility about one's work and one's framing of issues that they analyze and circulate through their research, including crucial existential areas of inquiry such as selfhood, embodiment, and sociality. US pragmatism thus becomes a means of expanding the sphere of responsibility for researchers and to view the task of academic analysis as an ongoing and dynamic process, rather than an attempt to master or control a given sphere of interpretation.

Turning to the work of Paula M. L. Moya, we can similarly see the influence of US pragmatism. However, rather than drawing from pragmatic semiotics, Moya analyzes what she describes as a "postpositivist" conception of objectivity from US pragmatism. In particular, she cites the work of Anglo-American authors such as Peirce, Quine, Donald Davidson, and Hilary Putnam as formative influences on the conception of objectivity that she develops in *Learning from Experience*.[21] Identities, she argues, "have a referential relationship to the world" and "refer outward—albeit in partial and occasionally inaccurate ways—to the social world within which they emerge."[22] Moya states that she endorses a "causal theory of reference in which linguistic terms (and identities) both shape our perceptions of and refer (in more or less partial and accurate ways) to causal features of a real world."[23] Among the references she cites in support of this theory of reference are Putnam's essays "The Meaning of Meaning" (1975), "Explanation and Reference" (1975), and his book *Reason, Truth, and History* (1981).[24] Moya also develops a discussion of linguistic reference in *Learning from Experience* and mentions in the same note about Putnam that she elaborates this conception of reference in her final chapter of the book through a reading of Chicana author Helena María Viramontes's *Under the Feet of Jesus* (1995).

Moya is among a group of theorists to extend some of Putnam's insights about natural kind externalism to social kinds.[25] Moya, for example, suggests that the form of realism that she defends is in dialogue with Putnam's semantic externalism.[26] Putnam, however, is notorious for revising his views regarding realism throughout various points in his career. Early work by the author could be characterized by a form of realism whereby the things our words pick out in the world bear causal relationships to the words we use to refer to them. This form of realism in Putnam's work is found in his collected works in *Mind, Language, and Reality* (1975), which contains two of the essays that Moya cites as influences on her thinking about her own causal theory of reference.[27] However, as Mario De Caro has argued, Putnam's work from roughly 1976 to 1990 shifted toward a somewhat antirealist position. This shift, De Caro notes, can be seen most forcefully in his 1981 articulation of what Putnam called "internal realism" in *Reason, Truth, and History*.[28] Moreover, Putnam appears to have changed his views again after 1990, claiming that his own version of internal realism was too idealistic.[29] Accordingly, there is significant debate in Putnam's work and about Putnam regarding questions of realism. To complicate matters, Moya also cites *Reason, Truth, and History* as formative for her work on linguistic reference and realism. Following her citations, then, we have her citation of Putnam's early work wherein a form of physicalism within his theory of reference was supporting his realist commitments; there is also a reference to Putnam's internal realist work, in which Putnam himself stated that he worried about the incipient relativism within his own account.[30] Given these tensions in Putnam regarding realism, it might be helpful to unpack briefly some of the terms on which Putnam shifted his philosophical views regarding realism, naturalism, and reference.

Regarding realism, we can look more carefully at Putnam's views regarding conceptual schemas. Putnam subscribes to what he calls a kind of "conceptual relativity," which he states does not bottom out in a denial of scientific or metaphysical realism. Putnam endorses the view that differing statements will have different truth conditions depending on the context and the speaker of the utterance, that "talk of criteria of existence and perdurance is metalinguistic talk on the face of it,"[31] and that "we renegotiate—and are forced to renegotiate—our notion of reality as our language and our life develop."[32] Putnam's views regarding the natural sciences, as a discourse that makes claims regarding existence in nature, is what De Caro, a scholar and compiler of Putnam's work, calls a "liberal naturalism." This view is "liberal" in that, unlike "strict" or "scientific" versions of naturalism in which everything that cannot be explained via a scientific worldview ought to be rejected, this conception of naturalism retains a pluralist stance toward commonsense views about existence.[33] According to De Caro:

> In [Putnam's] view, not all the real features of the world can be reduced to the scientifically describable features, and the natural sciences are not the only genuine source of knowledge to which all the other apparent sources should hand over their epistemic pretensions.[34]

In this sense, Putnam leaves space for realism about social kinds, as well as meaningful claims regarding non-natural objects. In this latter regard, De Caro writes as one of the principles of Putnam's liberal naturalism:

> Liberal naturalism, like all other forms of naturalism, should not make any supernatural assumptions. However, contrary to another very common opinion and in the spirit of the pragmatist tradition, according to Putnam this does not mean that all religious experience should be condemned as irrational or futile.[35]

Additionally, regarding claims within metaphilosophy that include questions regarding how philosophy will adjudicate epistemological matters, such as which beliefs are more justified or worthy of analysis, Putnam's pluralist approach to truth claims demonstrates a commitment to moral inquiry that cannot be subsumed under a scientific naturalist framework. On this point, De Caro notes:

> As to the epistemological status of philosophy, it should be noted that philosophy has a double face: one is the scientific face (which interacts with the natural and social sciences), and the other is the moral face (which "interrogates our lives and our cultures as they have been up to now, and that challenges us to reform both").[36] Both are essential. Pluralism plays a role also in metaphilosophy, then.[37]

Putnam's commitments to pluralism preserve important normative space for analyzing social conditions, including social kinds that involve identity claims. Moya's use of Putnam's work for her study of realism within analyses of social identity seem quite apt.

We can turn now to Moya's discussions of realism, reference, and causality to examine how Putnam's insights might play a role in her work. Moya argues that her conception of postpositivist realism defends a conception of identity that assumes that social identities are both constructed and real.[38] Against essentialist, transcendental, and supernatural conceptions of selfhood and identity, Moya wants to examine the ways in which identities are constructed through our social practices. However, against what she views as relativistic postmodernist tendencies to view identities as wholly arbitrary or fictional, she defends a realist commitment to the shared features of a social and natural world that people inhabit. Such features of the world, then, limit what we can say about each other and ourselves.[39] Moreover, she argues that such commitments to the seemingly arbitrary and "extreme linguistic constructivism" of such approaches (her main interlocutor here is Judith Butler) "impedes rather than enables the achievement of the liberatory political goals [postmodernist theorists] claim as their own."[40]

While we do not have space here to analyze Moya's treatment of "postmodernist" conceptions of identity, we can detect throughout her work a concerted critique of relativism. This concern was shared by Putnam as well and surfaced throughout his career and in his defense of internal realism. Similar to some of the criticisms Putnam proposed, Moya's direct critiques of postmodernist theory appear to be leveled against other philosophers of language regarding the potential truth value of any and all claims. If taken seriously, this implies an ontological expansionism that endorses a realist commitment to anything and everything. Additionally, both Moya and Putnam are committed to versions of fallibilism and pluralism, another initial feature that both views share regarding the status of truth claims.

To enrich Moya's view, we can look to how she understands identities as both constructed and real. She writes:

> Identities are constructed because they are based on interpreted experience and on theories that explain the social and natural world, but they are also real because they refer outwardly to causally significant features of the world. Identities are thus

context-specific ideological constructs, even though they may refer in non-arbitrary ways to verifiable aspects of the world such as skin color, physiognomy, anatomical sex, and socioeconomic status. Because identities refer—sometimes in partial and inaccurate ways—to the changing but relatively stable contexts from which they emerge, they are neither self-evident, immutable, and essential nor radically unstable or arbitrary.[41]

This approach seems at least partly compatible with Putnam's views. However, to clarify the relationship between Moya and Putnam, we would need to know more about how Moya conceives of reference, in particular, to determine the extent to which references to social kinds like "skin color, physiognomy, anatomical sex, and socioeconomic status" bear ontological claims regarding their relative social stability.[42]

Putnam's work from 1976 onward appears to offer a somewhat *more* pluralist approach than Moya. Namely, Putnam's conceptual relativism appears to actually be more ontologically liberal than Moya's approach to realism. In her analysis of Viramontes's novel, Moya makes a central claim regarding meaninglessness that appears to situate her perspective against Putnam's. She writes:

> Embedded within Viramontes's expanded notion of literacy is a thesis about the nature of language. *Under the Feet of Jesus* figures words as more or less powerful to the extent that they refer outward, beyond language as such, to actions or objects in the world. Where words lack a more or less determinate referent they are figured simply as noise.[43]

While much of this appears to be consistent with Putnam, the last sentence regarding a potential "lack of determinate referent" appears to conflict with his views. Moya's examples of meaningless language include unfulfilled promises made by a character in the novel: "His promises are meaningless; his words fail to correspond to lived behavior." Additionally, another character is a gossip, and "uses words carelessly." Moya states that her words are meaningless until they begin to refer to actions in the world: "My point is that when Maxine's [the gossiping character's] words start to refer, they cease to be noise and become words that can wound."[44] Lastly, she writes:

> In *Under the Feet of Jesus*, the power of language resides in the contextually determined meaning that becomes actualized in the process of human communication. Words in this novel are figured as noise until they serve the function of transmitting some (more or less determinate) meaning from one human consciousness to another.[45]

However, against this view, Putnam's version of conceptual relativism and internal realism does not defend the view that words are meaningless unless they refer to objects/actions within one given conceptual framework. In fact, Putnam is careful to argue that the conceptual worldviews entailed by physics or other natural sciences do not often answer the questions we are asking. Thus, no conception of the empirical world would be able to supervene on another in order to dismiss as meaningless or "noise" utterances that do not appear to satisfy some set of conditions within one conceptual framework.

To further clarify, let us consider Moya's and Putnam's respective views regarding verificationism. Moya, in defense of her theory of reference, relies on a conception of verification.[46] She states, as in the statements above regarding meaningless utterances, that utterances have meaning when they "refer to something verifiable" in the world.[47] Turning to Putnam, verificationism was another aspect of his work that shifted over time. Whether something is verifiable, according to Putnam, depends not simply on whether something can be reduced to a given empirical state of affairs. In fact, he writes the following on this point:

> When we speak of "states of affairs" what we normally think of are empirical states of affairs, ways the universe can be. And correspondence to such a state of affairs—one that actually obtains—is the standard of correctness for empirical statements. . . . [Yet, this statement] is misleading because said just like that it could be read as implying that there is one and the same kind of correspondence at stake no matter what the empirical statement is, and no matter what the occasion of its utterance may be. But that is not the case.[48]

In this sense, verificationism for Putnam does not reduce to whether one state of affairs obtains. Moreover, Putnam's liberal naturalism also implies a pluralism with respect to truth claims within differing conceptual schemes, which Moya does not analyze directly in her work.

As such, we see a deep engagement with pragmatic theory in Moya's work but also some notable differences between her work and that of theorists like Putnam who, by 1990, had dispensed with notions of verifiability and instead began relying on a kind of pluralism regarding truth claims. Accordingly, having more detailed elaborations from Moya regarding her views on realism, reference, and verification would be crucial for interpreting her stance on a number of these epistemological and ontological questions. However, from her engagement with pragmatist theory, we see that although she extends Putnam's work in directions attending to specificities of gendered and racialized existence, Moya may actually defend a more narrow version of realism than Putnam did in his own writings on the pluralism of states of affairs and practices of verification.

Lastly, we will briefly examine Linda Martín Alcoff's engagement with US pragmatism. Notably, Alcoff's oeuvre includes numerous engagements with pragmatist philosophy. Her first book, *Real Knowing* (1996), for example, offered chapter-length treatments of Davidson's and Putnam's work, respectively. However, rather than examine those various points of engagement, we will turn here to Alcoff's critique of Rorty's antirepresentationalism as an important site of engagement with neopragmatist insights.

Alcoff's main critical insight into Rorty's work is that his deflationary approach to truth and the proposal to eliminate forms of representationalism leave his view unable to account for the important veridical terms involved in cases of sexual assault and abuse. She begins by canvassing some of the major criticisms that Rorty has leveled against the representational paradigm in philosophy. Beginning in *Philosophy and the Mirror of Nature* (1979), Rorty eschewed the task of providing a theory of truth or a theory of reference. With respect to feminism, Rorty endorsed the goals of feminist philosophers such as Marilyn Frye and Catherine MacKinnon and interpreted them as creating new semantic authority for women. Also, he argued that their goals seemed more aimed at achieving social progress than an attempt to merely change truth claims regarding women. In this way, Rorty interpreted feminist philosophy as pragmatist in its efforts to improve the ways in which we live together. He writes in his 1990 Tanner Lecture:

> To be a pragmatist rather than a realist in one's description of the acquisition of full personhood requires thinking of its acquisition by blacks, gays, and women in the same terms as we think of its acquisition by Galilean scientist and Romantic poets. We say that the latter groups invented new moral identities

for themselves by getting semantic authority over themselves. As time went by, they succeeded in having the language they had developed become part of the language everybody spoke. Similarly, we have to think of gays, blacks, and women inventing themselves rather than discovering themselves, and thus of the larger society as coming to terms with something new.[49]

Rorty's concern here is that feminists need not make strong ontological claims regarding the truth value of women's agency or the ahistorical existence of the full personhood of women. Rather, the concerns are explicitly normative and thereby seek semantic shifts in the forms of meaning making that women create.[50] Rorty also argued that feminism would do well to leave universal claims and defenses of realism behind. Rorty offers pragmatism's critiques of universalistic claims and the abandonment of desires for absolutes as an approach for feminist theory.[51] In this way, he presents his views as more in line with the postmodernist critics who are critiqued by a number of feminist theorists, including Martinez, Alcoff, and Moya.

For Alcoff, this emphasis in Rorty's writings, including his writings about feminism, were misdirected primarily because there are ways of offering "modest and minimal versions of realism in which mirroring [has] no place."[52] Citing the work of Putnam, Roy Bhaskar, and Michael Williams, Alcoff argues that Rorty overlooks an entire thread of philosophical discourse that seeks to avoid correspondence and "mirror talk" and maintain commitments to realism (i.e., "that the universe is causally independent of us but not representationally independent of us.").[53] Alcoff clarifies this point:

> However, [such modest and minimalist realists] also tried to make sense of the commonsense idea that what we call true claims have a better relationship to that causally independent universe than do false claims, albeit relations that are oblique rather than isomorphic, connections without simple correspondences. This is why true claims build secure levees and false claims lead to global warming—not because the complete descriptions and concepts within true claims are carving nature at its joints but because in some sense, they are capturing some things about the world in some way.[54]

Alcoff's extended concern is whether these omissions in Rorty's critical approach to representation actually create a false dichotomy for feminist theory.

Given the plausibility of modified versions of realism, Alcoff analyzes whether Rorty's antirepresentational shift would work for feminist commitments to the pain and harm that oppressed peoples experience. In particular, Alcoff focuses on the nature of cruelty as something to be avoided within Rorty's progressive and optimistic picture for an expanded conception of the good life. Alcoff argues that without some reference to a better, more accurate characterization of pain, many forms of assault and cruelty against women would be minimized and dismissed. On this point, Alcoff writes:

> Imagine a scenario in which there is one discourse in which Rosie's pain from a sexual assault is invisible or unintelligible, or a second one in which it is considered justifiable or inevitable, and a third discourse in which it is visible as well as considered wrong and cruel. Rosie is inclined to prefer the third option as a more descriptively accurate characterization of the situation, since it articulates in a more accurate way what she has experienced. . . . Nonetheless, Rorty urges Rosie not to say that her preferred description is superior in its representational adequacy to a description in which the harm is either invisible or inconsequential.[55]

The concern expressed here by Alcoff is that Rorty's prescriptive move away from representational language and truth talk does not permit victims of sexual assault to claim that some forms of description are more accurate descriptions of the pain they have endured or the cruelty that others have inflicted on them.

Thus, Alcoff's proposal, contra Rorty, is that language such as "sexual violence," "date rape," and "marital rape"—rather than terms like "seduction" or "deflower"—are significantly different vis-à-vis their representational content.[56] Importantly, Alcoff argues that the need to refute claims about the inevitability of sexual assault or the naturalization of rape (e.g., claims that cisgender men are evolutionarily disposed to sexual violence) require representational responses. However, such uses of representational discourses need not refer to ahistorical, unchanging, infallible claims that appeal to "Nature," "Reason," "History," or "The Moral Law" (with absolutist and deterministic connotations). Put another way, feminists can rely on realist commitments to claims about the pain and cruelty of sexual assault and abuse without resorting to naive realist commitments about the way the world is regardless of our historical and interpretive practices.[57] As we can see in Alcoff's trajectory of research, her work does attempt to provide such a realist approach.[58]

Additionally, for Alcoff, using language like "rape" and "sexual assault" rather than "seduction" or "deflower" provides a more accurate depiction of the horrible events in question. She argues that the reason for this, in many cases, is "the rapist's point of view is probably riddled by self-delusion, ideological mystification, and self-justifying maneuvers that obscure perception."[59] Without an appeal to representationalism and realism, she argues, feminist accounts lose the ability to name such flawed beliefs and habits of thinking that perpetrators of violence hold.

Alcoff detects some potential critical oversights in Rorty's critique of epistemology. Namely, she argues that feminism is well supported by realist commitments to conceptions of how the world is. Like Moya, Alcoff is influenced by Putnam's style of internal realism. However, she distinguishes her approach from Putnam's by shifting the emphasis of conceptual schemes to contexts. Context-dependence, she claims, is different from Putnam's approach:

> Version-dependence involves being incapable of description outside of a theoretical version of reality with its own ontological categories; thus Putnam's realism is internal, or on *this side* of the man/world Kantian schema. Context-dependence involves a relationship not just to theoretical description but to a more inclusive context, which is also defined as including not only theory, version, and language game, but also historical, spatio-temporal, and social location. There are no properties of things that are context-independent, just as mass and extension change according to the nearest planet and the current velocity.[60]

Thus, for Alcoff, her version of realism is best captured through the term "immanent realism." Against notions of transcendence or an external/internal ontological divide (which characterizes Putnam's *internal* realism), Alcoff proposes that truth and falsity are derived from "the constellation of epistemic ingredients" about "the material world, the profane, the human real, without a God or an absolute knowledge."[61] Appearing to draw from a well-known pragmatist (and Peircean) methodology of eschewing debates about metaphysical realism, she describes veridical features of immanent realism as "an emergent property of all the elements involved in the context, including but not limited to theory."[62] As such, Alcoff's defense of representationalism draws from Putnam's realist commitments and critique of relativism to defend a conception of context-specific conditions regarding our epistemic claims.

Latina Feminist Decolonial Theorizing

Given this brief overview of several engagements with US pragmatism and neopragmatism by Latina feminist theorists, we can see a number of important overlapping concerns, as well as some points of divergence. Specifically, Martinez, Moya, and Alcoff share concerns with pragmatists regarding the impact of relativist frameworks on our understandings of meaning and truth. However, their critiques of relativism are often in the service of explicit normative commitments to the epistemic value of marginalized perspectives, rather than stemming from philosophical debates about scientific realism or the value of truth.

Additionally, Martinez traces the relationship between postmodernism and postcolonial critiques of Eurocentrism in her work, arguing that although the two threads of theoretical discourse are contemporaries, postmodernism does not engage with the same concerns as postcolonial theory.[63] In particular, Martinez argues that postmodernist theorists do not challenge individualism and liberalism directly and therefore do not defend practical commitments regarding theorization as a process. In this way, postcolonial theorists have the advantage of being in a position to enact better research practices across cultural and political divides, whereas postmodern theorists, on her reading, are less able to do so. Also, all three theorists defend versions of realism that seek to preserve intimate contact with the materially shared social worlds that they inhabit rather than abstract philosophical problems or debates within the academy. Martinez draws from Peirce and phenomenology but also from the works of Chicana and Latina lesbians such as Gloría Anzaldúa, Cherríe Moraga, Juanita Ramos, and Carla Trujillo to situate the cultural, gendered, and sexual stakes of her analysis.[64] Alcoff and Moya both engage the writings of Putnam and Davidson; however, their works also engage explicitly with Anzaldúa and Moraga as well.[65]

Martinez, Moya, and Alcoff also each develop trajectories of decolonial critique in their respective writings, which outline geopolitical problems that we do not find in the Anglo-American theorists they engage. Martinez's writings sustain an emphasis on analyses of US liberal individualism and the obstacles that commitments to liberalism create within a postcolonial context. Her 2003 article directly examines the creation and growth of individualism as a tenet of Eurocentric modernity. In particular, she argues that examinations of experience and identity by women-of-color feminists can often be dismissed as "essentialist" by postmodern critics.[66] However, such critics also end up perpetuating narrow framings of modernity, which leave the racist exclusions and practices of modernity unexamined. As such, critiques of rationality and representationalism, even from neopragmatist theorists like Rorty and Putnam, often ignore and thereby perpetuate patterns of exclusion within modernity.[67] Martinez's turn to semiotic phenomenology, which includes analysis of the inquirer's situated social locations and process of semiosis, becomes a way to navigate these efforts to critique global modernity and to retain a vested commitment to the lived experiences from people of color and peoples of the Global South.[68]

Alcoff also sustains a focus on critiques of Eurocentrism and the afterlives of colonialism. In *Visible Identities* (2006), she engages theorists such as Enrique Dussel, Walter Mignolo, and Ofelia Schutte, whose respective works challenge US imperialism and the dominance of Eurocentric modes of analysis within philosophy. Alcoff's development of a theory of Latina/o identity, as well as her framings of mixed-racial identities, and anti-Latina/o racism, are directly engaged in debates regarding the historical dominance of Anglo-American cultural norms and the political erasure of lifeways, languages, and epistemes of the Global South. As such, her work attempts to develop methodological commitments to overturning the conditions of coloniality.[69]

Likewise, Moya's corpus works against efforts to erase, neglect, or minimize the contributions of people of color. She argues that her commitments to a realist approach to identities is a critical stance against the Anglo- and Eurocentric belief that racial, ethnic, and gender identities are fictionalized obstacles to political solidarity. She argues that proposals to do away with identities or identity-based politics assume that people who argue from their situated social locations are merely "playing the victim" or making overgeneralizations about the intentions of the people around them.[70] Against such approaches, Moya reads identities as importantly linked to crucial sites of knowledge production and asserts that articulations of experience from nondominant identity positions are necessary for developing critiques of our social worlds.[71]

Furthermore, if we take the critical insights of Mariana Ortega (2017) and Elena Ruíz (2011) seriously (as I believe we should), Anzaldúa, Moraga, and other Chicana and Latina theorists, including Martinez, Moya, and Alcoff, are important participants in varied and plural decolonial movements within the academy. Given that these scholars developed critical tools from their training and experiences to examine the patterns of marginalization, stigmatization, and violence within their own lives and the lives of people of color (including those beyond the Global North), Latina feminist theory has been pivotal in the articulation of decolonial methodologies in the social sciences, literary theory, and philosophy.

As such, each theorist explored in this chapter has engaged with the critical insights of US pragmatism and neopragmatism, however, they do not assume an epistemic primacy or sufficiency of the Anglo-American theoretical frameworks that they engaged. For example, Alcoff, in a 1995 piece, explicitly takes up the "radical implications" of Putnam's writings in an effort to examine a way to negotiate tensions between "cultural imperialism and cultural relativism."[72] Specifically, Alcoff argues that Putnam did not extend the implications of his own thinking far enough to combat the dominance of cultural imperialism. While Putnam's work attempted to democratize processes of inquiry, including within the natural sciences, his writings on moral objectivity did not examine how desire and power influence what delimits the terms of rational deliberation. She writes on this matter in Putnam's work:

> I see a tension between these two tendencies in Putnam's work: the tendency to expand and complicate our understanding of what is involved in inquiry (to insist on what he calls its 'messiness') and the tendency to contain the forces of power and desire and to segregate these outside the domain of rational deliberation.[73]

Alcoff's approach to this tension is to examine how the desire and power to dominate others (including desires for epistemic mastery or finality in the academy) can shape our processes of inquiry. One concerted area of study in which she sees this possibility arising is in liberatory efforts to address global injustices, including structural oppressions and the forms of cultural imperialism that have long ravaged the resources, livelihoods, and epistemic resources of Black and Indigenous communities. Even in these early writings by Alcoff, we see direct criticisms of the elitist or progressivist narratives that frame the Global North's relationship to the Global South. Additionally, in another concise framing of this problem, Moya names this problem specifically and points to global capitalism and the destruction (and I would add appropriation and exploitation) of Indigenous knowledge systems as a function of the transnational flows of goods and resources between the Global North and South.[74]

Read in this light, we see important points of engagement with American philosophy, including, at times, critique and extension of pragmatist and neopragmatist thought and questions. Beyond this, however, we see a sustained body of literature from women-of-color theorists who remain committed to critiquing the academic institutions in which they themselves remain as participants. Through these lenses, we see Martinez, Moya, and Alcoff's engagements with US pragmatism and neopragmatism not so much as projects aimed at reevaluating or "saving" Anglo-American theory but rather as efforts to draw from their own forms of meaning making and processes of inquiry to develop a liberatory project dedicated to preserving and, moreover, enhancing the livelihoods of people of color and the tools available to continue engaging in decolonial praxis.

Notes

1. For another Latina feminist engagement with US pragmatism, see Edwina Barvosa, *Wealth of Selves: Multiple Identities, Mestiza Consciousness, and the Subject of Politics* (College Station: Texas A&M University Press, 2008).

2. Linda Alcoff, "New Apps Interview: Linda Alcoff," *New APPS: Art, Politics, Philosophy, Science*, April 4, 2012, accessed September 18, 2018, https://www.newappsblog.com/2012/04/new-apps-interview-linda-alcoff.html.

3. Kristie Dotson, "How is This Paper Philosophy?" *Comparative Philosophy* 3, no. 1 (2012), 13.

4. Dotson, "How is This Paper Philosophy?"

5. Quine's influence on feminist philosophy can be found through the work of authors such as Helen Longino, Lynn Hankinson Nelson, and Mariam Solomon.

6. Jaqueline Martinez, "Racisms, Heterosexisms, and Identities," *Journal of Homosexuality* 45, nos. 2–4 (2003): 109.

7. Martinez, "Racisms, Heterosexisms, and Identities"; Jacqueline Martinez, *Phenomenology of Chicana Experience and Identity: Communication and Transformation in Praxis* (Lanham, MD: Rowman & Littlefield, 2000); Jaqueline Martinez, "Semiotic Phenomenology and Intercultural Communication Scholarship: Meeting the Challenge of Racial, Ethnic, and Cultural Difference," *Western Journal of Communication* 70, no. 4 (2006): 292–310.

8. Martinez, "Semiotic Phenomenology," 293.

9. Martinez, 299–300.

10. Martinez, 300.

11. Martinez cites Vincent M. Colapietro's analysis of Peirce's categories: Vincent M. Colapietro, "Immediacy, Opposition and Mediation: Peirce on Irreducible Aspects of the Communicative Process," in *Recovering Pragmatism's Voice: The Classical Tradition, Rorty, and the Philosophy of Communication*, ed. Lenore Langsdorf and Andrew R. Smith (Albany: State University of New York Press, 1995), 30. For more on Peirce's categories, see Charles Sanders Peirce, "The Categories in Detail," in *Collected Papers*, ed. Charles Hartshorne and Paul Weiss, vol. 1 (Cambridge, MA: Belknap Press of Harvard University Press, 1958). Further references to Peirce's *Collected Papers* will be cited as "Peirce CP" with the volume and page number.

12. Peirce CP 1.342.

13. Peirce CP 1.358.

14. Peirce CP 1.339.

15. Martinez, "Semiotic Phenomenology," 301.

16. Martinez, 302.

17. Martinez, 302.

18. Martinez, "Racisms, Heterosexisms, and Identities," 121.

19. Martinez, 122.

20. Martinez, 123.

21. Paula M. L. Moya, *Learning from Experience: Minority Identities, Multicultural Struggles* (Berkeley: University of California Press, 2002), 12.

22. Moya, *Learning from Experience*, 13.

23. Moya, 15.

24. Moya, 15n21. She also cites Donald Davidson's "The Structure and Content of Truth," "On the Very Idea of a Conceptual Scheme," and "Thought and Talk" as formative of her views regarding an approach to cultural difference (Moya, *Learning from Experience*, 167n23). However, due to lack of space, I do not examine the relationship between Davidson's work and Moya's.

25. Other theorists include Tyler Burge and Sally Haslanger.

26. Moya, *Learning from Experience*, 16n23.

27. Moya, 15n21.

28. Mario De Caro, *Naturalism, Realism, and Normativity* (Cambridge, MA: Harvard University Press, 2016), 1.

29. De Caro, *Naturalism*, 2.
30. De Caro, 2–3.
31. De Caro, 84.
32. De Caro, 88.
33. De Caro, 11.
34. De Caro, 11.
35. De Caro, 12. See Hilary Putnam, "Wittgenstein on Religious Belief," in *Renewing Philosophy* (Cambridge, MA: Harvard University Press, 1992).
36. De Caro cites Putnam's "Science and Philosophy," in *Naturalism and Normativity*, ed. De Caro and MacArthur (New York: Columbia University Press, 2010).
37. De Caro, *Naturalism*, 13.
38. Moya, *Learning from Experience*, 86.
39. Moya, 10–12.
40. Moya, 12.
41. Moya, 86.
42. Moya, 86.
43. Moya, 180.
44. Moya, 180–181.
45. Moya, 183.
46. See, for example, Moya, 13, 41, 61, 86.
47. Moya, 182.
48. De Caro, *Naturalism*, 94–95.
49. Richard Rorty, "Feminism and Pragmatism," in *Feminist Interpretations of Richard Rorty*, ed. Marianne Janack (University Park: Pennsylvania State University Press, 2010), 37.
50. As an interesting aside regarding the relationship between Rorty and Latina feminism, Rorty does cite and briefly engage with the work of María Lugones in his Tanner Lecture as well. See Rorty, "Feminism and Pragmatism," 41n22.
51. Rorty, 25.
52. Alcoff, 137.
53. Linda Alcoff, "Rorty's Antirepresentationalism in the Context of Sexual Violence," in *Feminist Interpretations of Richard Rorty*, ed. Marianne Janack (University Park: Pennsylvania State University Press, 2010), 137.
54. Alcoff, "Rorty's Antirepresentationalism."
55. Alcoff, 142.
56. Alcoff, 145.
57. Alcoff, 147.
58. See, for example, Linda Martín Alcoff, *Visible Identities: Race, Gender, and the Self* (New York: Oxford University Press, 2006); and Linda Marín Alcoff, *Rape and Resistance* (Medford, MA: Polity, 2018).
59. Alcoff, *Rape and Resistance*, 149.

60. Linda Marín Alcoff, *Real Knowing: New Versions of the Coherence Theory* (Ithaca, NY: Cornell University Press, 1996), 218.

61. Alcoff, *Real Knowing*.

62. Alcoff, 219. For more on this point regarding Peirce's rejection of metaphysical realism, see Tom Rockmore, "On Classical and Neo-Analytic Forms of Pragmatism," *Metaphilosophy* 36, no. 3 (2005): 259–271.

63. Martinez, "Racisms, Heterosexisms, and Identities," 118.

64. See Martinez, "Semiotic Phenomenology"; Martinez, "Racisms, Heterosexisms, and Identities"; and Martinez, "Racisms, Heterosexisms, and Identities."

65. Moya, *Learning from Experience*; Alcoff, *Visible Identities*.

66. Jaqueline Martinez, "Racisms, Heterosexisms, and Identities," 119.

67. Martinez, 119.

68. Martinez, 112.

69. See, for example, Alcoff, *Visible Identities*; Linda Martín Alcoff, "Mignolo's Epistemology of Coloniality," *CR: The New Centennial Review* 7, no. 3 (2007): 79–101; and Linda Martín Alcoff, "An Epistemology for the Next Revolution," *Transmodernity: Journal of Peripheral Cultural Production of the Luso-Hispanic World* 1, no. 2 (2011): 67–78.

70. Paula M. L. Moya, "Who We Are and from Where We Speak," *Transmodernity: Journal of Peripheral Cultural Production of the Luso-Hispanic World* 1, no. 2 (2011): 79–94, 82–83.

71. Moya, "Who We Are," 79–94, 82–83.

72. Linda Martín Alcoff, "Democracy and Rationality: A Dialogue with Hilary Putnam," in *Women, Culture, and Development: A Study of Human Capabilities*, ed. Martha Nussbaum and Jonathan Glover (New York: Oxford University Press, 1995), 225, 230.

73. Alcoff, "Democracy and Rationality," 231.

74. Moya, "Who We Are," 82–83.

CHAPTER SEVEN

Dewey, Wynter, and Césaire

Race, Colonialism, and "The Science of the Word"

PHILLIP MCREYNOLDS

The theme of this volume is that American philosophy—which, for the purposes of this chapter means the classical American pragmatism of Peirce, James, and Dewey—needs decolonizing and can offer resources for said decolonization. While I realize that the sense of "American philosophy" as pragmatism is overly reductive (and the story of pragmatism, itself, is more complicated than one centered on the "Holy Trinity" of Peirce, James, and Dewey), Deborah Whitehead makes a strong case that pragmatism so understood has been, among other things, a very American story about America: "a mode of American cultural rhetoric and narrative, as a way of explaining America to itself at critical moments in U.S. history."[1] This seems to me a useful approach for the purposes of this volume.[2] It is appropriate and understandable that American pragmatism, as currently configured, presents this double aspect: while it is a colonizer's philosophy shot through with settler logic and related ideas, it is also the product of a rich encounter with indigenous philosophies that have distanced it from philosophies more typical of the western European tradition.[3] In this chapter I argue that both pragmatism and post-, non-, de-, and anticolonial thought stand to be mutually enriched by completing the transformations that are implicit in the hybrid nature of these traditions. My first claim is that while the pragmatism of John Dewey remains problematic due to its colonial baggage, it can be reconstructed by bringing it into contact with philosophies that actively resist, overcome, or otherwise respond to colonization and coloniality, specifically the ideas of Sylvia Wynter and Aimé Césaire. Second, I argue that Deweyan pragmatism can help us to better understand and concretize certain ideas found in Wynter and Césaire. Specifically, Dewey's idea of a "science of ethics" can help us to understand and implement Wynter and Césaire's call for a "science of the word" primarily due to deep but nonobvious affinities between these two approaches. Finally, an encounter between pragmatism and these philosophies—especially Césaire—is important for understanding and reinterpreting pragmatism in ways that distance it from its original humanist context within the discourse of modernity, which would otherwise undermine its emancipatory potential.[4]

It might at first seem strange to mention Dewey alongside Wynter and Césaire. Dewey was a New Englander reared on the philosophy of Hegel and is known for his scientific spirit as well as his advocacy of experimentally minded educational reforms in the United States. He seems worlds apart from the geopoetic and geopolitical vision offered by the Caribbean writers Wynter and Césaire. My rationale for linking these three thinkers is to highlight a set of abiding affinities that will create a space within pragmatism for opening a genuinely post-, anti-, and decolonial approach to race.[5]

Pragmatism's Colonial Legacy

First, it is important to acknowledge that pragmatism has a mixed and not entirely salutary record with regard to questions of race. Most significantly, the classical pragmatists themselves wrote very little on the subject. Moreover, while there has been some recent work in applying pragmatism in general, and Dewey in particular, to problems of race,[6] Thomas Fallace's 2010 book, *Dewey and the Dilemma of Race*, brings to light serious problems with this enterprise.[7]

John Dewey was deeply committed to working against "the injustice of racial discrimination and cultural imperialism," a commitment that he expressed throughout his long career both intellectually and practically (which amount to the same thing for Dewey).[8] As an example of a practical intervention, Dewey was one of the founders of the National

Association for the Advancement of Colored People (NAACP), and Dewey's interest in founding this organization can be traced directly to his conception of and approach to both democracy and inquiry. However, Fallace demonstrates that during the key period when Dewey formulated his most widely read works on development, democracy, and education, his position incorporated both a linear historicism and a genetic psychology that understood nonwhites to be inferior to whites. This was based on the eugenic myth that nonwhite/non-European cultures were evolutionarily and developmentally stunted compared with white/European culture. Thus, as Sullivan puts it, "The ethnocentrism of Dewey's linear historicism combined with the genetic psychology of his account of child development produce particularly racist results."[9] Moreover, this racism found in the educational philosophy of Dewey's middle period cannot simply be dismissed as an anachronism. Although he went on to develop a more multicultural approach to democracy and other matters, Dewey never disavowed his educational work, which was based upon these racially problematic theories. Indeed, as Fallace points out, as late as 1934 Dewey "essentially defended the linear historicist curriculum he developed" at the Laboratory School.[10] Fallace shows that far from being an isolated anomaly within his work, Dewey's ethnocentrism is a "weight-bearing structure" that any pragmatist concerned about race must squarely reckon with. Considering these problematic issues, Dewey's work itself needs reconstruction. Happily, as Westbrook notes, "'Reconstructing Dewey' has a decidedly Deweyan ring to it,"[11] and it is the beginning of a reconstruction of Deweyan pragmatism along postcolonial lines that I outline in this chapter. What I hope to show is how some promising ideas in Wynter and Césaire, ideas already geared toward a postcolonial approach to humanity and that resonate with some key ideas in Dewey's work, might open the way to a genuine postcolonial pragmatism.

Now, one might wonder—and I have been asked—why pragmatism? If Deweyan pragmatism is deeply racist in the ways that Fallace says it is, why not just skip over a problematic figure such as Dewey and go straight to the "good stuff" that one finds in writers such as Wynter and Césaire? My argument for sticking it out with Dewey and pragmatism is twofold: first, in my view, there are too many important resources in Deweyan pragmatism to merely leave it by the wayside. There are important ideas in this tradition that need to be remembered, recovered, and put to work in a viable postcolonial project. Among these ideas can be found a commitment to experimentalism, continuity, antifoundationalism, and the centrality of lived experience. Second, there are crucial similarities between important ideas and themes in Dewey and these two Caribbean thinkers that bring out the strengths of both traditions: attention to these commonalities can help, I think, to translate some of the more abstract ideas one finds in Wynter and Césaire into an idiom that one can apply practically toward concrete change in the contemporary world.

In pointing the way toward a postcolonial reconstruction of Deweyan pragmatism, I think is necessary to deploy Dewey's thought in thinking about a postcolonial idea of race. I turn to what might initially appear to be an unlikely source: Dewey's call for a "science of ethics." Many would consider this call to be one of the more outdated features of Dewey's philosophy and an unfortunate example of Dewey's scientism. Others simply view it as a call for experimentalism in ethics. Jennifer Welchman suggests that "it may even prove that [Dewey's] work is of greatest value for what now seems its most hopelessly outdated feature: his attempts to elevate ethics to the status of a natural science."[12]

Jennifer Welchman (and others) have pointed out that what Dewey meant by "science" in the early period in which he made these attempts was Hegelian science, whose synoptic aspirations Dewey soon abandoned. However, while Dewey abandoned Hegel's absolutism, he retained insights derived from Hegel's logic surrounding the basic continuity that underlies human experience. As T. C. Dalton explains:

> Dewey's deconstruction of Hegel was dedicated to the propositions that science, aesthetics, and ethics involve essentially the same processes of exercising human judgment under conditions of uncertainty, and that quantitative and qualitative values are intertwined in every act of moral commitment, aesthetic expression, and scientific generalization.[13]

Recent work by Mark Johnson, Tom Alexander, and Gregory Pappas underlines and augments this point: namely, that Dewey had in mind a mode of inquiry carrying no less authority than that of the natural sciences, a mode rooted in the aesthetic features of human experience.[14] I will argue that this idea is shared by Dewey, Wynter, and Césaire.

Dewey rejects Enlightenment faculty psychology, which is the view that human experience is partitioned into distinct spheres of influence: rational-scientific, moral-ethical, religious, and aesthetic. Instead, Dewey's philosophy articulates a fundamental continuity to all forms of human experience and endeavor, and the general thrust of his work is at least partly an attempt to call attention to this basic continuity and to follow up on its implications for inquiry. Drawing on Dewey as well as recent work in linguistics, cognitive science, and related fields, Mark Johnson argues that our basic conceptual categories—the categories that form the basis of all forms of judgment—are initially and characteristically both embodied and aesthetic. Calling attention to the "essential role of sensory-motor areas [in the nervous system] in our capacity for abstract conceptualization and reasoning" demonstrated by Lakoff and Johnson and elsewhere, Johnson argues that "human reasoning is inextricably tied up with emotions and feelings."[15] There simply is no reasoning without feeling and, hence, no pure reason, science, or instrumental logic that isn't always already thoroughly aesthetic. Johnson puts it as follows:

> The 'aesthetic' encompasses everything that goes into the possibility of a meaningful experience . . . Consequently *aesthetic sensitivity* makes it possible for us to be aware of, present to, and involved in what is happening and what is possible by way of experience and action.[16]

Similarly, Thomas Alexander has argued that Dewey's insistence "on the dynamic side of idealism while rejecting Hegel's dialectic for experimental psychology" moved Dewey to shift from a traditional, Western (European) "epistemology of *knowledge*" to a focus on an "aesthetics of *learning*" and that this shift constitutes "a radical break with the Western philosophical tradition."[17] The idea is that for a living, evolved creature that must cope in an uncertain world, learning is more important than knowing, and this learning is effected aesthetically, through our bodies and by means of feelings. Echoing Johnson, Alexander notes, "It is, after all, learning in which imagination, not merely reason, transforms our past into a meaningful future."[18]

One striking feature of this Deweyan approach, identified by Johnson and Alexander, that ties (e.g., scientific, ethical, and other forms of human) reason to feeling is its potential to explain Dewey's curious notion of a "science of ethics" that Welchman finds so promising. If all human judgment is rooted in, guided by, and carried out by means of a corporeal aesthetics, science and ethics are not so far apart after all, since there is no pure or even purely instrumental reason that is not rooted in what Susanne Langer called "the forms of human feeling," which is the province of aesthetics.[19] Another interesting and potentially helpful feature of this approach—helpful with respect to the (re)founding of a postcolonial pragmatic humanism—lies in its parallels with the poetic-scientific interests of Aimé Césaire and Sylvia Wynter, two writers who take the issues of racist colonialism and its legacy to be the foremost challenges of our time.

The problem that Wynter's writing is concerned with is "the code of symbolic life inscribed by the Color Line."[20] While this might strike some people as one specific problem (i.e., that of race), through careful analysis Wynter shows both how this code is constitutive of modernity as a whole—thus related to a whole host of issues, many of which might otherwise seem only tangentially (if at all) related to race—and the formative role that symbolic codes play in human life. Our contemporary world is organized around a conception of "Man" in which human beings are viewed as purely biological creatures.[21] Biocentric "Man"—"Man2," according to Wynter's nomenclature—is constituted by an origin tale in which He is the product of evolution by natural selection.[22] Far more than just a scientific theory or paradigm, the nexus of concepts that constitutes the idea of biological evolution *also* functions mythopoetically in our culture. Science can and does tell us about our world; however, science, particularly the science of humans, never does solely that. As Glynn L. L. Isaac explains, "Scientific theories and information about human origins have been slotted into the same old places in our minds and our cultures that used to be occupied by the myths."[23] What Wynter seeks to do is to expose the hidden codes that govern our goals and normatively shape our lifeworlds. As she puts it, "The rewriting of knowledge . . . must necessarily entail the un/writing of our present normative defining of the secular mode of the Subject."[24]

In a way, what Wynter has in mind is a kind of "talk therapy" for our culture. One might say that Wynter aims to disclose the social unconscious that supports and drives the neuroses of modernity so that they might be ameliorated.[25] And yet this characterization of Wynter's project, if accurate, is problematic because corresponding to the concept of a neurosis is a concept of well-being that is rooted in the very symbolic orders that Wynter hopes to upend. It is the very idea of being a healthy person (or a good Christian, an upstanding citizen, or a bourgeois "maker" instead of a proletarian "taker") that, according to Wynter, lies at the basis of the symbolic orders that undergird human life and culture. One of Wynter's key points is that "the induced desire for full being in terms of each order's governing code of symbolic life" is fundamental to human behaviors of generalized altruism. Other significantly social creatures, such as the social insects, it has been argued, are genetically programmed for generalized altruism.[26] Humans are not.[27] Moreover, behaviors such as generalized altruism are enforced and made concrete in humans by means of "the biochemical or natural opioid reward and punishment system of the brain."[28] Wynter proposes that humans *as human* divide the world into "same" and "other," marking the "other" as undesirable. It is "by means of these narratively encoded behavior-motivating schemata of 'lack of being' and redemption into 'true being' that the imperatives of the social order . . . enable the overriding of 'the dispositional products of biological evolution.'"[29] In other words, dividing the world into good (fully human) humans and bad (less-than-human) humans is "natural" insofar as it is a cultural adaptation that marks a break in the purely genetically encoded scripts of biological evolution.[30] What Wynter is up to here is what a Deweyan might call the "criticism of criticisms," which is Dewey's definition of philosophy.[31] If first-order criticism constitutes the social codes that govern social (and individual) norms and judgments, those norms and judgments will be maladaptive for some people, for example, in the form of a deeply rooted and culturally imbricated racism. What is needed is a criticism of this criticism that is funded by the aesthetic-corporeal basis of all human judgments. This, according to Johnson and Alexander, is Dewey's project as well. Moreover, recent research in human language and cognition, supplemented by Wynter's careful attention to the genealogies of racism, can only strengthen this project.

Much of Wynter's work is a recounting of the historical development of the culturally specific goal-defining distinctions during different historical epochs in such a way as to disclose the contingent nature of our current world order. Different symbolic orders have given rise to different "genres" of the human throughout history and across the world. Our current world order is one in which the Western, white, bourgeois, "developed" human is taken as the true model of human normalcy, whereas the non-Western, nonwhite, poor, underdeveloped human is understood to be its other. The Other to the Normal is implicitly (and sometimes explicitly) understood as inferior because it is, according to the current biocentric episteme, disselected by evolution and economics and therefore deserving not of resources but of domination. Importantly, this is not merely the perspective of the white Westerner. Rather, in colonial and neocolonial societies, because this perspective is introduced and constantly reinforced as the very basis for what is "good," this perspective gives rise to double consciousness. As Frantz Fanon observed, the colonized subject-body is taken from that subject and returned as an unrecognizable other. The thrust of Wynter's work is to provide specificity and concreteness to Fanon's "sociogenic principle."[32] When one looks at the socioeconomic nexus of modernity as a self-reproducing system in terms of codes that tell a man how to be a "good (or real) man" and a woman to be a "good (or real) woman," it becomes possible to understand why and how racism and its effects persist, despite pervasive and prevalent scientific challenges to biological race and other nonscientific efforts to undermine this idea and banish it from contemporary discourse. Above all, for the system (Europe, the West) to preserve itself, it must erect a symbolic boundary between itself and its other. It then constructs institutions internal to itself to support that boundary, meanwhile exporting disorder in the form of slavery, scarcity, and so on while expropriating resources from this Third World environment. As Fallace points out, Dewey's linear historicism and genetic psychology buy into and support this symbolic structure. As a result, this structure is carried over into Dewey's mature educational theory. Attention to this context and critique is one thing Deweyan pragmatism stands to gain from postcolonial thinkers such as Wynter.

I need to make clear here that in referring to the evolutionary biocentric episteme, Wynter is not taking up or promoting an antiscience stance. In fact, taking for example Wynter's discussion of opioid pathways and autopoiesis (not to mention communications theory and a whole host of other scientific findings and theories), she relies on science quite a bit in her critique. Rather, like Dewey, Wynter's relationship to "science" is complicated and cannot be reduced to either a simple scientism or an antiscience position. Indeed, like Dewey, Wynter embraces science while rejecting the reductive materialism that is often the unspoken and unchallenged philosophical assumptions of much supposedly objective and scientific writing about science. Wynter's position is that the notion of the human as a purely biological creature—that is, purely subject to evolutionary selection understood in terms of genetic determinism—is a product of the ideology of Western humanism that supplanted the prior theocentric model of the world. This conception is still operative in the biological sciences that Wynter employs to explain the hold that this ideology has over the current social order. Even so, there is ample evidence throughout Wynter's writings that she conceives of "the rise of the natural sciences" as giving rise to "the autonomy of human cognition with respect to the processes of functioning of the non-human orders of reality."[33]

However, Wynter is not content to abandon the field to a techno-scientific logic that places technics before the human. This refusal is, in fact, one of the important features that Wynter's philosophy shares with Dewey's.

One significant characteristic that characterizes our current world order, according to Wynter, is that we humans have entered what Hans Blumenberg has called "a phase of objectification." This is a situation in which

> events and their functioning spin out of the control of human motivation and purpose. At such times, a great counter-exertion is needed to bring these events back to serving the logic of human purpose rather than the reverse.[34]

If events are not under the control of humans, then who controls them? Wynter's answer is that humans have ceded their autonomy to a world of objects.

In an analysis of *Robinson Crusoe*, Wynter explains that when Robinson Crusoe names Friday, he simultaneously instantiates himself as master and Friday as servant while erasing Friday's previous life and world as an indigenous person.[35] Now in engaging in this naming, Crusoe thinks that it is he who has the authority, much like the authority given to Adam by God in the Garden of Eden. However, Friday recognizes that the only thing that authorizes Crusoe to (re)name him is Crusoe's gun—an object. Thus, it is an object that is responsible for ordering the minimal society of Defoe's novel, not a human being. Wynter asserts that today it is "the Absolute of the Technological Rationality, which, is increasingly directed to the purposes of its own goal-seeking rather than by human purposes [and] determine[s] Events that are once more out of the control of human motivation."[36] Along the same lines, it is worth noting here that Aimé Césaire equates colonialism with thingification.[37]

But note the event that transforms the power relationship between Crusoe and Friday: it occurs in the act of naming. Naming, according to Wynter, is fundamentally a poetic activity. Or, rather, poetry is the means by which we name and humanize the world and thereby invent ourselves: "Poetry is the agent and product by which man names the world, and calling it into being, invents his *human* as opposed to his 'natural' being," Wynter tells us.[38] Wynter's hope is that, as Katherine McKittrick puts it, "poetics might disrupt the habitability of the normal,"[39] a "normal" that heretofore has been structured in terms of objectification. Such a poetics might open up "a new worldview from the perspective of the species—that is, from outside the logic of biocentric models: not as *genre* or *mode* of human but as human."[40] It is not a question of breaking the bonds of the we/other circle of naming. To be human is to humanize, and Wynter is calling for a poetics of humanization. The first step in developing such a poetics involves a critical phase identifying the cultural codes that give dominance to the object and result in Man's alienation from the human. The second step involves constructing a new science of the human that is rooted in this poetics. In this she recalls Césaire's call for a new "science of the word." Wynter seeks to harness the biological and human sciences: *not* to reveal the truth or create a knowledge about humanity but to create a new humanity beyond the dehumanizing knowledges and practices of the current epoch.

Wynter uses the scientific findings of systems biology and neurophysiology to supplant the biocentric ideology in which the white, Western bourgeoisie is opposed to its other: natives, the poor, the nonwhite. Through the employment of a new poetics, she is calling for what she calls a "Second Emergence." The "First Emergence," according to Wynter, was the freedom of human beings from determination by purely genetic codes. The cost of the First Emergence was subordination to culturally specific symbolic codes. Thus, the Second Emergence will involve the recognition of these codes and identification of the ways in which they function, together with a creative transformation of these codes such that Man is no longer alienated from the human. With Césaire, Wynter is seeking not human*ism*, the ideology of Man, but "a true humanism, made to the measure of the world."[41]

Thus, while the specifics of this poetics of the new human need to be articulated, what should be clear is the way in which Wynter's project is much more a question of production than representation, a project whose parallel we find in pragmatism.[42] As Foucault argued, the currently dominant biocentric ideology produces specific types of human beings by producing their truth, that is, in producing knowledge about them.[43] The first part of Wynter's strategy is to undermine the universal truth claims of this ideology to make room for different habits of thinking, habits that can produce different sorts of human beings. Wynter hopes to open a space for the human *as such* (in contrast to Man), which is not governed by *genres* of the human but is rather a space for a genuine, nonhierarchical multiplicity.

There are some important parallels between Césaire's, Wynter's, and Dewey's understandings of the role of the transformative nature of aesthetic modes of experience. For Dewey, "meaning is not . . . a psychic existence; it is primarily a property of behavior."[44] When one recognizes that this is not a form of behaviorism but rather an appreciation of the necessarily embodied character of meaning, one begins to see the resonances between Dewey's view and the perspectives of Wynter and Césaire.

Gregory Pappas explained the often-overlooked roles of qualitative experience in guiding and controlling inquiry in his analysis of Dewey's essay "Qualitative Thought," *Logic: The Theory of Inquiry*, and elsewhere.[45] The idea of "situation" is central to Dewey's philosophy, and according to Pappas, one cannot make sense of this idea without understanding the idea of qualitative experience. Dewey is quite adamant throughout his writings that one generally cannot aver to cookie-cutter solutions to genuinely problematic situations. This is because each situation is unique. What makes each situation unique, according to Dewey, is the fact that each situation has its own distinctive, pervasive quality. That quality, which is not primarily cognitive and cannot be reduced to symbolic formulae (linguistic or otherwise), is what controls inquiry into that problematic situation from its earliest stages in, for example, identifying and formulating the problem to the qualitative transformation of that situation into a new situation.[46] It is important to note that for Dewey "inquiry" is not restricted to signifying "scientific inquiry." There is inquiry in areas as diverse as art, morals, and education, as well as the sciences. And qualitative thought, according to Dewey, plays no lesser or greater role in any of these forms of inquiry than any other.[47] Importantly—especially when one is tempted to reduce to scientific investigation what Dewey says about inquiry—we must understand that Dewey's understanding of inquiry is not reducible to Peirce's doubt-belief structure but rather involves a qualitative transformation of one situation into another. That is, according to Dewey, inquiry is not just "problem solving," that is, the transformation of an indeterminate cognitive situation into one that is determinate. Rather, for Dewey, inquiry transforms noncognitive experience as well, changing the whole tenor of the preinquiry situation into a new situation with a different flavor or character.[48]

Dewey's emphasis on the role of qualitative thought stems from his understanding of knowers as embodied agents and from the fact that "in inquiry knowing, acting, *and feeling* are intimately related."[49] It is important to understand that this appeal to feeling does not amount to the claim that there is some sort of irreducibly subjective factor in cognition. For Dewey, qualities are neither subjective nor objective but are rather the product of the relationship—Dewey would say "the transactions"—between the knower and her environment, an environment that is at once material, mental, natural, and cultural. To summarize Dewey's position with respect to the significance of qualitative thought, I offer Dewey's own words: "The immediate existence of quality, and of dominant and pervasive quality is [a] the background, [b] the point of departure, and [c] the regulative principle of all thinking."[50]

Compare Dewey's understanding of the role of qualitative, embodied experience in thinking to Césaire's account in *Poetry and Knowledge* of "an entire experience" as the controlling factor in poetry:

> What presides over the poem is not the most lucid intelligence, or the most acute sensibility, but an entire experience . . . the whole weight of the body, the whole weight of the mind. All lived experience. All the possibility.[51]

It is important to recognize that Césaire is not writing here about poetry alone. Rather, he's talking about a poetic mode of inquiry or, we might say, poetic thinking. In modernity, Césaire argues, the world has been split into the scientific view and views guided by feeling, a bifurcation that deprives us of a coherent and original relation to the world (see Emerson, for instance):

> Just as the new Cartesian algebra permitted the construction of theoretical physics, so too an original handling of the word can make possible at any moment a new theoretical and heedless science that poetry could already give an approximate notion of.[52]

According to Wynter, the natural sciences "had remained 'half-starved' because they were unable to make our human worlds intelligible"; in its place Césaire calls for "a new order of knowledge, specific to human forms of life, a science, therefore, of the Word."[53] Anyone familiar with Dewey's work will (I think) sense a resonance here with Dewey's persistent concern that our prowess in science and technology has outpaced our ability to reasonably determine how we should put them to work.

I argued earlier that despite common misunderstandings, neither Dewey nor Wynter is against science. One problem in bringing all three figures together in a common project united by what we might call a "science of ethics" (Dewey) or a "science of the Word" (Césaire/Wynter) is that of the three, Césaire can be plausibly read as being antiscience. Whereas Dewey is self-consciously an experimentalist, Césaire comes off as *against* experimentalism when he writes, for example, the following:

> It is an error to believe that knowledge to be born, had to await the methodological exercise of thought or the scruples of experimentation. I even believe that man has never been closer to certain truths than in the first days of the species. At the time when man discovered, with emotion, the first sun, the first rain, the first breath, the first moon. At the time when man discovered in fear and rapture the throbbing newness of the world.[54]

Césaire goes as far as to say that "poetic knowledge is born in the great science of scientific knowledge," putting the scientific in opposition to the poetic, an opposition that Dewey would never sanction.[55]

Angela Last, however, argues that Césaire is not antiexperimentalist or even, as one might plausibly conclude, antiscientific. What Césaire is proposing is a different kind of experimentation than is prevalent in modern scientific inquiry. Césaire is arguing instead for poetic experimentation. Last explains, citing A. J. Arnold, that "this view of poetry [is] as an experimental ground for exploring a 'fundamental unconscious unity in nature.'"[56] Césaire took this position, according to Last, because "especially in Césaire's time, science remained noticeably silent about common materiality and preferred to create artificial boundaries in the service of imperialism."[57] Last's article is, in part, an exploration of similarities between the critiques of capitalist rationality and destructive globalization offered by Aimé and Suzanne Césaire and Simone Weil, three authors who were not critical of science as such but of its role in imperialist domination. Dewey, one should observe, shared these concerns about the uses of science. Thus, if we properly understand Césaire's context and the object of his critique, it might be rationally argued that he is not antiscience *as such* but is rather critical of the development of science in the context of a world-dominating colonialism. His project is to offer an alternative way of thinking about human-world relations than those assumed and reinforced by that project.

Last explains, "Suzanne and Aimé Césaire's geopoetics experiment with changing human-world relations in order to context the capitalist view of nature and naturalized humans as a resource."[58]

The affinities between Dewey and the Césaires go even deeper. Dewey famously was critical of various dichotomies and, in particular, the one traditionally erected between nature and culture. Dewey, rather, was keen to attend to the continuity at the heart of all experience and was always insistent upon the importance, noted above, of situation and context. Compare with Last's account of the Césaires: "In their focus on the body as a construct of universal nature/culture, but also a location of response to a particular nature and culture, they refuse a 'disembodied universalism' in favour of advancing a universalism that is rich with all that is particular.'"[59] Moreover, just as Dewey refused to cede values to scientific determinism or to understand the normative as being separate from nature, for Césaire, "the physical world does not constitute the ontological source of ethics or politics, but is represented in a way that would enable a new view of it—and of our relation to it."[60] This is precisely the pragmatist approach to the relationship between "facts" and "values." Césaire and Dewey share a common set of beliefs and concerns—beliefs about the relationship between "science" and labor and concerns about the relationship between science and human values.

None of this is to say that Césaire's and Dewey's positions are identical with regard to science, poetics, or anything else. Césaire and Dewey occupied different cultural and historical landscapes and, as such, had different perspectives and concerns. One thing that Césaire's critique provides Deweyan pragmatism is an antidote to a modernist humanism that is rooted in colonial tropes. As Last explains, the Césaires' "play with stereotypes of colonized peoples and landscapes as savage entities to be domesticated results in ironic transformations that question the supposedly 'universal' European values."[61] For Césaire, poetics is a means of exploring alternative universalisms.[62] This project has much in common with Dewey's commitment to and understanding of continuity and the role of the qualitative in thought. Césaire's project and his perspective move beyond Dewey's, however, in significant ways in his appreciation of the pernicious role that the tropes of modernist humanism continue to play in structuring life in what is, fundamentally, an unbalanced and destructive ecological and economic order.

The primary claim I make in this chapter is that for Césaire, Wynter, and Dewey, the layered, textured, and thoroughly cultural and encultured quality of human experience, when recognized for what it is and its role in human life and culture, can give rise to what we might call "a new science" based upon what Susanne Langer called "the forms of human feeling."⁶³ Césaire, in noting the layered nature of human experience where archaic structures are never abandoned but built upon and repurposed, is calling attention to what Dewey called "the principle of continuity."

This "new science" should be important to us now because, according to Wynter, it is the only way of dealing adequately with "the code of symbolic life inscripted [sic] by The Color Line."⁶⁴ In the context of the history and present reality of racism, this is the only way to proceed because of the bodily enacted historical rupture of colonialism, both for colonizer and colonized. John Drabinski explains that

> if history and memory are nothing but the historical experience of disaster and its bearing on the body, and if survival is nothing but an assemblage (not bricolage) of memory-fragments wanting retrieval and reactivation, then the relation of the past to future cannot be settled.⁶⁵

Pragmatists are sometimes accused of not paying sufficient attention to the past, but for both Dewey and Césaire we cannot return to the past. (Nor should we want to.) Yet, to paraphrase a famous James Baldwin line, the past is, if anything, the present. A pragmatist will likely agree that the most (and perhaps only) promising way of dealing with the reality of racism and the legacy of colonialism, as with any problem, is inquiry. Wynter writes, "With the destruction of these barriers (barriers, in Césaire's terms, between the 'study of nature' and the 'study of words'), the 'narrative order of culturally constructed worlds, the order of human feelings and belief will become subject to scientific description in a new way."⁶⁶ It is my view (and the thesis of this chapter) that what we might call "a new science of the human," one not rooted in the deliberate subjugation and inferiorizing of vast swaths of humanity, is a good way to understand what Dewey was calling for in his hopes for a "scientific ethics." Reconstruction along these lines is what is needed to put pragmatism to work on the wicked problems of race and decolonization.

Notes

1. Deborah Whitehead, *William James, Pragmatism, and American Culture* (Bloomington and Indianapolis: Indiana University Press, 2015), 5–6.

2. That said, this chapter is about pragmatism as one component of American philosophy, not American philosophy in its entirety. My purpose here is to draw out links with other forms of philosophy of the Americas.

3. For pragmatism as a hybrid philosophy heavily influenced by indigenous traditions, see Scott Pratt, *Native Pragmatism: Rethinking the Roots of American Philosophy* (Bloomington: Indiana University Press, 2002).

4. In this chapter I identify humanism with modernism—the discourse of modernity—insofar as I accept Wynter's critique of both. In this critique, Wynter argues that modernity as a discourse develops precisely out of the creation of the notion of humanity at the heart of humanism.

5. I am not equating these approaches, but they are related. As McCall and I argued in the introduction, it is important to think of decolonization as a process, not a product. It is not fruitful to think of it as something that can be achieved once and for all but as a struggle whose history is as long as that of the very processes of colonization. I shall, for simplicity's sake, refer to all of these approaches as "postcolonial" for the remainder of this chapter.

6. See, for example, Shannon Sullivan, *Revealing Whiteness: The Unconscious Habits of Racial Privilege* (Bloomington: Indiana University Press, 2006); and Shannon Sullivan, *The Physiology of Sexist and Racist Oppression* (New York: Oxford University Press), 2015.

7. Thomas Fallace, *Dewey and the Dilemma of Race: An Intellectual History, 1895–1922* (New York: Teachers College Press, 2010).

8. Robert Westbrook, foreword to *Dewey and the Dilemma of Race: An Intellectual History, 1895–1922* by Thomas Fallace (New York: Teachers College Press, 2010).vii–viii.

9. Shannon Sullivan, "Review of *Dewey and the Dilemma of Race*," *History of Education Quarterly* 51, no. 4 (2011), 558–561.

10. Fallace, *Dewey and the Dilemma of Race*, 168.

11. Westbrook, foreword, viii.

12. Jennifer Welchman, *Dewey's Ethical Thought* (Ithaca, NY: Cornell University Press, 1995), 6.

13. Timothy H. Dalton, *Becoming John Dewey: Dilemmas of a Philosopher and Naturalist* (Bloomington: Indiana University Press, 2002), 9.

14. Mark Johnson, *Morality for Humans: Ethical Understanding from the Perspective of Cognitive Science* (Chicago: University of Chicago Press, 2014); Thomas Alexander, *John Dewey's Theory of Art, Experience, and Nature: The Horizons of Feeling* (Albany: State University of New York Press, 1987); Thomas Alexander, *The Human Eros: Eco-ontology and the Aesthetics of Existence* (New York: Fordham University Press, 2013); and Gregory Pappas, "John Dewey's Radical Logic: The Function of the Qualitative in Thinking," *Transactions of the Charles S. Peirce Society* 52, no. 3 (2016): 435–468.

15. George Lakoff and Mark Johnson, *Metaphors We Live By* (Chicago: University of Chicago Press, 1980); Johnson, *Morality for Humans*, 24.

16. Johnson, 68.

17. Alexander, *The Human Eros*, 34.

18. Alexander, 52.

19. Susanne Langer, *Feeling and Form: A Theory of Art* (New York: Charles Scribner's and Sons, 1955).

20. Sylvia Wynter, "'Genital Mutilation' or 'Symbolic Birth?' Female Circumcision, Lost Origins, and the Aculturalism." *Case Western Law Review* 47, no. 2 (1997): 501–553, 128.

21. Far from a sexist pseudo-universalization, Wynter's use of "Man" is a technical term that she uses to denote the rise of a specific conception of the human, a conception that excludes vast swaths of humanity from its definition. Specifically, Wynter details how a specific conception of humanity she refers to as "Man1" arose from the medieval theocentric episteme and how this conception was later replaced by "Man2," which arose from the more recent biocentric episteme. See, for example, Sylvia Wynter, "Ethno or Socio Poetics," *Ethno-Poetics: A First International Symposium*, ed. M. Benamou and J. Rothenberg (Boston: Boston University, 1976), 78–94.

22. While one might worry that Dewey's naturalism could fall victim to this critique, it is important to keep in mind a couple of factors. First, "naturalism" has many meanings and one of them is simply, "materialism." If this is what one means when referring to Dewey's philosophy, he is clearly not a materialist. Second, Dewey's philosophy sounds very biologistic in the sense that Wynter criticizes it—that is, a sense that reduces human life to an economy of deterministic matter-energy relations. This is mainly because of Dewey's language, which is adopted from Spencerian evolutionism. But such an account is far from Dewey's actual position. Dewey's philosophy is anything but reductionistic and, importantly, his notion of the "live" creature emphasizes the transformative potential and creativity of living organisms, as does Wynter's use of DNA-coding and biological systems theory. Dewey and Wynter both take up the best biological science of their day without committing themselves to the implicit metaphysics that is assumed to (and often does) accompany it.

23. Quoted in Wynter, "Genital Mutilation," 113.

24. Sylvia Wynter, "The Ceremony Must Be Found: After Humanism," *Boundary* 2, nos. 12-13 (1984):19–70, 21.

25. This is something like the characterization offered by Paget Henry; see Paget Henry, *Caliban's Reason: Introducing Afro-Caribbean Philosophy* (New York and London: Routledge, 2000).

26. W. D. Hamilton, "The Genetical Evolution of Social Behaviour," *Journal of Theoretical Biology* 7 (1964): 1–52; Laurent Lehmann, and Laurent Keller, "The

Evolution of Cooperation and Altruism—A General Framework and a Classification of Models," *Journal of Evolutionary Biology* 19, no. 5 (2006): 1365–1376.

27. Susan Oyama, *Evolution's Eye: A Systems View of the Biology-Culture Divide* (Durham, NC: Duke University Press, 2000).

28. Wynter, "Genital Mutilation."

29. Wynter, "Genital Mutilation."

30. Oyama challenges the notion of purely gene-encoded anything (all ontogeny, including behavior) for nonhuman organisms as well, but this only strengthens Wynter's argument that "culture" interacts with "biology" in complex ways.

31. John Dewey, *Experience and Nature, The Later Works, 1925–1953*, ed. Jo Ann Boydston, vol. 1 (Carbondale: Southern Illinois University Press, 1925).

32. Frantz Fanon, *Black Skin, White Masks*, trans. Charles Lam Markmann (London: Pluto, 2008), 4.

33. Wynter, "Genital Mutilation," 153.

34. Blumenberg quoted in Wynter, "The Ceremony Must Be Found," 21.

35. Daniel Defoe, *Robinson Crusoe* (New York: W. J. Black, 1941); Wynter, "Ethno or Socio Poetics."

36. Wynter, "The Ceremony Must Be Found," 22.

37. Aimé Césaire, *Discourse on Colonialism*, trans. Joan Pinkham (New York: Monthly Review, 2000), 42.

38. Wynter, "Ethno or Socio Poetics."

39. Katherine McKittrick, *Demonic Ground: Black Women and the Cartographies of Struggle* (Minneapolis: University of Minnesota Press, 2006), 132.

40. McKittrick, *Demonic Ground*, 135.

41. Césaire, *Discourse on Colonialism*, 73.

42. Richard Rorty, *Philosophy and the Mirror of Nature* (Princeton, NJ: Princeton University Press, 1979).

43. Michel Foucault, *The Order of Things* (New York: Vintage, 1994).

44. Dewey, *Experience and Nature*, 1925, 141–42.

45. Gregory Pappas, "John Dewey's Radical Logic: The Function of the Qualitative in Thinking," *Transactions of the Charles S. Peirce Society* 52, no. 3 (2016), 435–468.

46. Pappas, "John Dewey's Radical Logic."

47. According to Dewey, all thinking is controlled by the quality of the situation in which it emerges, and qualitative thinking does not have a separate logic for different kinds of situations. See Pappas, "John Dewey's Radical Logic," 438.

48. Pappas, 440.

49. Pappas, 441.

50. John Dewey, "Qualitative Thought," *The Later Works, 1925–1953*, ed. Jo Ann Boydston, vol. 5 (Carbondale: Southern Illinois University Press, 1988): 244–263, 261.

51. Aimé Césaire, "Poetry and Knowledge," in *Lyric and Dramatic Poetry, 1946–82*, trans. Clayton Eshleman and Annette Smith (Charlottesville: University of Virginia Press, 1996), xlvii.

52. Césaire, "Poetry and Knowledge," xlix.

53. Wynter, "Genital Mutilation," 176.

54. Césaire cited in Nick Nesbitt, "Antinomies of Double Consciousness in Aime Cesaire's *Cahier d'un retour au pays natal*," *Mosaic* 33 no. 3 (2000): 114.

55. Césaire, "Poetry and Knowledge," xlii.

56. Angela Last, "We Are the World? Anthropocene Cultural Production between Geopoetics and Geopolitics," *Theory Culture & Society* 33, nos. 2–3 (2017): 157–168, 156. While this might strike the reader as the speculative metaphysics of German Idealism, which Dewey criticized, the point is that both Dewey and Césaire were advocates of experimentation. For Césaire this experimentation was an exploration of the "unconscious unity of nature" while for Dewey it involved a transformation of "experience."

57. Last, "We Are the World," 156.

58. Last, 158.

59. Last, 158.

60. Last, 158.

61. Last, 157.

62. Last, 159.

63. Langer, *Feeling and Form*.

64. Wynter, "Genital Mutilation," 175.

65. John Drabinski, "Césaire's Apocalyptic World," *South Atlantic Quarterly* 115, no. 3 (2016): 567–584, 581.

66. Wynter, "Genital Mutilation," 180, quoting Heinz Pagels.

PART THREE

EXPANDING THE AMERICAN CANON

CHAPTER EIGHT

The Social Ontology of Care among Filipina Dependency Workers
Kittay, Addams, and a Transnational Doulia Ethics of Care

CELIA T. BARDWELL-JONES

Relationships of dependency are an essential feature of the human condition. These relationships of dependency are characterized as intimately social insofar as the material and physical requirements toward our well-being require the love, care, and nurturance of another person. In this chapter, I want to focus on how dependency and care situate notions of the cross-cultural self within embedded transnational relationships and how these new constructions of the self work against and within colonial systems of oppression. These relationships offer more concrete ways to think about the nature of the multicultural self situated in between contradictory claims of empowerment and enslavement, such as the case of Filipina dependency workers. In an age of globalization, in which travel and migration become the outcomes of global market economies motivated by imperial desire, decolonization as a methodology and theoretical framework extends into transnational contexts of migration in which a critique of colonizing systems of power becomes the backdrop of agency formation among Filipina dependency workers. If we are to decolonize American thought, it is essential to center our analysis away from a rigid domestic narrative that secures borders, claiming entitlements to the identity of America but perhaps thinking about our transnational relationships that intricately make up the American social fabric.

As the world becomes more connected through transnational global markets, more attention needs to be paid to how transnational relationships of dependency are fundamentally relationships of dependency. An ethics of care provides both an important resource for critically examining the ways in which social life is predicated on relationships of dependency and an important contribution toward understanding questions of obligation and responsibility within transnational relationships of dependency. One example that has not received much attention in care ethics is the case of transnational dependency workers,[1] including many women from the Philippines who leave their country of origin to work in First World households such as in the United States. In my view, attending to the nested dependencies of transnational dependency workers reveals a more concrete and embedded perspective in care ethics, which can then be used to address the concerns of globalization and international relationships.

The need for dependency workers in First World countries has taken its toll in countries such as the Philippines. This need has generated the largest amount of foreign revenue in the Philippines, totaling approximately US$7 billion, mostly coming from migrant domestic workers. Care work in the Philippines is considered to be the country's largest export to other countries. In fact, the Philippine government has identified a care crisis in the Philippines, as more and more Filipinas leave home seeking better wages in order to care for their families back in the Philippines.[2] It is important to understand how dependency work has expanded into a global context and theorized as global care chains.

Global care chains, as initially theorized by Parreñas, identify the limiting conditions of Filipina dependency workers imbricated within systems of imperial market economies that carry over into the inescapable demands of care work. Global care chains also carry an emotional toll on Filipina dependency workers. Barbara Ehrenreich and Arlie Hochschild identify a few challenges transnational Filipina mothers face. First, constant contradictory emotions besiege the transnational mother. She cares for her First World charge while her own children are left with family members in the Philippines. The complex experiences of loneliness and yearning for her own children at home inform the kind of care the First World charge receives. This, of course, has disastrous effects on the children who continually yearn to be with their transnational mothers. One Filipina woman Parreñas interviewed gave the following tearful lament:

> When the girl I take care of calls her mother Mama, my heart jumps all the time because my children also call me "Mama." When I pack her lunch . . . that's what I used to do for my children . . . I think I should be taking care of them instead of another child. . . . If I had wings, I would fly home to my children. . . . Just for a moment, to see my children and take care of their needs, help them, then fly back over here to continue my work.[3]

Arlie Hochschild characterizes this social reality as "globalization's pound of flesh."[4] The emotional experience of loss, felt by both mother and child, is an effect of the global market economy.

Second, while it is clear that transnational dependency workers are dependent on employment in First World countries, the reciprocating dependency of the First World on this dependency work largely remains invisible. As Ofelia Schutte has argued, on a macro level, global market economies directed by neoliberal policies do not incorporate dependency work in the gross national product of the country.[5] Dependency work is often seen as a service in which the employee's obligation to the employer is limited to an economic relationship, thereby masking the nature of the relationship. Since this dependency is not recognized among many First World employers, the responsibility to their workers is also concealed.

Third, care work, paid or unpaid, is continually undermined and further devalued. The invisibility of the work and of the care workers themselves underscores the modes of valuation of reproductive labor in our society. This labor does not produce products but instead sustains people. In a market-driven economy, however, it is difficult to assess the value of this kind of work, and thus it is valued much lower than work that manufactures goods for sale. Hochschild argues, "The low value of care keeps the status of women and those who do it, and ultimately all women, low."[6]

Eva Kittay has also problematized the situation of care ethics within the lives of Filipina dependency workers in addressing their well-being and agency. Working against systems of oppression, Kittay strives to articulate political solutions to make space for Filipina women's agency.

> If, as many feminists have argued, women cannot exercise the freedom to pursue their various aspirations as long as they retain the primary responsibility of caring for dependents, structures must be in place to ease the responsibilities that have traditionally fallen on the shoulders of women, or women will be hindered in their quest to share this world equally with men.[7]

Kittay advocates a change to the oppressive ethical and political structures that perpetuate the suffering and harm to all women, including Filipina dependency workers. This involves moving our ethical and political considerations into the concrete transnational relationships that connect diverse social lives. However, it is important to recall the concerns of Parreñas and others that "housework is not a 'bond of sisterhood' but a 'bond of oppression.'"[8] Solidarity cannot be grounded on a narrow perspective of housework given the complex hierarchies that emerge from the global care chains.

Alison Weir, keeping this challenge of transnational solidarity in mind among women, also considers how care ethics can be framed to address the lives of Filipina dependency workers. In her view, a relational model of freedom, as opposed to an individual model of freedom, is essential in effectively transforming the ethical and political structures cross-culturally. Kittay has recognized that a public ethos of care must go beyond a domestic narrative and recognize the global circumstances that underlie the experiences of dependency workers: including remittances that are sent back to support their families in their countries of origin. Both authors tacitly acknowledge that space between national boundaries emerges and situates an ethics of care that can speak to the lives of Filipina dependency workers who must navigate their agency within oppressive colonial structures.

In extending the discussion of Kittay and Weir to address the concerns of Filipina dependency workers, I understand our global situation as fundamentally characterized by transnational relationships of dependency, which demands an ethics of care that pays closer attention to concrete moral responses to those who are culturally different and, despite appearing foreign and distant, are living and working close at hand. Like Kittay and Weir, I also center my analysis of care ethics by focusing on the lives of Filipina dependency workers. My basic strategy is to offer a model of care ethics inspired by an expansion of Eva Kittay's notion of the doulia principle to transnational relationships of dependency through

Jane Addams's conception of care and dependency within the context of her social work with immigrant communities. Decolonizing American conceptions of care requires refocusing the subject of care within the contradictory and complex social ontology of colonial transnational relationships of dependency. Following Gerwal and Kaplan, the practices that connect us with distant others occur within the transnational boundary spaces determined by forces of globalization. It is in this third place that our moral orientation of care should operate: negotiating the maze of economic markets, citizenship rules, language barriers, remittances, and the translation of cultural value systems. Thinking about distant others requires attention to the boundaries that connect us to one another in an international context. It requires that we look closer to home in thinking about our responsibilities to others abroad. Nel Noddings has recognized this move in care ethics as "starting at home."[9] However, it is important to understand one's home as occupied by culturally different others, making one's caring response less parochial and more transnational. This allows us to understand our responsibilities to more distant others by recognizing transnational relationships of dependency that fundamentally characterize the human global experience.

In the next section, I will articulate an ethics of care within transnational boundary conditions to address the concerns of the Filipina dependency worker. In effect, this analysis generates a transnational public ethos of care situated within the complexities and contradictions of transnational relationships of dependency. These dependent transnational relationships serve as the context many Filipina dependency workers must navigate. My basic strategy will be first to examine Eva Kittay's argument about dependency and how it generates a public ethos of care known as a doulia principle. Next, I will expand this notion of the doulia principle to a transnational context through Jane Addams's conception of care and dependency in her work with immigrant communities.

Examining the Social Role of the Doulia Principle

Kittay argues that dependency is an "inescapable" reality that conditions the "life history of each individual." She understands this reality as manifest in "early childhood, illness, disability and old age."[10] By virtue of our biological reality, we are inevitably dependent on others for care and sustenance and for our very survival and growth. It is important to note that the "incapacity" that characterizes one's dependencies is established "neither by will nor desire."[11] In other words, one is constrained by these relations of dependency in lived experience, and it is impossible to remove oneself physically and willfully from these relationships. It is also worth noting how these unavoidable dependencies are determined not only by biology or the physical facts of one's body but also by the social circumstances that determine what counts as being old, frail, ill, or disabled. Ultimately, the cultural dimensions in combination with one's physiological constraints condition what can be thought of as dependent, shaping the very concept of dependency.

In this sense, one's condition of dependency cannot be understood as an exceptional circumstance. For Kittay, to conceive of dependency in this manner "dismisses the importance of human interconnectedness," which is necessary for survival and "the development of culture itself."[12] Not only does dependency constitute our physical lives, it also percolates into human social relations. To this extent, relations of dependency cross the lines of the prepolitical or familial realities of our lived experience into the social and political institutions governing our public lives. In fact, dependency, "as a feature of the human condition, has crucial bearing on the ordering of social institutions and on the moral intuitions that serve to guarantee adherence to just institutions."[13]

Moreover, relations of dependency imply a responsibility to care for and form moral attachments with others within dependent relationships. This capacity to care is a mark of one's humanity.[14] The moral upshot of this claim is that one cannot thrive if this capacity is not cultivated within the moral and political practices of society. Nel Noddings views the notion of growth in care ethics as one that rejects rigidity. This commitment to growth overlaps nicely within the pragmatist tradition. In the context of education, a child's growth must stem from her interests as an individual and must not be blocked by confining expectations from parents or the larger society.[15] Noddings argues that growth requires "time and care" from the individual. This notion of growth resonates with Kittay's claim that society cannot thrive if exploitation is a norm. Since the growth of the individual is tied to the growth of society, an exploitive society is one that blocks an individual's growth and in turn prevents society from achieving its own growth. Kittay seems to suggest the need for an attitude of caring that ultimately cares for the process of caring itself—that is, if society is to thrive and grow. The growth of the individual and that of society are both dependent on the capacity to care. Thus, as Kittay argues, "At the nexus of these relationships of dependency is a moral responsibility."[16] In this sense, the moral responsibility involves an attitude of caring for caring in order to ensure that society continues toward growth.

In this respect, Kittay emphasizes the relationship between the dependency worker and her charge as a paradigmatic case of a dependency relationship. In this relationship, there remains an obvious vulnerability that is experienced by both the dependency worker and her charge. Not only is the charge vulnerable and in need of the dependency worker's care work, but because the nature of dependency work requires selfless acts from the dependency worker, there is a chance that the care needed to sustain this dependent relationship will be inadequate. The dependency workers' vulnerability exposes society's obligation in caring for the process of caring. Kittay argues:

> A system that pays adequate attention to the dependency relation will be one seeking both to empower the dependency worker with respect to her own interests and whenever possible, to decrease the dependency of the dependent as well. By relegating dependency to the status of an afterthought, neither caregiver nor charge is well-served.[17]

By focusing on the dependency relation, our responsibility is understood as one of responsiveness, care, and trust, which solidifies our bonds to the human community and the wider environmental community we are in a relationship with. Viewing our responsibility as an activity of sustaining dependent relationships provides us with a picture of ethics congruent with the "unassailable fact" of our dependencies.

Thus, Kittay offers a model of reciprocity, developing a doulia system in thinking about how social responsibility is viewed if the dependency relation is seen as foundational to the ordering of just social institutions. A doula is "a postpartum caregiver who assists the mother, and at times relieves her."[18] Rather than understanding the doula as replacing the mother's role as caregiver to her infant, "the doula assists by caring for the mother as the mother attends to the child."[19] While the early Greek conception of the doula's service is related to the work done by slaves, which occurs within exploitative relationships, Kittay wishes to redirect the doula's notion of service as one of interdependence "that recognizes a relation—not precisely of reciprocity but of nested dependencies—linking those who help and those who require help to give aid to those who cannot help themselves."[20]

According to Kittay, an ontological model of interdependence based on the doulia system recognizes our need for care as human beings, and this should be made available to everybody, including those who do the work of caring. This principle of the doulia as defined by Kittay implies an extension to the public domain. This extension emphasizes a public ethos of care. The larger society must play a role in ensuring the well-being of the dependency worker. The need for care of the dependency worker signals a moral response from the society she is a part of. The doulia principle establishes a principle of connection and attentiveness to relationships essential for the growth and well-being of society. This principle characterizes the responsibility of society to its dependency workers.

The principle of the doulia, understood as a public ethos of care according to Kittay, establishes two important tasks for society. First, it develops a specific "social responsibility (derived from political justice realized in social cooperation) for enabling dependency relations satisfactory to dependency worker and dependent alike."[21] The principle of the doulia recognizes the value of relationships of dependency as necessary for the health of all human beings. Second, the principle of the doulia as a public ethos of care would encourage social institutions to "foster an attitude of caring and a respect for care by enabling caregivers to do the job of caretaking without becoming disadvantaged in the competition for the benefits of social cooperation."[22] By respecting the dependency workers' well-being, society ensures that the work of care continues under more favorable conditions for the dependency worker. In caring for the dependency worker, society cultivates an attitude that values the work of caring.[23] A public ethos of care, articulated through the doulia principle, would focus on the dependency worker's well-being because she embodies the dependency relation.

Kittay is committed to preserving the caring-for relation of the dependency worker by establishing a doulia principle that cares about the demands of dependency work. By establishing the requirements of care as fundamental in society, Kittay recognizes the social ontology of dependency and develops an ethics of care that allows one to *care-about* while avoiding the pitfalls of abstraction or unwanted charity. However, how might we understand this doulia principle within transnational relationships of dependency, particularly in the case where the Filipina dependency worker is considered a foreigner, maintaining commitments to distant countries, yet nonetheless is proximate? Moreover, if we look at the transnational dependency worker as paradigmatic of international societies, what might global responsibilities look like? Addressing the needs of the transnational dependency workers would reveal our inevitable transnational relationships of dependency and direct our associated global responses of care closer to home. *Caring-about* must be tied to concrete practices of care, which involve more face-to-face interactions. Rather than viewing *caring-about* as an attitude that can be applied in international contexts, such as giving money to starving children in Somalia without even realizing how we might directly relate to their experiences, it is best to view this moral orientation within one's familiar engagements with culturally different others. This will encourage a moral orientation of care to be more flexible (less parochial) and less prone to instances of caring imperialism or paternalism/maternalism. In the next section, I show how Jane Addams's notion of care and dependency is informed by her work with immigrant communities. Addams ultimately provides us with a flexible understanding of a moral orientation of care conceived within transnational relationships fostering interaction. This will lead my analysis to a formulation of a transnational doulia principle.

Addams and the Social Ethics of Dependency

Maurice Hamington understands Addams's work at Hull House as exhibiting a social habit of care. For Hamington, Addams "provides what care ethics has often been accused of lacking: a strong social-political element."[24] It is my contention that Addams provides a unique contribution to care ethics by offering a social ontology to the social and political concerns surrounding the global context of care and dependency. I will examine how Addams's notion of affectionate interpretation or sympathetic understanding implies a notion of the *space-between* that fosters social interaction. A social ontology that emphasizes interaction can serve as a way of thinking about how Addams's relational model of ethics can extend into a public ethos of care.

Affectionate Interpretation and Sympathetic Understanding as a Public Ethos of Care

The notion of sympathetic understanding has often been cited among Addams scholars as an important feature that links her philosophy and work at Hull House to feminist care ethics.[25] Sympathetic understanding is usually viewed as highlighting an epistemological or moral orientation that values care in moral judgments. Affectionate interpretation appears in Addams's essay "A Modern Lear" and is used to articulate the notion of sympathetic understanding. However, I focus on the terminology of affectionate interpretation because I think her use of this term in "A Modern Lear" highlights her social ontology, which can similarly be understood within her notion of sympathetic understanding. In this way, her notion of sympathetic understanding is broadened to include questions of ontology as well as epistemology and values. This has implications for thinking about transnational relationships of dependency.

While the pragmatist and feminist traditions do not assume a rigid distinction between ontology, epistemology, and ethics, it is important to see how sympathetic understanding has usually been theorized as a moral orientation of care rather than as an explanation of the ontology of relationality. Hamington understands Addams's notion of sympathetic understanding related to questions of knowledge. He writes, "Knowledge is a prerequisite for embodied care because one cannot care for something about which one knows nothing."[26] For Hamington, how we know has much to do with the body. Sympathetic understanding brings us into relation with the communal needs of society by sympathetically engaging the lives of others, rather than being limited to one's individual or parochial experiences. Sympathetic understanding is understood as an orientation of care that enables us to become more socially engaged and more related to others.

Seigfried understands Addams's notion of sympathetic understanding as a social habit that we learn by directly engaging "on a day-to-day basis" with people who are culturally, politically, or ethnically diverse.[27] It operates within the realm of action. In this way, our sympathies for one another break down rigid attitudes that suggest a singular access to morality. Morality, in this sense, necessarily seeks the diverse perspective that can only be attained by actually interacting with culturally different others, rather than assuming prior to the interaction a single principle of morality. Seigfried understands sympathetic understanding as a moral orientation that values care, which is important in thinking about what constitutes a just community.

In this way, Seigfried suggests that a commitment to diversity is essential in cultivating a nonexploitive society:

Through the mediation of sympathetic understanding, a space can be opened in which the viewpoint, values, and goals of others can become part of moral deliberation and social transformation. Only by letting them speak for themselves and not projecting our viewpoints on them or thinking we can unproblematically enter into their worlds through imagination can such collaboration take place without coercion or co-optation.[28]

It is important to recognize that a boundary space emerges between people such that mutual recognition is possible. The *space-between* need not be limited to individuals since it also affects the commitments of the communities that individuals are a part of. Social awareness begins with individuals, but the possibility of social transformation is realized when communities are open to the influences of culturally different others. In this way, rather than viewing an ethics of care as an individual moral orientation that one can apply to distant others, Addams's notion of sympathetic understanding underscores a social orientation of care by underscoring communities' flexibility for social change through encounters with communities that are culturally different. This boundary space becomes an important feature in Addams's work in thinking about larger social relationships that extend beyond one's individual or parochial relationships.

Sympathetic understanding, called *affectionate interpretation* here, is introduced in Addams's discussion of the Pullman Strike of 1894. The Pullman Palace Car Company factory workers, working with the American Railway Union, led a strike against the Pullman Company seeking better wages. The strike ended unsuccessfully without arbitration for the factory workers and resulted in the federal government intervening in order to open the railways. Furthermore, Pullman received broad public criticism regarding his paternalistic policies toward his workers, particularly his policy that required his employees to live, pay rent, and buy food in the company town. In this case, the conflict was between the workers of the Pullman Company and the employer, who thought of himself as a benefactor to his employees. But Pullman's workers had expressed their disapproval through a strike after he raised their rents to pay dividends to his investors. Addams compares the tragedies of the industrial relationship surrounding the workers' strike to the tragedies of the familial relationship in Shakespeare's *King Lear*. In the context of family obligations, Addams is able to identify the problems of the Pullman strike by recognizing relationships of dependency between both the employees and Pullman.

Much like King Lear, the president of the Pullman Company felt that the workers' strike was a sign of ingratitude for his acts of generosity. However, Addams comments that Pullman lost the ability to attain "a simple human relationship with his employees." Addams identifies this faculty as *affectionate interpretation* and argues that this quality was lost to King Lear and Pullman, who both succumbed to egoistic interpretations of the situation. This prevented both Lear and Pullman from affectively interpreting the concerns of Cordelia and the workers, respectively. Trapped in their own narrow perspectives, both Lear and Pullman lacked the means to understand how other people in the relationship can play a role in shaping their own experience. Moreover, Addams also felt the workers (and Cordelia) possessed a "narrow conception of emancipation," which prevented them from finding a meaningful relationship with their employer. Because both sides of the relationship lacked the capacity to interpret the situation affectionately, there was "no mutual interest in a common cause."[29]

Addams suggests that affectionate interpretation brings the individual out of her narrow perspective to seek a diversity of viewpoints. However, this move toward culturally and socially different others entails an element of suffering. Addams argues:

> It sometimes seems as if only hardship and sorrow could arouse our tenderness, whether in our personal or social relations; that the king, the prosperous man, was the last to receive the justice which can come only through affectionate interpretation.[30]

Addams seems to suggest that a requirement of affectionate interpretation demands that one must undergo a sense of suffering or loss of one's familiar beliefs and customs. Suffering opens one to the possibility of social transformation. It signals a departure from one's narrow or parochial conceptions and brings one into relation with other kinds of social experience. Consequently, affectionate interpretation not only suggests the embedded character of relationships of dependency, particularly in family relationships, but also underscores how the interaction is fraught with tension between one's individual desires and one's commitment to communal and social relationships. The departure prompts an inquiry into the meaning of one's social relationships. One's choices are dependent on how meaningfully and authentically we understand our relationship to others.

Placing oneself in between one's individual perspective and one's commitment to others requires that one must exhibit the virtue of humility in order to achieve a sense of social justice.[31] Reflecting on the old Hebrew Prophets' three requirements, Addams reformulates the *caring-for* and *caring-about* distinction through an understanding of the virtue of humility as the middle ground between the requirements of "loving mercy" and "doing justly." Solely fulfilling the requirement of loving mercy by giving indiscriminately without understanding the concerns of others would lead to a form of unwanted charity. One merely *cares-about* in an abstract manner, and how one *cares-for* others might lead to paternalism/maternalism or possibly a caring imperialism. Solely fulfilling the requirement of doing justice would lead to dogmatic rules and strict policies governing our relationships with others without any sort of sympathy. In other words, one does not consider how care plays an important role in justice and, in effect, does not care at all.

Between these two requirements, Addams suggests that we should

> "walk humbly with God," which may mean to walk for many dreary miles beside the lowliest of His creatures, not even in the peace of mind which the company of the humble is popularly supposed to afford, but rather with the pangs and throes to which the poor human understanding is subjected whenever it attempts to comprehend the meaning of life.[32]

"Walking humbly" requires us to engage with others regardless of the diverse perspectives that constitute the larger society and one's more personal and familiar relationships. In other words, Addams views *caring-about* as grounded within the practices of *caring-for*. This requires work and effort. As Seigfried understands Addams's project of social ethics, "the transformation is personal, but the means are social."[33] Affectionate interpretation suggests that we find meaning in our moral orientation of care by traveling with others, walking humbly for many miles, and experiencing the pain of maintaining this social relationship. This can only be done by recognizing a third place or a boundary place of social experience that both displaces us from our narrow conceptions and opens us to the possibility of understanding those from different locations of social experience.

The need for a social morality in ethics is prompted by anxiety among individuals seeking "their actual relations to the basic organization of society."³⁴ For Addams, a basic yearning for connection with others moves questions of ethics into social experience. Understood within a social realm, ethics is conceived relationally through the daily experience of living with one another. Addams writes, "We are learning that a standard of social ethics is not attained by traveling a sequestered byway, but by mixing on the thronged and common road where all must turn out for one another, and at least see the size of one another's burdens."³⁵ The common road represents a boundary place constituted by travel, displacing the subjects from their familiar environments and thrusting them into a situation ready for transformation. It is the common road of experience that meaningfully brings us into relation with one another. This assumes that ethics is not about applying principles generated outside of specific interactions but requires that moral guidelines emerge within actual day-to-day engagement with the lives of others within the boundaries of social experience characterized by our common efforts with one another. Addams exemplifies the pragmatist commitment to experience and social experimentalism that considers the messiness and ambiguity of a rich, complex, and culturally diverse social context.

Interacting with culturally different others becomes a necessary requirement for Addams in order to generate meaningful social relationships. Care is situated within an experimental method in which one learns how to become open to the diverse perspectives that make up social life. In this way, affectionate interpretation proposes a relational moral attitude that emphasizes the need for reciprocity within social relationships. According to Seigfried in the introduction to *Democracy and Social Ethics*, Addams understands the social relation as reciprocal.³⁶ Addams thinks that one's personal transformation, which occurs within the boundaries of social experience with socially and culturally different others, fosters an attitude of care that cares for caring, much like Kittay's doulia principle. Once one is transformed through the process of affectionate interpretation, one develops, according to Addams, a public ethos of care, which seeks "the betterment of humanity."³⁷ As Nodding describes growth in the process of *caring-about*, Addams develops a notion of growth in social ethics requiring that communities be flexible and experiment with the diversity of experiences. Being closed to experience and to others prevents one from engaging in social transformation, as Addams argues:

> A man who takes the betterment of humanity for his aim and end must also take the daily experiences of humanity

for the constant correction of his process. He must not only test and guide his achievement by human experience, but he must succeed or fail in proportion as he has incorporated that experience with his own.[38]

Caring for caring, understood as a public ethos, is grounded upon the daily experiences of those who affectionately interpret the lives of others in social experience. Addams's view of reciprocity extends to a larger public attitude that values the work of care in our day-to-day interactions with others so that the well-being of society is well served. Attending to relationships of dependency in our daily lives through an attitude of caring for caring becomes a way of achieving the "betterment of humanity." Addams's sense of reciprocity cultivates a public ethos of care by opening up for transformation one's own social ideals relative to the daily interactions with socially and culturally diverse others.[39] It is important to emphasize here that the commitment to social experimentalism within the context of cross-cultural encounters offers a critical perspective that might undermine global colonial forces within the context of transnational relationships of dependency.

In addition, Addams's argument for the subjective necessity for social settlements views the individual's well-being as tied to the well-being of society:

> It is always easy to make all philosophy point to one particular moral and all history adorn one particular tale; but I may be forgiven the reminder that the best speculative philosophy sets forth the solidarity of the human race; that the highest moralists have taught that without the advance and the improvement of the whole, no man can hope for any lasting improvement in his own moral or material individual condition; and that the subjective necessity for Social Settlements is therefore identical with that necessity, which urges us on toward social and individual salvation.[40]

Affectionate interpretation makes a necessary synthesis, understanding the concerns of the individual as related to a wider social process. Being attentive to connections and relationships of dependency secures the possibility for social transformations. Affectionate interpretation offers a relational method for understanding the continuity, or relationships of dependency, between the individual and the wider society.

Affectionate Interpretation as a Transnational Public Ethos of Care

Affectionate interpretation can be seen as a public ethos of care that pays particular attention to the ways in which the individual is connected to and ensconced in social activities and communities. Additionally, it serves as a way of bringing this public ethos of care out of its parochial limitations within nation-state boundaries by recognizing that the individual's relationship to a social life necessarily percolates into international social activities. As a notable peace activist, Addams's view of social ethics extends beyond nationalisms. The features of affectionate interpretation that generate a public ethos of care can be extended to international social life. However, this transition is deeply rooted in the daily activities that we choose to engage in with culturally different others.

For Addams, narrow perspectives lead to critical misunderstandings. The individual perspective prevents the possibility of seeing other points of view and how one can find meaning in social life. Social relationships imply the assumption that we are all dependent on each other, not only for sustenance and care but also to understand ethical life. Without engaging with others, the individual perspective lacks moral meaning in the sense that the individual's views are not properly socialized. Hamington comments that this feature in Addams's thought "is a demanding moral imperative."[41] In fact, Addams finds it necessary to engage with others who are culturally different. Since our experiences are partial, it is of utmost necessity that we engage others who are culturally different in the communities in which we live. Caring for distant others risks the inability to *care-for* others concretely and makes the moral orientation of *caring-about* seem abstract and empty. Addams views this problem of caring for distant others close to home. She sees the work of caring practiced within the crowded urban cities where the clash of cultural difference is lived and experienced every day through the lives of immigrants. The crowdedness of social experience suggests that the work of caring is done in a proximate context. Addams is attentive to the transnational social relationships located in the immigrant quarters of Chicago, which greatly influence her notion of cosmopolitanism.

Immigrants become important in Addams's conception of what it means to be internationally minded. In *Newer Ideals of Peace*, immigrants embody the faculty of affectionate interpretation due to their social position in society as newcomers facing the demands of the host country's processes for becoming a citizen. These insights into the lives of immigrants prompt Addams to develop what I take to be a transnational public ethos of care based on the experiences of immigrants as they emerge in her interactions. Immigrants are not distant others in the sense that one need not travel outside the United States to meet Italians, Russians, or Poles. For Addams, one can travel quite locally to encounter Italian, Russian, or Polish culture. While Robinson characterizes the shrinking world as a "disembedding place" due to globalization, Addams directs our attention to concrete embedded places that are transnational, such as cosmopolitan urban centers, particularly immigrant neighborhoods.

Given the features of affectionate interpretation, it is important to understand the motivation behind Addams's emphasis on immigrants in relation to developing a more internationally minded way of thinking that will lead to international peace. First, Addams begins with the assumption that social morality has an "origin in social affections."[42] Affectionate interpretation demands that one be sympathetic to the concerns of others. King Lear lacked this capacity and failed to understand the plight of his daughter. Likewise, Pullman saw himself as a benefactor to his employees, which prevented him from seeing their concerns. For Addams, social morality emphasizes emotion. In the context of international or cross-cultural experiences, this requires a cultivation of moral sentiment that is cosmopolitan in affection. Addams understands our international ethical relationships in the context of our more tribal or domestic relationships.[43] She argues that a double conception of morality divides our ethical actions. The first conception is the relation within a "tribe" or social group. The second is the relation to "outsiders." However, these must be combined in order to develop an international model for peace. Otherwise, these divided sets of ethical actions will take on militarizing habits that will ultimately lead to war.[44]

In combining these two ethical postures, what we ought to do in our country and what we ought to do with "outsiders," Addams argues that we should "naturally seek for [the synthesis of the two ethical postures] in the poorer quarters of a cosmopolitan city."[45] In seeking the development of this cosmopolitan social sentiment, we should look to more concrete social experiences that address cross-cultural relationships, such as the life of immigrants. Addams recognizes that "emotional sentiment runs high among newly arrived immigrants,"[46] due to their own displaced status in a new country. Displacement cultivates "an unusual mental alertness and power of perception."[47] Immigrants have traveled, in the sense that they are willing to revise their cultural habits and renounce social customs practiced for many generations. In other words, they are willing to open themselves up for transformation. They are willing to participate in a larger social life that sometimes demands casting aside accepted customs and habits. Immigrants are also in a unique position to settle or "seek companionship in a new world" and thus "inevitably develop the power of association which comes from daily contact with those who are unlike each other."[48] Immigrants embody epistemic locations that can provide insight into the relationship between the domestic and the international. These epistemic locations take on the character of the *space-between* and inhabit the interactions of immigrants and their host community. Through these interactions, immigrants contribute to the very makeup of their host community. Addams argues that just as immigrants' hopes and dreams can be instructive in shaping city government, education, and charity work, "so their daily lives are a forecast of coming international relations."[49]

Addams's commitment to experience can launch our inquiries into a cosmopolitan social morality in crowded cities. Crowded cities require a "deeper and more thoroughgoing unity" that only could be had among a "highly differentiated people,"[50] rather than more stable and homogenous social collectivities. A "commingling" of many different kinds of people expresses a type of unity that negotiates a balance of opposing views and forces. The unity "gravitates" toward the common road or the daily interactions of people. According to Addams, resolution of differences can only be accomplished through social means:

> It is natural that this synthesis of the varying nations should be made first at the points of the greatest congestion, quite as we find that selfishness is first curbed and social feeling created at the points where the conflict of individual interests is sharpest.[51]

Addams believes that through these daily encounters, narrow nationalist perspectives can be challenged, providing us with important insights into the development of an international public ethos of care toward peace.

At times, it is clear that Addams in these passages of *Newer Ideals of Peace* romanticizes the possibilities of cultivating a cosmopolitan sentiment for a social morality through the figure of the immigrant. She refers to them as "humble harbingers of the Newer Ideals of Peace" or the "kindly citizens of the world."[52] In fact, one might argue that she places an unusual degree of responsibility on the immigrant, particularly in that the difficult task of living in a host country usually occupies their priorities, rather than becoming saints of cosmopolitanism or the bearers of international peace. More critically, Rivka Shpak Lissak argues that Addams's strategy of incorporating immigrants has assimilationist motives rather than making a place for their specific ethnic traditions to play a role in American life.[53]

Addams, however, is too entrenched in the daily lives of immigrants through her work in Hull House to make this idealistic and romanticized judgment. It is not their political positions regarding war and peace that make their situation promising. In fact, Addams suggests that many immigrants have advocated for war and not peace. The importance for Addams lies in the fact "that they are really attaining cosmopolitan relations through daily experience."[54] Through interactions with immigrants, Addams believes there is hope in uncovering the "vital relation—that of the individual to the race."[55] This task is not just for immigrants. It is a mutual task that involves a caring attention, which involves utilizing the faculty of affectionate interpretation and recognizing a transnational space of interaction that encompasses the realities of the immigrant's life.

Addams employs a version of affectionate interpretation by highlighting the social interactions within transnational relationships that bring us into relation with culturally different others that extend outside our nation-state borders. Both the lives of immigrants and one's specific interactions with immigrants serve as transnational relationships where one's work of care is placed between social relationships that are not limited to the dichotomy of ethical postures, either focusing on relations within a domestic polity or with foreign others. By highlighting these social relationships with immigrants, Addams directs our analysis of cosmopolitanism to a realm of action and experience that pays particular attention to one's relationship with those who are considered both outside of and a part of a domestic polity.

Addams calls upon our skills of affectionate interpretation toward immigrants in the areas of the "Americanization" of immigrants and the education of immigrant children. According to Addams, rather than assimilating immigrants in the United States through abstract concepts, such as rights or mere memorization of phrases of the US Constitution, we need to listen to their experiences of living in their country of origin. She argues, "We believed that America could be best understood by the immigrants if we ourselves, Americans, made some sort of a connection with their past history and experiences."[56] In this sense, Addams encourages us to stake ourselves and become open for transformation, as Americans, in our engagement with immigrants, thereby developing a new national narrative alongside the narrative of the immigrant. This would lead to widespread discussion of what it means to be an American in relation to the experiences of culturally different others.

In the case of the education of immigrant children, Addams encourages teachers to learn about the cultures of their students. In "The Public School and the Immigrant Child," Addams redirects the destinations of travel to more local situations. For Addams, the shrinking world is apparent in our own communities. One must seek these interactions and help restore to immigrants the knowledge of their culture, rather than viewing knowledge of other cultures as to be found strictly outside of the nation-state boundary. In these two instances, Addams encourages social habits of cosmopolitanism and brings the public ethos of care to international contexts. These two processes in understanding the immigrant highlight the transnational spaces that determine the immigrant's life, as well as invite new forms of international relationships to emerge in a domestic context—at home. In other words, the result of a social synthesis of domestic and international relations occurs within transnational social relations between nations. What I take to be Addams's transnational social ethos of care encourages Americans to develop cosmopolitan affectionate interpretations by achieving the sense of a common ground between culturally different others.

The common ground is a wider context of social experience that can facilitate mutual understanding between culturally different others. This notion of a common ground emerges in Addams's work with immigrants in understanding cosmopolitan artwork and the formation of the Labor Museum. In one scenario at Hull House, Addams recounts an encounter with an "old pioneer," who was "fiercely American" and thought the decline of the neighborhood was the fault of the rising numbers of "foreigners" settling into the cities. The old man complained to Addams of the many "foreign" artworks that decorated the walls of Hull House. Addams responds with a decolonial sentiment:

> I endeavored to set forth our hope that the pictures might afford a familiar island to the immigrants in a sea of new and strange impressions. The old settler guest, taken off his guard, replied, "see; they feel as we did when we saw a Yankee notion from Down East,"—thereby formulating the dim kinship between the pioneer and the immigrant, both "buffeting the waves of a new development."[57]

The Labor Museum, which featured many crafts from the immigrant's country of origin, facilitated presentations and workshops to help restore to the immigrants their past histories and traditions and bring them into relation with American cultural experiences. Addams thought the Labor Museum could be a model for that "educational enterprise which should build a bridge between European and American experiences in such wise as to give them both more meaning and a sense of relation."[58] In this way, cultural misunderstanding could be mitigated once a larger relation or a common ground was established between the immigrant and American culture. Both instances strive to facilitate mutual understanding and synthesize international and domestic relations by providing the context, defined by certain practices and action such as artwork and the Labor Museum, in which citizens can be brought into relation with one another. This relationship forges a new sense of what American life means.

Addams adds to an ethics of care a way of envisioning our relationships of dependency nested within transnational spaces of interaction, particularly in the case of immigrant neighborhoods. She understands the moral orientation of care to distant others closer to home by emphasizing the ways in which we concretely relate to culturally different others through interactions with immigrants. By situating the problem of caring for distant others within the context of one's day-to-day encounters with culturally and ethnically diverse immigrants, one is able to develop a more cosmopolitan spirit based in concrete and embedded relationships with culturally different others, rather than abstractly *caring-about* geographically distant others. Addams's social experimentalist empathetic approach provides the possibility of challenging colonial norms that produce attitudes of American exceptionalism that rigidly define American conceptions of the self. Moreover, Addams emphasizes the transnational relationships that are conditioned by our choices to attend to these diverse perspectives and that anchor our moral orientation to distant others within concrete and embedded social relationships within our specific interactions with immigrants. Her public ethos of care as characterized by her notion of affectionate interpretation is transformed into a cosmopolitan sentiment as she seeks unity with other nations to further her activist goals of peace.

In the following section, I would like to bring together Kittay's insights on the principle of the doulia and Addams's transnational public ethos of care in order to address the concerns of transnational dependency workers. By looking at these workers' concerns, I argue a transnational doulia principle develops, which has implications for thinking about the nature of international communities.

Toward a Transnational Doulia Principle: Making Visible Transnational Responsibilities

In her important contribution to feminism and globalization, Ofelia Schutte argues in her essay "Women, Dependency and the Global Economy" that neoliberal policies are incapable of assessing dependency work as a type of productive labor in developing countries for two reasons. First, the unpaid care work is rendered invisible "and not considered productive itself."[59] Second, women are forced to go back home to offset the cuts in social services. According to Schutte, neoliberal policies fail to account for the time the woman would be engaging in had she been free from dependency work.[60] This has serious effects on the "life projects" of many dependency workers. Schutte links the ability to form life projects for oneself, which requires time and energy, as essential for the health of the country. Policies should be geared in "raising the quality of people's lives (including women's lives), not undermining it."[61]

Developing this sentiment into transnational contexts, it is important to recognize the nested transnational dependencies of the Filipina dependency worker. The example of the Filipina dependency worker signals an opportunity to understand how *caring-about* distant others can be done in the context of *caring-for* the Filipina dependency worker in a transnational context. Given Addams's insights about immigrants, one's moral orientation of care to distant others should be predicated upon one's attention to the closer transnational relationships that establish further connections to international or global communities. In fact, the commitment to growth requires that individuals also need the time and care to develop their own life projects. In the context of Filipina dependency workers' growth, a transnational relationship of dependency exposes our responsibility to others beyond the nation-state. Since the lives of Filipina dependency workers are connected to their country of origin, our resulting care for distant others is anchored to the more proximate relationship we have with the Filipina dependency worker. This might change how transnational relationships are conducted.

Understanding our moral orientation of care to distant others within a transnational context recognizes the pervasiveness of transnational relationships in our global lives. One might argue that a more appropriate solution to the lives of care workers would be to abolish this practice altogether. First World nations must wean themselves off the labor of Third World women. Rather, monetary aid should be directed to needy countries so as to prevent mothers and fathers from leaving their children for economic reasons. While these solutions do address the structural problems that compel many Filipinas to work as overseas dependency workers, a transnational framework begins within relationships that can often be oppressive to those who are marginalized. Beginning from this framework would envision solutions that recognize the Filipina dependency worker's agency rather than treating them like subjects of oppression to be given aid. Solutions within a transnational doulia system would consider the agency of all participants within these complicated and unequal relationships.

By focusing on the dependency relation, First World responsibility is understood as one of responsiveness, care, and trust, which forges social bonds in the human community and the wider global community. Some recommendations by Arlie Hochschild to address the "care crisis" among Filipina dependency workers in order to ensure the overall well-being of the dependency worker, her First World charge, and her own children in the Philippines include: provide paid visits to return home by the employer, liberalize immigration laws to allow the dependency worker to sponsor their children, create domestic violence shelters for women in their country of origin, find ways in which the children of dependency workers can also come and live in the host country, more men could also help in the household, and finally, care should be valued more in society.[62] Though better state welfare programs to support care work might be seen as a step in the right direction, Parreñas insightfully reminds us how state support can often benefit employers and not the Filipina dependency worker.[63]

These recommendations highlight a transnational doulia principle, which seeks to address the human dependency claims of transnational dependency workers. There are three requirements the transnational doulia principle demands of ethics and international relationships. The first emphasizes the visibility of obligations beyond nation-state boundaries through attention to encounters with foreign dependency workers. In this sense, transnational relationships are experienced closer to home. The recommendation of creating domestic violence shelters in the country of origin of the transnational dependency workers highlights one's ethical attention to politics in another country. However, this global awareness of domestic violence is predicated on more local interactions.

The second requirement of a transnational doulia principle not only recognizes that the transnational Filipina dependency worker is constrained by the dependency work itself but also recognizes that emotional loss and suffering besiege the transnational dependency worker due to responsibilities in maintaining multiple homes and the pain of family separation. Hochschild and Kittay refer to this special harm as the *global heart transplant*. This experience of loss, even though not directly experienced by the citizens of the host country, prompts an inquiry into sustaining transnational relationships of dependency. The work of care, in this sense, contains a sense of yearning and connection that transcends geographical distance. Placing one's ethical obligations within this transnational context exposes one's responsibility toward developing a more meaningful internationally minded community. The transnational doulia principle would attend to the dependency relation between multiple international homes. This may involve employer-paid visits back to the Philippines or permitting visa sponsorships of children. It may mean employers allowing more time for the dependency worker to stay connected with her children and families; or it could politicize the host families' obligations to advocate for better quality of life in the Philippines. None of these solutions will fully address the problems of the global care chain, but a transnational ethos of care can help guide the necessary action by focusing on maintaining and sustaining homes across borders.

Addams understands our social ethics to be narrow and isolated if we don't seek out a variety of diverse experiences. The experimental approach Addams practices in her work at Hull House demands flexibility in one's individual and social lives in order for personal and social transformation to take place. Following Addams, a third requirement of the transnational doulia principle would direct everyone to seek out the diverse range of experiences that mark nested relationships of dependency. This would make visible a large range of social experiences and ethical responsibilities currently made invisible by neoliberal policies. The transnational doulia principle develops a *caring-about* attitude through a focus on local experiences with "strangers" living in one's neighborhood and doing dependency work in one's home. The transnational doulia principle requires that practices of care be more flexible and open to the transnational context pervading social life. It is these local interactions that disrupt narrow conceptions of American identity and bring one into a relationship with an internationally minded community.

Notes

1. I understand *dependency worker* and *care worker* in the same way. However, following Kittay's terminology in *Love's Labor*, I use the term *dependency worker* to emphasize the fundamental character of human social relationships marked by one's inevitable dependencies. A dependency worker is attentive to the dependency relation through acts of care. In characterizing the foreign care worker as a dependency worker, I want to emphasize the work these women do to attend to the claims of transnational relationships of dependency, which become more visible in a growing transnational context.

2. Rhacel Salazar Parreñas, "The Care Crisis in the Philippines: Children and Transnational Families in the New Global Economy," in *Global Woman: Nannies, Maids and Sex Workers in the New Economy*, ed. Barbara Ehrenreich and Arlie Hochschild (New York: Henry Holt, 2002).

3. Rhacel Salazar Parreñas, *Servants of Globalization: Women, Migration, and Domestic Work* (Stanford, CA: Stanford University Press, 2001), 119.

4. Arlie Hochschild, "Love and Gold," in *Global Woman: Nannies, Maids and Sex Workers in the New Economy* (New York: Henry Holt, 2002), 26.

5. Ofelia Schutte, "Women, Dependency, and the Global Economy," in *The Subject of Care: Feminist Perspectives on Dependency*, ed. Eva Feder Kittay and Ellen Feder (Lanham, MD: Rowman & Littlefield, 2002).

6. Hochschild, "Love and Gold," 29.

7. Eva Kittay, "The Global Heart Transplant and Caring across National Boundaries," *Southern Journal of Philosophy* 66 (2008): 138–165, 139.

8. Rhacel Salazar Parreñas, *The Force of Domesticity: Filipina Migrants and Globalization* (New York: New York University Press, 2008), 43.

9. Nel Noddings, *Starting at Home: Caring and Social Policy* (Berkeley: University of California Press, 2002).

10. Eva Kittay, *Love's Labor: Essays on Women, Equality, and Dependency* (New York: Routledge, 1999), 29. My discussion here and over the next two pages draws on my earlier work, "Dependence and Care in Peirce's Training of Reasoning" in *Synesthetic Legalities: Sensory Dimensions of Law and Jurisprudence*, ed. Sarah Marusek (New York: Routledge, 2017), 147–162.

11. Kittay, *Love's Labor*, 29.
12. Kittay, 29.
13. Kittay, 37.
14. Kittay, 38.
15. Noddings, *Starting at Home*, 185.
16. Kittay, *Love's Labor*, 50.
17. Kittay, 37.
18. Kittay, 106.

19. Kittay, 107.
20. Kittay, 107.
21. Kittay, 109.
22. Kittay, 109.
23. Doula shares the same root as the word *dulia*, which refers to the attitude of reverence to the Virgin Mary. I thank Scott Pratt for pointing this out to me. It seems that Kittay's principle of the doulia as a public ethos of care implies a kind of reverence, not in a religious sense to the Virgin Mary (although it does seem that the Virgin Mary may have signified an idealized notion of the dependency and caring relation that inspired reverence in her followers) but as a reverence to the dependency and care relation the dependency worker embodies.
24. Maurice Hammington, *Embodied Care: Jane Addams, Maurice Merleau-Ponty, and Feminist Ethics* (Urbana: University of Illinois Press, 2004), 103.
25. Charlene Haddock Seigfried, *Pragmatism and Feminism: Reweaving the Social Fabric* (Chicago: University of Chicago Press, 1996); Marilyn Fischer, "Jane Addams's Pragmatist Pacifism," in *Peacemaking: Lessons from the Past, Visions for the Future*, ed. Judith L. Pressler (Atlanta: Rodopi, 2000); and Hamington, *Embodied Care*.
26. Hamington, *Embodied Care*, 99.
27. Seigfried, *Pragmatism and Feminism*, 217.
28. Charlene Haddock Seigfried, "Introduction," in Jane Addams, *Democracy and Social Ethics*, ed. Charlene Haddock Seigfried (Chicago: University of Illinois Press, 2002), xxi.
29. Jane Addams, "A Modern Lear," *Survey* 29 (November 2, 1912): 131–137.
30. Jane Addams, *Democracy and Social Ethics*, ed. Charlene Haddock Seigfried (Chicago: University of Illinois Press, 2002), 5.
31. Addams, *Democracy and Social Ethics*, 33.
32. Addams, 34.
33. Seigfried, "Introduction," xx.
34. Addams, *Democracy and Social Ethics*, 6.
35. Addams, 7.
36. Seigfried, "Introduction," xxi.
37. Addams, *Democracy and Social Ethics*, 79.
38. Addams, 79.
39. Addams discusses an example of the charity visitor who visits tenement homes in Chicago. Addams identifies the charity visitor's failed attempts to help these families as a problem of not being open herself to social transformation. The charity she gives becomes empty and abstract to the lives of the tenement families she visits. Addams argues that "the young woman who has succeeded in expressing her social compunction through charitable effort finds that the wider social activity, and the contact with the larger experience, not only increases her sense of social obligation but at the same time recasts her social ideals." See Addams, *Democracy and Social Ethics*, 33.

40. Addams, 68.
41. Hamington, *Embodied Care*, 105.
42. Jane Addams, *Newer Ideals of Peace* (London: Macmillan, 1907), 11.
43. Addams, 11.
44. Addams thinks that a morality built upon a rigid separation between our relations with our domestic polity and our relations with outsiders cultivates a militaristic attitude since there is no common ground that can be shared between the two social relationships. In the chapter "Democracy or Militarism," in the *Newer Ideals of Peace*, Addams makes the case that peace is the "unfolding of life processes which are making for a common development" (1). Without an understanding of how we, as a domestic polity, might relate to foreign others, a militaristic spirit develops.
45. Addams, 12.
46. Addams, 13.
47. Addams, 14.
48. Addams. 14.
49. Addams, 16.
50. Addams, 16.
51. Addams, 17.
52. Addams, 18, 19.
53. Rivka Shpak Lissak, *Pluralism and Progressives: Hull House and the New Immigrants, 1890–1910* (Chicago: University of Chicago Press, 1989), 9. Seigfried argues in a footnote to the introduction to Addams's *Democracy and Social Ethics* that Lissak misunderstands Addams's philosophical project and thus misreads Addams's analysis of immigrants. See Seigfried, "Introduction," xxxv.
54. Addams, *Newer Ideals*, 18.
55. Addams, 19.
56. Jane Addams, "Americanization," in *Jane Addams Reader*, ed. Jean Bethke Elshtain (New York: Basic Books, 2002), 240–247, 244.
57. Jane Addams, *Twenty Years at Hull House* (Woking, UK: Dodo, 2006), 58.
58. Addams, *Twenty Years*, 127.
59. Schutte, "Women, Dependency," 143.
60. Schutte, "Women, Dependency," 143.
61. Schutte, 144.
62. Hochschild, "Love and Gold," 29.
63. Parreñas, *The Force of Domesticity*, 60.

CHAPTER NINE

Creolization and Playful Sabotage at the Brink of Politics in Earl Lovelace's *The Dragon Can't Dance*

Kris Sealey

In this paper, I offer the theoretical framework of Creolization as a tool through which American philosophical thought might theorize moments of resistance at the level of the everyday. My approach is explicitly transatlantic, insofar as Earl Lovelace's *The Dragon Can't Dance* is my anchoring literary text in this endeavor.[1] One of the most prominent Caribbean storytellers, Lovelace writes from the geopolitical location of the Americas and hails from Trinidad and Tobago. As such, his work underscores an Afro-diasporic sensibility that has always been a shaping force in thought from the Americas. In other words, Lovelace's literary works (particularly *The Dragon Can't Dance*) are ultimately meditations on meaning making and self-definition for black subjectivity in the Americas, given the legacy of the plantation and the lingering forces of neocolonialism. The goal of this chapter is to name such meaning-making practices *creolizing* practices, which, to my mind, has particular significance for how American philosophy might engage with questions pertaining to resistive acts of self-determination, political agency, and alternative futures. In other words, this chapter puts forth Creolization—its conceptual grid, analytics, organizing frame—as "indispensable to any effective analysis of the politics of *making newness* and empowering social change."[2] It is a politics at the heart of the idea of the Americas. In this vein, my understanding of Creolization joins H. Adlai Murdoch's conception, as he describes the phenomenon as one of "exchange and transformation that is indispensable to understanding New World experience."[3]

In offering Creolization as an important practice of resistance, and as a practice through which a different future might emerge, I hope to position it alongside conceptual formulations like George Ciccariello-Maher's decolonizing dialectics and María Lugones's formulation of plural sociality.[4] I do so not to propose that Creolization usurps the efficacy of these other modes of theorizing resistance and the possibility of social change but rather to offer practices of Creolization as a much-needed interlocutor of these critical orientations. This is because, through Creolization, we not only find a mechanism for describing the unfolding of a Caribbean history but more significantly for giving an account of how everyday negotiations of a violent lifeworld produce ground for alternative and more liberatory ways of being human. Theorizing in terms of Creolization allows us to uncover the "hidden poesis," to which María Lugones refers, in her development of a streetwalker tactics. These tactics are transgressive negotiations of the social order, at the level of the everyday, that "[manipulate] the mechanisms of discipline [to] conform to them in order to *evade* them."[5] Like Lugones's streetwalker tactician, the creolizing subject transgresses the spatial boundaries prescribed by the logic of domination in a way that responds to her will to resist that domination.

Creolization's conceptual frame also urges us to see these transgressive negotiations at the level of the everyday (in the intimate spaces of the home, in spiritual worship, and in community formations) as, indeed, critical. That is to say, these are encounters with the discursive manifestations of oppression that precisely call into question the codes for living put forth in those discursive manifestations. Through the alternative pathways they generate, creolizing practices are ultimately about denaturalizing these oppressive codes and about finding, in the folds of what appears to be a totalizing dominant structure, other more liberating possibilities. As I will demonstrate through Earl Lovelace's fictional account, these sorts of transgressions rarely rise to the level of change in *political* ground. But, through the alternative conceptions of human living that they rehearse, the dominant political ground is unable to account for them and therefore is not as totalizing a system as it appeared to be.[6] This "new content"—from the quotidian moments of everyday life—has the potential to jostle the political as it remains outside (below or beyond) politics.[7] Attention to practices of Creolization allows us to see the political implications of this jostling effect—an effect of the imaginative capacities of subjects determining more liberatory ground for living.

Beginning with the frame of Creolization also allows us to consider those quotidian and critical negotiations as necessary conditions for imagining different futures.[8] Hence, in offering Lovelace's fictional account of this playful jostling, my claim is not that Creolization's poetics are sufficient for explicit political usurpation. To be sure, my analysis shows that the efficacy of these playful poetics lies in their *failure* to rise to the level of the political.[9] Instead, my argument is that we have better knowledge about New World acts of resistance against structural violence when we include these creolizing capacities for imagining alternative futures as a necessary condition for change at the political level. To borrow from Frantz Fanon, the possibility of "introducing invention into existence" is to be found at the level of the everyday.[10] And as I will show in this chapter, it is in their nonteleological and nonnormative status that these everyday acts constitute inventions of this radical (Fanonian) sort. The performative parodies of Lovelace's dragon dance are without *telos* (their liberatory capacities go no further than the performance itself) and thus fail to offer any political prescriptions for life. But like the inventions for which Fanon calls at the end of *Black Skin, White Masks*, these playful performances register in open-endedness; they rehearse the possibility of the future *as* open-ended). And in so doing, they foreground what is most "human" to the human dimension—its incalculability and unpredictability. This open-endedness locates these creolizing performative moments beyond the political, but it also accounts for the newness (inventiveness) of their content, content for which politics cannot fully account. Faced with this limitation, mainstream politics is jostled, forced to bear witness to the fact that not everything comes from its domain. It is in this sense that creolizing poetics are able to *affect* the political from a position *outside* politics.

In using Earl Lovelace's novel to illustrate this, my specific orienting questions are as follows: What is an experience of belonging and self-determination, when that experience is situated as it is in the Caribbean, in a sociality and a politics of impurity? How does self-determination unfold when it must unfold out of the fragmented histories and broken cultural lineages of which the Caribbean past consists? How might identity be alternatively constituted when the boundary between "here" and "elsewhere" is blurred, when fluidity and transience informs intersubjective life, and when border transgression is the foundation for practicing not only adaptive but also *resistant* modes of belonging?[11] Creolizing practices have long constituted the social ontology of the Caribbean archipelago. Lovelace's *Dragon* offers a rich opportunity for making this clear, bringing to life what Creolist scholars aim to capture through their use of Creolization, which is that Antillean American capacity to refashion fragments of a colonial past for the sake of self-determination in a present and future that is both impure and decolonial, and that conditions liberatory existence in the face of colonial hegemony/oppression. Ultimately, my reading of Lovelace's novel aims to uncover ways in which Creolization has historically named moments of resistance against colonial (and postcolonial) domination across the Americas in general, and in the Antilles in particular.[12]

Creolization as Bricolage

To think Creolization is think about the Caribbean and about the plurality of its life worlds and syncretic cultural modes. It is to also think about the amalgamation of historical events that brought people together (their languages, "origin" stories, and identity narratives) in a place that really should never have witnessed their meeting. These markers of the communities that would be named "Creole" call our attention to two signifying factors. Firstly, societies in the Caribbean grow out of a specific history of rupturing, as a consequence of the brutalities of the Middle Passage. As such, memory recuperation/repair is one register of Creolization. And (or, perhaps, *but*) secondly, the Middle Passages' historical rupture makes way for the discursive and cultural inventions that define the creolizing process. That is to say, what emerges from the fragmented memories of Caribbean pasts is not so much an attempt to restore or return to lost and unchanged origins but rather articulations of what Stuart Hall would call certain translations of these fragments: translations that signify in the living contexts of Caribbean life. As a consequence of this signifying, these translations speak to the concrete exigencies of that Caribbean space. Hence, in what are recognizably Creole artifacts, language phrases, food, and religious symbolism, one finds this undercurrent relationship between old and new, between the past and its invented transmutations in the present. In this sense, Heather Smyth's words are apt when she describes Creolization as a production of "de-essentialized cultures" and "beautiful inauthenticities."[13]

Wendy Knepper notes the ways in which the role of bricolage facilitates deessentialism in the creolizing artifact. As "a mode of interpreting and adapting existing materials to new circumstances or needs,"[14] bricolage accounts for the ongoing, adaptive, and fluid processes through which Creole identity formations develop. To say this otherwise, to situate bricolage at the center of Creolization, is to mark its products (as well as their implications for the life worlds in which they are produced) as perpetually open, diametrically opposed to calloused conceptions of meaning making and world formation.[15] Hence, in offering a reading of Creolization as bricolage, Knepper is able to show that as a theory of identity, Creolization is ultimately a process of adaptive improvisation, which is to say it moves in response to the urgencies of the concrete, creatively refashions at the level of the local for the sake of the "now," and works toward futures whose meanings are obliquely horizonal instead of expressly intentional. That is to say, as bricolage, "[Creolization] should be understood as an unending, fluid process that cannot be reduced to a single path or principle [as it brings about] unpredictable results and transformative potential."[16]

To be sure, this open-ended improvisation at the heart of Creole worldmaking comes out of historical necessity. It is a practice that is a consequence of loss. That is to say, "[Creolization] *always* entails inequality, hierarchization, issues of domination and subalterneity, master and servitude, control and resistance. Questions of *power*, as well as *entanglement*, are always at stake."[17] To reiterate, the systematic dehumanization that conditioned plantation economies included the annihilation of the cultural and social memory of the stolen Africans who would provide the chattel labor for New World capitalism. As such, slave communities' efforts toward reconstituting their humanity (and there were plenty) necessarily began in disparate fragments that retained only as echoes their cultural origins. As such, efforts toward constituting memory could not support any project geared toward the full restoration to the origin. As Knepper points out, there were always holes to fill as these improvisatory acts of bricolage produced creolizing conditions for the possibility of human life.[18]

Creolization as improvisation not only made this possible but also made it so that world constitution and identity formation in this Antillean context has always been "open, fluid," and with plurality at their core.[19] This constitution points to the complex relationship between creolizing practices and the rigid dominant structures out of which they emerge. As improvisation, Creolization works with what is immediately available in the space and time of the local while importantly remaining unrestricted by normativities meant to make unavailable the possibility of free self-determination in these life worlds. Hence, world formation is open, via Creolization, insofar as "[it] can be seen enacted . . . as the art of the disparate and fragmentary . . . transforming and supplanting the reason of the [social] engineer."[20] What makes Creolization a practice of "de-essentialized cultures and beautiful inauthenticities" is its reliance on bricolage—on patching together from local resources what is necessary for the adaptive and critical work at hand in the "now," in a continuously resistant relationship with the structures of not only the modern slave plantation but also of contemporary metropoles constructed out of colonial legacies of migration and transplantation. Wendy Knepper opposes this bricolage against a more "rationalized plan," the kind that would require articulating in advance of the concrete significations of existence on the ground, one's vision for meaning making, subject-formation, and the overall organization of the social world. Instead, the bricolage at the heart of Creolization calls for adaptation in real time, not for the sake of staying true to a pregiven order but precisely in readiness to work around or against that order should the need for making meaning in the world call for it.[21]

My motivations in reading Earl Lovelace's *The Dragon Can't Dance* through the lens of Creolization are twofold. Firstly, I am interested in how these trademarks of Creolization allow us to read the everyday practices of Creole communities—the slave communities on the plantation as well as those postcolonial outposts of empire, as politically meaningful acts of sabotage. And secondly, I am interested in the ways in which, alongside and despite the openness of Creoleness, worlds that become possibilities for self-definition to such communities emerge. To pose this latter point differently, I am interested in how Creolization, as the production of "identity as something profoundly incoherent [given its openness and fluidity]," nevertheless offers grounding and orientation needed for self-definition.[22] To my mind, these two aspects are connected to each other, since in these Creole contexts, the mechanisms through which homemaking practices enact themselves are very much against (despite, or perhaps alongside) mainstream structures that code for the estrangement (or home*less*ness) of the communities in question. All of which is to say, in the context of the Creole, the very act of self-definition can be understood as an act of politically meaningful sabotage.[23] In her description of the informal practices that often characterize the Creole economies of communities working against neocolonial structures, Michaeline Crichlow writes that the features of such economic transactions "do not appear to violate existing regulatory frames [even though they] cannot be said to comply with them either."[24] That is to say, such activities surreptitiously undermine the universalizing legitimacy of normative positions, insofar as they attest to other possibilities for living (possibilities for which the more normative positions cannot account). In this sense, Creolization supports the production of newness in a space-time grid that appears closed off to alternatives and does so in a way that is neither fully visible nor fully invisible. These alternative ways remain underground (so to speak), under the cover of hegemonic norms; however, out of that subterranean space, they expose the cracks in those norming structures out of which creolizing communities determine alternative (and, indeed, more emancipatory) modes of belonging.

It is in this sense that Patrick Chamoiseau names Creolization as "a system of counter-values, or a counter-culture, that reveals itself as both powerless to achieve complete freedom and fiercely determined to strive for it nonetheless."[25] This will be important for my reading of *Dragon*, insofar as Chamoiseau's account forces us to determine what (if anything) in creolizing practices are political in nature. Do the syncretic, inventive improvisations of Creolization offer the possibility of any *political* resistance?[26] In my reading of Lovelace's novel, I highlight how through Aldrick's dragon dance (and its surrounding plots) we are prompted to consider the political differently, particularly when the goal at hand is to determine possibilities for the emergence of the radically new—what, in an important sense, must engage with the political as its radical "Outside." In her account of the deployment of myth and counternarrative by the Creole storyteller, Wendy Knepper uses the language of "jostling" to describe the effect of Creolization's adaptive, "hole-filling" improvisations on what we might name the official accounting of things. This image of the jostled or liminally contested status quo will be important for my engagement with *Dragon* and for the question of what possibilities for political resistance, if any, does Creolization offer.

Creolization as a Liminal Dialectic

Decentering the normative value of authenticity is central to creolizing practices. In other words, in the bricolage of piecing together fragmented cultural memory in the making of new sense (out of the vestiges of an old sense), little attention is paid to being faithful to the idea of an original (founding) culture. At the same time, there is a desire to mark, in its absence, the memory that was lost as a consequence of historical violence. In other words, in the midst of bricolage's "re-membering" (piecing together some new articulation of the world out of pieces of what was) is a remembering, or preserving—in bricolage form—traces of what was.[27] One encounters this in Caribbean religions like Voodoo and Santeria, and in cuisine whose Caribbeanness is precisely because it alludes to the palates of regions in West Africa and India (to name a few).[28] This means that despite their newness, creolizing practices (and their products) rest in a historical specificity—a "submarine" history, to borrow from Kamau Braithwaite[29], submerged below the violence of the Middle Passage. This submarine history persists as the fluidity of Creole formations move toward new life worlds, which is to say that the newness of the Creole artifact is not ahistorical, even though its relationship to and signification within the social ontology at hand is not determined by the historical narrative. Out of the adaptive improvisation of bricolage, this historical narrative of rupture and violence is refashioned in a way that, through counterstories, "jostles" its claim to having the last word. The original loss and violence remain (and so, creolizing practices are not about an erasure of that history). But the implications of that originary loss, for what it means to be human, and for what it means for homing and belonging, is contested.

My turn to Lovelace's *Dragon* is to highlight such an account of refashioning historical loss and rupture, out of a generated space—one grounded in communal agency—that facilitates that refashioning. In other words, out of Lovelace's story emerges the so-called miracle of Creolization[30] whereby the spatiality and temporality of the social shows up not as a flat and homogeneous consolidation of the status quo but rather as already differentiated by certain fault lines or cracks that mark alternative possibilities for self-determination and personhood. Michaeline Crichlow reminds us that in thinking about the workings of governmentality in the context of Creolization, we ought not to think only "statecraft or governance, but rather . . . a discursive field in which exercising power is rationalized."[31] As we think about how, in creolizing spaces, there is a jostling of the social ontology supported by mainstream structures, we should identify this jostling effect as a contestation of the legitimacy of prescriptions of personhood, meaning, relation, and world constitution. In other words, through Creolization, the rationality of these prescriptions for living is derationalized (if you will), so that they signify for what they are: prescriptions for the social that entrench governmentality's power to produce the subject. In destabilizing these prescriptions, Creolization works to offer alternative modalities (pockets of alterity) against and within the discursive spaces in which "power is rationalized." In these alterities, power and reason are decoupled so that power encounters itself as contingent.

It is in this sense that the creative determinations in creolizing practices avail strategies for how to "dwell with power."[32] That is to say, space is made for ruptures within the sociality engineered by the mainstream, so that the social is really a coexistence between (a) such moments of *the otherwise* (moments of critical alterities) and (b) the sociality of the mainstream. Or, as Stuart Hall asserted, "The low invades the high, blurring the hierarchical impositions of order," without completely undoing the order in question.[33] We are reminded here of Crichlow's account of those informal economies in which transactions "do not appear to violate existing regulatory frames [even though they] cannot be said to comply with them either."[34] In a similar and broader vein, creolizing enactments of rupture dwell within those social systems that remain, despite (and alongside) such ruptures. These mainstream systems remain in a condition of being jostled by Creolization's overall effect on power's capacity to rationalize itself.

It is in this sense that, creolized, the social is given over as heterogeneously textured, much like what María Lugones describes in her conception of ontological plurality.[35] In both accounts of the social, attention to the everyday, local conditions of social life reveals an entangled web of multiple engagements with power and multiple enactments of the effects of power on the lives of subjects. For Lugones, ontological plurality affords a critical vocabulary for understanding how the lives of marginalized subjects are not solely ones of dispossession under mainstream structures but are actually rich with moments of resistance against the codes put forth by the mainstream. In describing Creole societies, Wendy Knepper similarly draws attention to multiple negotiations with the rationalities of power within the social in her distinction between "place" and "territory." She writes, "As opposed to territory, associated with nation-state, monolingualism, and a theory of a single race, language and religion, the [place] is multi-interracial, multi-intercultural, and multi-interreligious."[36] Although this Creole differentiating (or "rhizoming"[37]), which results as a consequence of the adaptive work of bricolage, does not rest on the explicitly political stakes found in Lugones's picture of ontological pluralism, both conceptions point to the tension (and even contradictory relationship) between place/locality/everyday interstices and territory/mainstream/official codifications of the human. In both cases, these contradictions point to local manifestations of working with/around structures of domination for the sake of self-determination, self-definition, and agency. These local manifestations complicate the story of what it means to live alongside structures that foreclose such possibilities so that out of that complication we get a picture of social and cultural sabotaging of the rationalities of power.

In order to make sense of this social heterogeneity, we are called to understand such acts of sabotage in terms of liminality and thresholds. In other words, creolizing practices, liminally enacted, result in the social as cracked and fissured and as jostled in its legitimacy to determine codes of conduct. In this sense, the newness in the world made possible through Creolization is positioned to respond to what Homi Bhabha refers to as "the problem of 'beginning' outside the question of 'origins.'"[38] That is to say, in locating the "transformation and/or transmutation"[39] of Creolization in the limen of the social, we are able to make sense of what it means for world constitution, meaning production, and subject formation to emerge anew (as a beginning), out of history's totality (as a beginning *again*).

In her exegesis on new modalities of the human, Sylvia Wynter establishes the extent of the totality against which this problem of beginning again, of thinking the human anew, must work.[40] Her argument establishes the "master code"[41] of Western modernity, a code that relies on a fundamental line of ontological division whose manifestations throughout the unfolding of the project of modernity vary only in degree and not kind. Said otherwise, Wynter establishes the ways in which divisions between the realms of "lunar and sublunar," "spirit and flesh," "clergy and lay," "rational and irrational," and ultimately, "first world and third/fourth world" all sustain an ontology of the human out of which difference (newness/beginning) can only signify as the "non" (or "not") of the human. Wynter argues that these master codes of modernity have become "overrepresented" so that their provincial constitution of the human as Man is encountered as the *only* possible constitution of the human as Man. In other words, this overrepresentation means that modernity shows us no alternatives for human life. But this is because "the subjects of these orders . . . experience their own placement in the structuring hierarchies . . . as having been extrahumanly . . . designed and/or determined, rather than as veridically or systematically produced by [their] collective human agency."[42] In other words, modern Man's agency is opaque to him, insofar as the provincialism of modernity's overrepresentation is disavowed and given over as ordained from elsewhere.

It is with this question of agency in mind that I offer practices of Creolization as a possible avenue for rethinking the human and for repositioning the social for the sake of such alternative conceptions. In her essay, Wynter provides an extensive quotation from Mikhail Epstein, whereby he offers "transculture" as "a space in, or among cultures, which is open to all [cultures]." He writes, "Culture frees us from nature; transculture frees us from culture, from any one culture."[43] This notion of transculture—as a space that is not only part of culture but also a space from which there can be agency to *break free from* culture—aligns with the liminal thresholds that locate the jostling effects of Creolization. Much like Epstein's view that "[culture] . . . is what a human being creates and what creates a human being at the same time,"[44] Creolization offers a set of social and cultural practices that are not only constituted in mainstream normativities but that also *unsettle* those very normativities. In other words, we are called to understand these liminal contestations as "turning social transgression toward, or even into, creative patterns of community expression," expressions that underscore the dialectical relationship between human agency and the stasis of institutional culture.[45] Operational in the threshold spaces of the social is this dialectical scrambling of the lines that determine where "created" begins and "creator" ends. But it is precisely through this scrambling—this liminal blurring—that Creolization founds "the emergence of qualitatively new desires, social relations and modes of association."[46] To put this another way, in destabilizing the prescriptions of modernity's master code, Creolization works to offer alternative modalities against and within the discursive spaces in which "power is rationalized." In these new cultural contexts, power and reason are decoupled, so that power encounters itself as contingent (no longer overrepresented) and human agency reveals itself as such. Hence, through the work of Creolization, sociality is heterogeneous, always already a plurality of local wombs,[47] each simultaneously crack and fold, so as to facilitate everyday ruptures of the hegemonic totality of the same.

In this vein, Creolization gives us the conceptual tools to think about the present in terms of a generative time and to think about space as creatively constituted by/through living adaptations, which improvise from a place of human agency and *for the sake of* human agency. But for this to emerge in frames of liminality and threshold, these everyday ruptures must signify as open ended, as movements toward a not-yet-determined *otherwise*. Were this not the case, it would have to be true that a departure from rationalities of power would be nothing other than establishing some other closed-off system, another rationality of power. In other words, "rupture" would not yet be sufficiently radical, since "radical" points to something more than replacing one totality with another. But in the creolizing sense, this replacing is precisely what "rupture" never means. This is precisely *not* how those everyday acts of sabotage signify in their adaptive bricolage. When the Creole jostles the rationality of power, *gateways* onto alternative subject formations are produced as open-ended possibilities that are both outside of and unnameable by *not only* a particular mainstream rationality but outside and unnameable in an absolute sense. That is to say, these "gateways toward" must remain as such, and the liminally constituted subject formations founded at these thresholds must remain as such (at the threshold). Because it is through this liminality and open-endedness that the capacity for sabotage signifies. It is through the openness of the gateway that power's power to rationalize and totalize finds its limitation. Indeed, in its unnameability, the mode of being of these gateways is able to answer the question, posed by Homi Bhabha, of how something radically new emerges, to then engage with the totality of power nonetheless, in and despite its newness.[48]

For these reasons, I identify the comportment of performative play as what accounts for the particular kind of sabotage constitutive of creolizing practices. In the sabotage of play, the subject and her articulations of the world are both squarely within and radically outside political signification such that it remains power's unnameable remainder with which politics must nevertheless contend. To be constituted as play (or as carnivalesque, if you will) these acts are, at best, obtusely included as participatory factors in world constitution and meaning making or at worst, outright nonbelonging antisense. What this means is that insofar as her pursuit for self-determination begins in structures whose rationalities of power offer her sociocultural erasure and economic disenfranchisement, the creolizing subject "actively pieces together different signs and produces sometimes new (*and sometimes unsanctioned*) meanings."[49] As they are unsanctioned, these improvisational productions destabilize sanctioned norms from their position outside of/beyond the discursive regions of such sanctioning, critically calling into question the very posture of closure that is most essential to the political power of the status quo. In the context of Caribbean Creolization, it is often through this playful contestation of power—this playing with and alongside power—that we bear witness to this destabilization of closure. To this end, how might we understand these playful contestations—this Carnival poetics—as not only a process of Creolization but perhaps, more importantly, as *the* grounding mode of what it means to creolize? And secondly, in what sense can this Carnival poetics enact a mode of sabotage that is politically meaningful?

Creolization as Carnival/Play

In Curdella Forbes's reading of the fiction of Caribbean writer George Lamming, she notes the ways in which his novels trace the recurring motif of grief and loss that emerges in response to the Caribbean's "unique birth."[50] This birth comes out of past rupture and fragmentation and carries into the genealogical construction of its identity this original loss of its African cultural memory. Using Lamming's fiction as her archetype, Forbes points out that because the project of constructing a postcolonial Caribbean sense of identity never aims to reverse such lost origins, the poetics of the Caribbean narrative is neither teleological nor atavistic. The nation's articulation of its identity is neither with some final terminus in mind nor motivated by some origin to restore. But because the loss in question is encountered as irretrievable, its absence is generative, clearing the way for an orientation toward possibility, invention, and openness. Hence, a significant portion of Caribbean fiction is driven by an account of identity as performative—an identity that emerges in the nonlinearity and immediacy of a performative moment. Given the ways in which authenticity/faithfulness to a retrievable origin is impossible and therefore decentered, these performative identity constructions emerge to precisely unwork or unsettle themselves. As Forbes writes, "[The] inscription of possibility rather than teleology can be envisaged as the ground of the Caribbean dynamics of syncretism and creolization."[51] The absent origin constitutive of Caribbean history thus makes room for invention and for new to emerge out of old in ways that trace back to a drowned origin that is impossible to restore.

It is in this sense that processes of Caribbean Creolization manifest as a playful poetics, through which narratives of identity (communal and individual) emerge as performative inventions of self. Play enacts the possibility of moving beyond the scripts of loss and dispossession that one finds in the plot of the transatlantic slave trade and the plantation economy. In other words, to think about Creolization in terms of playful contestation is to find, in the resistance against those scripts, a playing that undoes a teleology of the colonial subject (a teleology that pronounces death as the last word). Rather, the power of the normative is put in relief, in a suspended unworking, or perhaps, in a liminal dialectic that says to the normative, "Nothing is final, no version of the story is settled."

To describe this playful contestation as a sabotage of mainstream structures is to situate the Carnival poetics of Creolization in oblique relation to the political. That is to say, play is not so much a full-frontal political stance but rather an unsettling *of* the political from those liminal sites of cultural everydayness. Natasha Barnes reminds us of the importance of attending to such sites in the Caribbean context, not only because they are sites of "the ritual of transformation whereby tragedy is disguised, diffracted and diffused"[52] but more significantly because they condition the possibility for "a new positive citizenship . . . a new civil religion."[53] In other words, although it is the case that the contestations in creolizing play cannot constitute overt political resistance, they do rehearse a community's capacity to imagine a new, postcolonial conception of itself. Though these rehearsals are at the cultural level, Barnes reminds us that they are vital for the kinds of living metamorphoses called for in that move from colonial dispossession to a *de*colonized national emancipation.[54] Hence, we are able to find political *possibilities* in such playful contestation and in attending to them, "draw on the informal, chaotic transcripts from below" to find new demands made *to* the political for more liberatory ways of being human.[55]

Dancing the Dragon on the Brink of Politics

In his interview with Maria Grau-Perejoan, Earl Lovelace reflects on the significance of his choice, as a Caribbean writer, to remain in the Caribbean: "I think one value of staying is that you don't have to write of a remembered place. The value of staying is that I have been present to see everything unfold not just as a spectator but as a participant as well."[56] In staying, Lovelace's meditations on Caribbean "whatness"—its identity or way of being—comes from living with a sense of the Caribbean as never finished, a Caribbean that continues to create itself toward an open future in a living present. In choosing to remain and write from there, Lovelace is able to tell his story from the perspective of this living present, with the kind of vibrant hope that emerges only from the complexity of that

Creolization and Playful Sabotage at the Brink of Politics | 219

living present.[57] Indeed, in writing the Caribbean in this modality of the "not-yet-complete," his work is particularly attuned to the real-time, performative constitution of that Caribbean identity. His novels offer a notion of the Caribbean (of what it means to be Caribbean) not as frozen in a remembered time but as alive with the vitality of making and remaking again, with the open-ended movement of a future horizon whose obscurity nevertheless conditions the possibility of rupturing the totality of the "now," by a "from below" liminal agency.[58] This dynamic conception of what it means to be Caribbean—a Caribbeanness that is continually opened up, through play, in performativity—is what, for Lovelace, the Caribbean writer is called to give an account of. S/he must "explain the society to itself." But, in that accounting—one operating in an alive unfolding—the writer is to explain Caribbean society to itself even though "[the] Caribbean was not a place you knew really, it was a place you were [always] getting to know."[59] That is to say, the explanation left room for the unexpected and for a future not coded for in the status quo. As such, it is never to be offered as the last word. In other words, Lovelace is careful that the "what" of Caribbean identity always remained open to the performative jostle of Creolization's playful poetics. He also notes that such a "playing with" or "playing in" identity constructions was never for its own sake but rather to disguise those comportments of rebellion that challenged the (neo-)colonial status quo. In other words, playful contestation here is both critical and politically meaningful, despite its remaining beyond the reach of the political's capacity to define or categorize. In Lovelace's words, we might understand these playful poetics as the unfolding of a Caribbean identity beyond colonialism, in the "[establishing of] a new and humane society."[60]

I turn now to his 1979 novel, *The Dragon Can't Dance*, as a fictional account of this subversive power in Carnival poetics. What looks like complete social and economic dispossession in the lives of the characters of Lovelace's novel is punctuated by and broken up into playful contestations of the administrative powers of the state. Through masquerade, the characters invent, in order to perform, full and human selves. H. Adlai Murdoch points out that such a reclaiming of cultural identity and social positionality through the performativity of Carnival has historically marked Caribbean identity. "[These] creolized Caribbean societies ultimately effected a complete transformation of carnivalesque principles . . . appropriating and refashioning their potential for subversion and liberation into the polysemic contemporary round of revelry that is now an icon of [Caribbeanness]."[61] In his novel, Lovelace offers such a story of subversive refashioning through the performative modality of play and for the sake of articulating a sense of belonging in the midst of social and economic alienation.

Set in a predominantly Afro-Trinidadian community in the outskirts of the capital of Port-of-Spain, the Hill is known for its contending (warring, to be precise) steel bands that descend into the streets of the city on Carnival Monday and Tuesday, partaking in what is really a music-driven enactment of power, self-definition, and visibility.[62] My focus is on Aldrick, the only character Lovelace marks with some "submarine" lineage back to African slaves. On Carnival Monday and Tuesday, Aldrick's charge is to dance the dragon dance, a performance that is really a placeholder for a subaltern unsettling of capitalist structures and its ethic of property ownership and family values. Aldrick quietly refuses it all. Indeed, we might hear in the echoes of his character development the "I would prefer not to" of Melville's Bartleby. Aldrick's gentle refusal of all things proper (love interests, family ties, a job) is juxtaposed alongside his menacing performance of the dragon dance. Natasha Barnes writes, "While wearing his dragon masque and dancing his dragon dance, Aldrick is assured a personhood, however ephemeral the terms of its representation."[63] Parodying the debased morality and evil in the colonial stereotype of the African slave (indeed, mocking the stereotype's epistemological authority), Aldrick's dragon mas consists of chains, horns and tail, and greased-black skin against the bright red of the costume's wings. Parading/dancing in this costume during Carnival means to move through a crowd of spectators as a menace (their menace), until perhaps one is given money as payment for moving on. Aldrick treats his responsibility to perform this dragon dance as a spiritual ritual and as an obligation he has to the community on the Hill to perform the collective scream that will proclaim their personhood on these two days of the year. This scream—neither political nor without political register—works against the feeling of dispossession that marks the other days, between Ash Wednesday and Carnival Monday.

In Lovelace's novel, through the lens of this festive/playful reversal of the social order, we witness the community on the Hill searching for a self that they will create out of their collective play. In other words, the self is invented in order to be performed. In this sense, the trajectory in the poetics of the play grows out of an absent self (a sense of nobodyness, if you will) toward an ephemeral anchoring in a Caribbean world not yet free from colonial subordination. The following passage describing Aldrick's love interest, Sylvia, is perhaps a good demonstration of this: "Then he [Aldrick] saw Sylvia, dancing still with all her dizzying aliveness . . . refusing to let go of that visibility, that self that Carnival gave her . . . lifting up her arms and leaping as if she wanted to leap out of herself into her self, a self [that] she could *be* forever."[64] The self that Sylvia finds is performed, and as with Aldrick's dragon dance, it is performed in order to be found. More importantly, there is the desire to be in flight *toward* this self in such playful contestations (contestation that, I hold, characterize the movement of creolizing processes in general). In one sense, we should see in Aldrick's dragon dance (and Sylvia's revelry) attempts to become a "somebody," stand in the visibility of public recognition that one, indeed, is a person.

But in another sense, I want to propose that Aldrick's dragon dance—these Carnival poetics—retains the spirit of antiessentialism that characterizes Creolization's syncretism. As performance, these flights toward identity are located in an absolute "now" and signify concretely in the living time and place of the communal performance. Aldrick's dragon dance lives *as* it is performed and shared and bears truth in (and not beyond) the shared experience of that performance. To be sure, out of that living, communal moment, the power of the dragon is both invented and found so as to fill the void of (selfless) dispossession that marks Aldrick's life 363 days out of the calendar year. But because it lives in the singularity of the performative experience and does not outlive this performative experience, this self is not at the level of the normative. Indeed, it is this antinormativity that makes *political* failures out of these Carnival contestations of power. This is the heart of Aldrick's political disappointment toward the end of the novel: after his band of friends hijack two police offers and their truck in an attempted coup d'état of Port-of-Spain, they are sentenced to prison. Aldrick moans, "They [the Port-of-Spain police] knew we was just some fellas with guns who jump off the Corner and drive into town and shout liberation . . . even with no police to stop us we couldn't do nutten. . . . They allow us to run loose until we give we self up so that we could see for weeself that all we could do is a dragon dance; all we could do is to threaten power, to show off power we have but don't know how to organize, how to use."[65]

Indeed, there is power in the unworkings of this Carnival poetics in how it unsettles the political. But the relationship between this contestation and the political is, we might say, ambiguous, liminal, and even sometimes contradictory. We are reminded here of the scene playing out in Trinidad in 1970 between national politics and calypso culture. Throughout Trinidad's history, and as a consequence of what I mark as an ambiguous relationship between the political and the poetic, mainstream politics has adopted multiple stances toward Carnival revelry, calypso, and steelpan, varying from explicit censorship/curtailment to outright disinterest. In 1970, this all seemed to come to a head when then prime minister, Dr. Eric Williams, in an attempt to be flippant about calypsonians' scathing critical commentary of his political party, seemed to actually belie his own wariness about their criticisms. When asked to comment about the calypsonian known as Mighty Chalkdust, Williams pronouncement was, "Let the jackass sing." That year, Mighty Chalkdust's calypso titled "Let the Jackass Sing" was all the rave in Trinidad.

I offer this anecdote to stress the ambiguous entry of creolizing critical practices into the political, to show that what, at the level of play, shows up as a "critical category of Caribbean resistance"[66] becomes at the level of politics a joke not even worth a response by law enforcement. (Aldrick and his band weren't even stopped by the police as they drove around the city shouting "liberation!"—truly, they were jackasses who were allowed to sing.) I propose that we do not see these ambiguous enactments as failures but rather as precisely the locus and enabling mechanism of the subversive power of these playful (creolizing) contestations. Enacting contestations outside of/oblique to the political, these Creole poetics sustain themselves as nonteleological and as nonnormative. In other words, what might be regarded as the limits of their playful reversals and mockeries of political structures is ultimately what safeguards the promise and possibility within their narrative productions. Wrapped perpetually "in the mode of their possibility,"[67] these playful inventions of self-determination/identity are never actualized in a moment of political revolution. But it is in this "circumvention [of] the business of frontal political engagement" that we must locate their political efficacy.[68]

Concluding Remarks

My hope is to have offered an argument for including Creolization into philosophical accounts of the Americas. As a conceptual frame, it allows us to pose important questions about the making of modern subjects, about the possibility of the "new" emerging from the old and about thinking through the politics of temporality in terms of obscure futures. Primarily coming out of the Antillean region of the Americas, creolizing practices engage with the present and offer possibilities for the future in ways that are both impure and obfuscating of origins, and in so doing, allow decolonial possibilities to emerge out of structures of coloniality. To be sure, this all happens at the level of the everyday. But what this means is that in attending to these liminal sites, it becomes possible to develop an analysis of the political power and political knowledge that emerges in/through the local. It is at this level that one finds (so as to acknowledge) the creative agency that enacts ruptures in what Sylvia Wynter names the "master code" of modernity's overrepresentation of Man.

Through the Antillean American capacity to refashion a colonial past—for this sake of alternative futures—those plantation communities were able to "adapt, resist, and accommodate the slave regime."[69] As critical practices of personal survival, Creole modes of being in the world were not simply a matter of finding ways to stay alive in the midst of everyday violence. More significantly, it was also about performing (inventing) a life worthy of living and, in that performance, contesting the finality of that everyday violence by refusing its fate.[70] In the spirit of Michaeline Crichlow's proposal for understanding Creolization as a conceptual category that might have relevance beyond the plantation, I have proposed an account of creolizing practices that continue to refashion the social and jostle the political in order to generate liberating possibilities and new subjectivities in the age of neocolonial hegemony. In this spirit, Earl Lovelace's *The Dragon Can't Dance* invites us to understand resistance and everyday sabotage in this way, despite the oblique and nonfrontal relationship between these resistive gestures and the political. Through my reading of his novel, I have shown that it is in this circumvention of the categorical work of politics that the playful poetics of Creolization unworks the closures and callouses of dominant structures. There is no settled version of the story of self-determination (hence the significance, for Lovelace, that he writes from the space of the Caribbean, and not outside of it). And it is out of this open-endedness that practices of Creolization are, indeed, rehearsals of hope. The story that Lovelace tells ends with a failed coup d'état, but in the midst of that explicit political failure is a note that is radically anticipatory, open and rich with a promise of transformation. Much like Lovelace himself, his readers are called to continue to believe.

Notes

1. Earl Lovelace, *The Dragon Can't Dance* (New York: Persea, 1979).
2. Michaeline Crichlow and Patricia Hothover, "Homing Modern Freedoms: Creolization and the Politics of Making Place," *Cultural Dynamics* 12, no. 3 (2009): 283–316, 283.

3. H. Adlai Murdoch, "Créolité, Creolization and Contemporary Caribbean Culture," *small axe* 52 (March 2017): 180–198, 181.

4. George Ciccariello-Mahar, *Decolonizing Dialectics* (Durham, NC: Duke University Press, 2017); Maria Lugones, *Pilgrimames/Peregrinajes: Theorizing Coalitions Against Multiple Oppressions* (Lanham, MD: Rowman & Littlefield, 2003).

5. Maria Lugones, *Pilgrimames/Peregrinajes*, 213, emphasis added.

6. In Frantz Fanon's assessments of the cultural changes pertaining to the use of the transistor radio in post-1954 Algeria, he identifies a similar critical significance of these everyday transformations. He writes that as the radio transforms from an instrument of colonial domination to one of revolutionary struggle, French colonialism is presented with "new content" that forces it to see itself as a system that is never completely closed. See Frantz Fanon, *A Dying Colonialism* (New York: Grove, 1965), 19. In my book, *Creolizing the Nation* (Evanston, IL: Northwestern University Press, 2020), I read Fanon's accounts of how Algeria's cultural transformations supported its political revolution in terms of Creolization.

7. Fanon, *A Dying Colonialism*, 19.

8. Anthony Alessandrini makes a similar claim in bringing Jamaica Kincaid's work into conversation with Fanon's (particularly the creative nonfiction of *Black Skin, White Masks*). He describes the power of Kincaid's and Fanon's imaginary writing as the power to create conceptual space in which a new version of the human might be articulated. In other words, these imaginative, critical projects "bring into being a (not yet) post-colonial category of the human." See Anthony Alessandrini, *Frantz Fanon and the Future of Cultural Politics: Finding Something Different* (Lanham, MD: Lexington, 2014), 128. Perhaps we might read Lovelace's story of the dragon in this register. But, more than this, I propose that we read the playful sabotage of creolizing practices as living texts themselves, operating not only as a critique of colonialism's legacy but also grappling with an articulation of what a possible postcolonial future would be.

9. I note this aspect of Creolization as one of its important distinctions from Ciccariello-Maher's conception of decolonizing dialectics.

10. Frantz Fanon, *Black Skin, White Masks*, trans. Charles Lam Markmann (London: Pluto, 1967), 229.

11. At its etymological origin, "Creole" (and the Spanish *criollo*) signifies the ambiguity involved in being native to the New World without being indigenous to the place that has become (as a consequence of displacement and/or transplantation) one's home.

12. "Indeed, because they are marked by an extermination of the original population and became totally dependent on the metropole because of their plantation economies, the Caribbean archipelago witnessed the extremes of the New World experience." See J. Michael Dash, *The Other America: Caribbean Literature in a New World Context* (Charlottesville: University of Virginia Press, 1998), 5.

13. Heather Smyth, "The Black Atlantic Meets the Black Pacific: Multimodality in Kamau Brathwaite and Wayde Compton," *Callaloo* 37, no. 2 (Spring 2014): 389–403, 399.

14. Wendy Knepper, "Colonization, Creolization, and Globalization: The Art and Ruses of *Bricolage*," *small axe* 21 (October 2006): 70–86, 71.

15. This points to the important distinction between *Créolité* as an articulation of an (essential) Caribbean identity and Creolization as a sociocultural process that "[stresses] principles of exchange and combination rather than the mythic singularities of a single origin." See Murdoch, "Créolité, Creolization," 187.

16. Murdoch, 188.

17. Stuart Hall, "*Créolité* and the Process of Creolization," in *Creolizing Europe: Legacies and Transformations,* ed. Encarnación Gutiérrez Rodríguez and Shirley Anne Tate, Liverpool University Press, Liverpool, 2015, 16.

18. "The group replaces rites or myths that are missing with elements that can fill the same function. This explains the presence of Christian elements in voodoo, elements that fill in the holes." See Knepper, "Colonization, Creolization, and Globalization," 76.

19. Knepper, 79.

20. Knepper, 73–74.

21. Curdella Forbes describes such creolizing modes of social organization as "a constellation, not a synthesis, a polyphony, not a symphony, a perverse, sacred transversality, not a teleology." See Curdella Forbes, "The End of Nationalism? Performing the Question in Benitze-Rojo's *The Repeating Island* and Glissant's *Poetics of Relation*," *Journal of West Indian Literature* 11, no. 1 (2002): 4–23, 14.

22. Patricia Marie Northover and Michaeline Crichlow, *Globalization and the Post-Creole Imagination: Notes on Fleeing the Plantation* (Durham, NC: Duke University Press, 2009), x.

23. I pursue this in more detail in *Creolizing the Nation* (Chicago: Northwestern University Press, 2020). Specifically, one of its chapters brings the homing practices of Creolization into engagement with Mariana Ortega's account of "hometactics," which she develops in *In-Between: Latina Feminist Phenomenology, Multiplicity, and the Self* (Albany: State University of New York Press, 2016).

24. Northover and Crichlow, *Globalization and the Post-Creole Imagination*, 37.

25. Patrick Chamoiseau, *Creole Folktales*, trans. Linda Coverdale (New York: New Press, 1994), xiii.

26. I pursue this question elsewhere, by bringing together Fanon's account of the decolonial nation together with Glissant's account of the composite community. See Kris Sealey, "The Composite Community: Thinking Through Fanon's Critique of a Narrow Nationalism," *Critical Philosophy of Race* 6, no. 1 (2018): 26–57.

27. In this context, "[cultural] identity . . . belongs to the future as much as to the past." See Stuart Hall, "Cultural Identity and Diaspora," *Identity: Com-*

munity, Culture and Difference, ed. Jonathan Rutherford (London: Lawrence and Wishart, 1990), 225.

28. H. Adlai Murdoch's account of the musical form of *zouk* also underscores this across Caribbean musical modalities. See Murdoch, "Créolité, Creolization," 194–196).

29. "The unity is submarine." See Edward Kamau Braithwaite, *Caribbean Man in Space and Time: A Bibliographical and Conceptual Approach* (Mona, Puerto Rico: Savacou, 1974), 1.

30. Northover and Crichlow, *Globalization and the Post-Creole Imagination*, 284.

31. Northover and Crichlow, 286.

32. Northover and Crichlow, 284.

33. Stuart Hall, "For Allon White: Metaphors of Transformation," *Stuart Hall: Critical Dialogues in Cultural Studies,* ed. David Morley and Kuan-Hsing Chen (New York: Routledge, 1996), 292.

34. Northover and Crichlow, *Globalization and the Post-Creole Imagination*, 37.

35. María Lugones, *Pilgrimages/Pereginajes: Theorizing Coalition against Multiple Oppressions* (New York: Rowman & Littlefield, 2003).

36. Knepper, "Colonization, Creolization, and Globalization," 79.

37. Knepper, 79.

38. Homi Bhabha, "How Newness Enters the World: Postmodern Space, Postcolonial Times and the Trials of Cultural Translation," *Location of Culture*, 2nd ed. (London: Routledge Classics, 2004), 334.

39. Northover and Crichlow, *Globalization and the Post-Creole Imagination*, 288.

40. Sylvia Wynter, "Unsettling the Coloniality of Being/Power/Truth/Freedom: Toward the Human, After Man, Its Overrepresentation—An Argument," *New Centennial Review* 3, no. 3 (Fall 2003): 257–337.

41. Wynter, "Unsettling," 323.

42. Wynter, 315.

43. Wynter, 285–286.

44. Wynter, 285.

45. Murdoch, "Créolité, Creolization," 196.

46. Northover and Crichlow, *Globalization and the Post-Creole Imagination*, 308.

47. Northover and Crichlow, 285.

48. Bhabha, "How Newness Enters the World," 303–337.

49. Knepper, "Colonization, Creolization, and Globalization," 79, emphasis added.

50. Curdella Forbes, *From Nation to Diaspora: Samuel Selvon, George Lamming and the Cultural Performance of Gender* (Kingston, Jamaica: University of the West Indies Press, 2005), 151.

51. Forbes, *From Nation to Diaspora*, 155.
52. Forbes, 89.
53. Natasha Barnes, *Cultural Conundrums: Gender, Race, Nation and the Making of Caribbean Cultural Politics* (Ann Arbor: University of Michigan Press, 2006), 21.
54. To recall Frantz Fanon again here, this is the hope in his demand for inserting invention into existence.
55. Natasha Barnes, *Cultural Conundrums*, 75.
56. Earl Lovelace, "The Day Is Not Yet Done," interview by Maria Grau-Perejoan, *Atlantis: Journal of the Spanish Association of Anglo-American Studies* 38, no. 2 (December 2016): 203–213, 204.
57. To this end, I will share the following anecdote. At the 2012 Trinidad and Tobago Boca Literary Festival, Lovelace was at a dinner with an impressive cadre of Caribbean writers. When asked by either Lorna Goodison or Mervyn Taylor why he never left Trinidad, unlike so many others at the table, his response was simply, "Because I believed." I thank Lauren K. Alleyne for this potent account.
58. This brings to mind Fanon's conception of the kind of national culture out of which, subsequent to independence from colonial rule, a nation can hope to move beyond the Manichean stasis of colonialism. Of this kind of living, open-ended culture, Fanon writes, "[The] characteristic of a culture is to be open, permeated by spontaneous, generous fertile lines of force." See Frantz Fanon, *Toward the African Revolution* (New York: Grove, 1964), 34.
59. Lovelace, "The Day Is Not Yet Done," 204.
60. Lovelace, 207.
61. Murdoch, "Créolité, Creolization," 196.
62. For an extensive account of both the historical emergence and contemporary relevance of Caribbean Carnival, see Peter Mason's *Bacchanal! The Carnival Culture of Trinidad* (Philadelphia: Temple University Press, 1998).
63. Barnes, *Cultural Conundrums*, 83.
64. Earl Lovelace, *The Dragon Can't Dance*, 127. Speaking to the origin of Carnival in slave communities, Rex Nettleford points out, "[The] sustaining lifeblood of these events was the creation by the participants of masks to disguise, of music to affirm, or dances to celebrate, as well as the germination of ideas beyond the reach of those who brutishly supervised them for the rest of the year." See Rex Nettleford, "Implications for Caribbean Development," *Caribbean Festival Arts: Each and Every Bit of Difference*, ed. John W. Nunley and Judith Bettelheim (Seattle: University of Washington Press, 1988), 184.
65. Lovelace, *The Dragon Can't Dance*, 185–186.
66. Barnes, *Cultural Conundrums*, 23.
67. Barnes, 23.
68. Barnes, 76.
69. Northover and Crichlow, *Globalization and the Post-Creole Imagination*, 29.

70. See Lovelace, "The Day Is Not Yet Done," 207: "Colonialism is not all that happened to these islands and those who people them."

CHAPTER TEN

Decolonizing Mariátegui as a Prelude to Decolonizing Latin American Philosophy

SERGIO ARMANDO GALLEGOS-ORDORICA

Though his work has had a lasting influence on Peruvian and Latin American philosophy, José Carlos Mariátegui (1894–1930) remains a rather marginal figure in the twenty-first-century English-speaking philosophical world, since only a few contemporary philosophers have addressed his thought.[1] Nowadays, considering that Mariátegui was heavily influenced by Marxist ideas, his philosophical contributions may seem to be *dépassées* just as those of other Marxist thinkers from the first half of the twentieth century such as Rosa Luxemburg or Antonio Gramsci. However, I believe this assessment is mistaken, insofar as Mariátegui's thought contains valuable insights for such contemporary philosophical projects as those involving the articulation of a decolonized philosophy.[2] But just as I believe that Mariátegui's thought is important for projects aimed at the decolonization of philosophy, I also think that Mariátegui should not be read uncritically. To be more specific, the thesis I defend in this chapter is that Mariátegui's thought is ambivalent (very much like the thought of John Dewey)[3]: on one hand, it contains the philosophical resources needed for the articulation of a decolonizing philosophy; on the other hand, it needs to be decolonized itself, as it is underpinned by a series of assumptions that can be traced back to the Eurocentric and colonial intellectual framework that Mariátegui criticizes. If this argument is valid, at least two interesting upshots emerge from my assessment of Mariátegui's thought. First, my argument would help to vindicate the idea that the ambivalent status of Mariátegui's thought in that it provides resources for decolonizing movements but also needs to be decolonized itself, is not anomalous in Latin America. In fact, some authors have persuasively argued that this same trait also emerges in other prominent Latin American philosophers of the period such as José Vasconcelos, whose work has been used by Chicano activists to resist oppression in the United States despite its disparaging views of Amerindians, blacks, and Asians.[4] Second, my argument would provide the basis for a careful recovery and use of the main insights present in Mariátegui's thought, thus allowing the development of a more solid groundwork for decolonizing philosophical projects.

This chapter is organized as follows. In the first section I present the philosophical antecedents from which Mariátegui's thought emerges, focusing on the influences in his work of certain Marxist thinkers (in particular, Georges Sorel) and of Peruvian *indigenistas* such as Manuel González Prada. In the second section, I argue that Mariátegui's thought contains sufficient intellectual resources to be used in decolonizing projects. To show this, I offer a brief analysis of his most important work, *Seven Interpretive Essays on Peruvian Reality* (in particular, of the second and fourth essays, which are respectively titled "The Problem of the Indian" and "Public Education"), and I argue using textual evidence that Mariátegui articulates some important ideas that can be used to further decolonization projects: specifically, the claim that Peru's "Indian problem" is not racial but economical (to the extent that the misery and ignorance of the Peruvian masses are the result of an unjust economic system and not of the racial composition of Peru's population) and the claim that the division and hierarchization of human beings into races is a "tawdry sham" of white men to justify imperialist projects and establish colonial regimes. Having done this, I contend in the third section that Mariátegui's thought needs to undergo decolonization insofar as Mariátegui subscribes to certain claims that stem from the Eurocentric intellectual framework that he criticizes. To show this, I offer a brief analysis of his essays "The Religious Factor" and "Literature on Trial," and I argue using textual evidence that Mariátegui subscribes to the division of human beings into races—a division he criticizes elsewhere—as well as to the view that races stand in a certain hierarchy. Having done this, I propose in the fourth section a way to decolonize Mariátegui's thought, and I show how this decolonization can be used to further other philosophical decolonization projects. Finally, I offer a brief conclusion.

The Genealogy of Mariátegui's Thought: Sorelian Marxism and Peruvian Indigenism

Though the work of Mariátegui has not been extensively addressed by Anglophone philosophers, those who have engaged with his work, such as Ofelia Schutte, have pointed out that his philosophy seems to have emerged as the product of at least two different intellectual traditions. Following one tradition, which can be traced back to certain European Marxists (in particular, to Georges Sorel), Mariátegui defended the importance of myth as a political tool for the transformation of society.[5] However, while Sorel maintained that myths (and, in particular, the Marxist myth of the general strike) are primarily useful in fueling antagonism between bourgeois elites and the working masses—and promoting a sense of class consciousness and unity among the proletariat—Mariátegui went further than Sorel in the sense that he incorporated another dimension into Sorel's proposal. Indeed, while Sorel viewed the myth primarily in terms of its power to generate a social revolution through the exacerbation of class divisions, Mariátegui articulated a conception of myth as a political tool that was not grounded in fostering divisions. Rather, his conception was about promoting unity among social classes through the development of a national consciousness based on the contributions and perspectives of the masses of disenfranchised Peruvians (who were overwhelmingly Amerindians):

> The myth of [Mariátegui's notion of] the social revolution results from this new consciousness, a consciousness through which people are united rather than separated, as in Sorel's case. In particular, the myth operates to unite all those who wish to contribute to the new society. It transcends rigid class distinction. Most importantly, it incorporates the forgotten masses of Peruvians. . . . Finally, in Mariátegui, the concept of the nation is not formed prior to the myth of the general strike, as it was in Sorel's France. The nation is something to be forged through the new consciousness and through the myth of the social revolution.[6]

Thus, while advocating (following Sorel and Marx) for a social revolution that would transform the appalling material conditions in which the impoverished masses of Peruvians lived and toiled, Mariátegui integrated a nation-building or nationalist component into the Marxist project he pursued. This nationalism is manifested in his comparison of the Spanish colonial regime with the Peruvian republican government. Mariátegui emphasizes that "while the [Spanish] viceroyalty was a medieval and foreign regime, the republic is formally a Peruvian and liberal regime."[7] For Mariátegui, the republican government is only formally or nominally Peruvian to the extent that "the Republic has impoverished the Indian, has aggravated its oppression and has deepened its misery."[8] Thus, since Mariátegui considers the republic as a prolongation of the colonial regime insofar as republican elites have systematically oppressed and exploited the Amerindian population, he then argues that the socialist project of liberating these masses of Amerindian workers and peasants must be nationalistic. This is because, as he maintains in his essay "Nacionalismo y Vanguardismo en la Ideologia Política," "for [economically or politically] colonized peoples, socialism acquires, given the circumstances, a nationalistic attitude without negating any of its principles."[9] In this respect, his thought diverges from that of European Marxists who sought to separate social revolutions from nation-building or nationalistic projects, which were often considered reactionary endeavors spearheaded by bourgeois elites and geared toward the undermining of class solidarity among workers in different countries.[10] In contrast to European Marxists such as Luxemburg and Liebknecht, Mariátegui's socialist project is nationalistic in nature because, in his view, Peru had only formally become independent (since its socioeconomic structures remain medieval and foreign) and, given these conditions, his socialist project is nationalistic because "the idea of a nation—as an internationalist has stated—embodies at certain historical periods the spirit of freedom."[11]

The nationalistic project that aimed to turn Peru into a genuinely (as opposed to a formally) independent nation by ending the systemic labor exploitation and the political and economic marginalization that Amerindians were subject to had been defended, prior to Mariátegui, by other distinguished Peruvian intellectuals. The essayist and critic Manuel González Prada, in a classic essay titled "Nuestros Indios" (Our Indians), asserted that the ignorance, abject poverty, and vicious habits (e.g., alcoholism) manifested by Amerindians in Peru were the result not of innate "racial" dispositions but rather the product of their oppression within the framework of a quasifeudal system imposed by landowners (*gamonales*) that had never been substantially modified after the end of the Spanish colonial period.

To be more specific, according to González Prada, the backwardness, disunity, and lack of civic virtue that plagued Peru (and which had been patently manifested in the calamitous defeats of Peru at the hands of Chile during the War of the Pacific) were the result not of an inherent inferiority of Amerindians but rather of the material conditions of deprivation endured by the Peruvian masses. Thus, in opposition to the highly influential views of European thinkers such as Herbert Spencer and Gustave Le Bon (who suggested that the political instability and the underdevelopment of Peru and the rest of Latin America were chiefly due to the racial makeup of their populations), González Prada's *indigenismo* was manifested through his claim that the "the problem of the Indian is economical and social more than educational."[12] Thus, one of the central ideas of the version of *indigenismo* stemming from Gónzalez Prada is that Amerindians are not physically, mentally, or morally inferior to Europeans: their ignorance, misery, and moral degradation are the product of what Aníbal Quijano has recently labeled the "coloniality of power," which is a socioeconomic system in which "the racist distribution of new identities was combined . . . with a racist distribution of labor and the forms of exploitation of colonial capitalism."[13] In his writings, Mariátegui acknowledges the importance of González Prada's *indigenismo* as an antecedent to his own views when he writes that González Prada "makes judgements that signal him as the precursor of a new social consciousness."[14]

However, since González Prada ends his essay claiming that "the Indian will be redeemed through his own efforts, and not through the humanization of his oppressors" but then leaves unaddressed the question of how effective social change can be carried out in Peru, his *indigenismo* remains a utopian aspiration. In contrast to this stance, Mariátegui's position is far more programmatic: although he agrees with González Prada that "the solution to the problem of the Indian must be a social solution [and] its enactors must be the Indians themselves,"[15] he also argues that the desire for social change of the forgotten Amerindian masses can only be properly harnessed and effectively channeled through socialism. Indeed, for him, "the spread in Peru of socialist ideas has brought forth a strong movement of Indigenous demands" and the beginnings of a national coordination of Amerindian efforts has created a situation wherein "for the first time the government has been forced to accept and proclaim *indigenista* perspectives."[16] Thus, as the previously cited passages show, Mariátegui's intellectual influences blend Sorelian Marxism (which relies on the importance of myth as a political tool and is voluntaristic in nature, insofar as it stresses the key importance of strikes and other direct activities to bring about the revolution) and Peruvian indigenism (which is a nationalistic ideology that, in Mariátegui's own words, "advocates for the reconstruction of Peru on the basis of the Indian").[17] Having highlighted the intellectual genealogy of Mariátegui's thought, I want to now explore which decolonizing tools and strategies Mariátegui uses.

Decolonizing Strategies and Tools in Mariátegui's Works

Prior to exploring what decolonizing strategies and tools Mariátegui deploys, it is important to be clear on what decolonizing consists of (or, to be more precise, how the notion will be understood here). In order to do this, one should bear in mind an important distinction that Aníbal Quijano has made between colonialism and coloniality. For Quijano, colonialism is "a product of a systematic repression, not only of the specific beliefs, ideas, images, symbols or knowledge that were not useful to global colonial domination, while at the same time the colonizers were expropriating from the colonized, specially in mining, agriculture, engineering as well as their products and work."[18] In contrast, coloniality (or the "coloniality of power," as he also calls it) is characterized as a specific form of global domination where "the social category of 'race' [is] the key element of the social classification of colonized and colonizers."[19] Thus, coloniality is, according to Quijano, a far more resilient system of domination because it justifies specific divisions of space, labor, and resources among various groups on the basis of something that purports to be a natural category. This leads Quijano to assert that "coloniality is, then, the most general form of domination in the world today, once colonialism as a political order was destroyed."[20]

Building upon Quijano's insights, Walter Mignolo and Catherine Walsh draw another crucial distinction between two notions of decolonization. The first notion of decolonization, which is tied to the notion of colonialism, is usually defined in terms of "freeing a colony to allow it to become self-governing or independent; to build the former-colonized own nation-state," and therefore this notion is "connected with liberation struggles in Asia and Africa."[21] The second notion of decolonization, which is tied to the notion of coloniality, involves "the recognition and undoing of the hierarchical structures of race, gender, heteropatriachy, and class that continue to control life, knowledge, spirituality, and thought, structures that clearly are intertwined with and constitutive of global capitalism and Western modernity."[22] In the analysis that follows, my aim will be to assess whether Mariátegui's thought offers the resources to be used in decolonizing projects that involve the recognition and undoing of coloniality. And I will leave aside their potential use to tackle colonialism.

On this issue, even a brief reading of Mariátegui's most important pieces (in particular, his *Seven Interpretive Essays on Peruvian Reality*) shows that Mariátegui is extremely aware of how the notion of race (and other notions such as those of ethnicity, class, and gender) have been used in Peru and globally, both historically and in recent times, to separate different populations in a hierarchical fashion and to justify divisions of space, labor, and resources in accordance with a colonial framework. For instance, in one of the most forceful passages of his essay "The Problem of the Indian," Mariátegui writes the following lines:

> The assumption that the Indigenous problem is an ethnic problem stems from the oldest repertory of imperialist ideas. The concept of inferior races helped the white West in its task of expansion and conquest. To expect Indigenous emancipation from an active mixing of the aboriginal race with white immigrants is an anti-sociological ingenuousness, conceivable only in the rudimentary mind of an importer of Merino sheeps. The Asian peoples, to which the Indian people is not inferior in the least, have assimilated the most creative and dynamic aspects of Western culture without transfusions of European blood. The degeneration of the Peruvian Indian is a tawdry sham of pettifoggers of the feudal table.[23]

This passage is remarkable insofar as Mariátegui recognizes different ways in which coloniality has traditionally operated, and he attempts to undo them. First, he explicitly says that the notion of *inferior race* (which has been used historically as a category to indistinctly lump very different Amerindian groups into) has been deployed in order to support the imperialist endeavors of various European nations and to justify the imposition and the maintenance of colonial institutions (e.g., the *encomienda*) on Amerindian populations. Secondly, he suggests that claims of racial degeneration used to put down Amerindians are not only shoddy lies, but they are lies created by the legal system. In doing this, he makes clear that the notion of race is not a natural category but a social one: it has been created by the law. Thirdly, contrary to other prominent Latin American intellectuals such as Venezuelan historian Arístides Rojas (1826–1894) or the Mexican anthropologist Manuel Gamio (1883–1960), who advocated for European immigration and *mestizaje* (i.e., racial mixing) as a way to progressively assimilate Amerindians in Venezuela and Mexico (and thus alleviate their material oppression and cultural marginalization), Mariátegui denounces *mestizaje* as an utterly misguided strategy. Mariátegui argues that *mestizaje* assumes that biology, culture, and morality are indissolubly joined (or, at least, that cultural and moral traits of human groups are directly influenced by their biological features). By mentioning the case of Asian groups and then pointing out that their moral and cultural achievements have been obtained without mixing with Europeans, Mariátegui aims to undo coloniality by showing that the moral and cultural characteristics of human groups are independent of their biological makeup.

In addition to underscoring how the notion of inferior race was used by Europeans to justify imperialist endeavors and the imposition of colonial regimes across the Americas, Mariátegui also points out in his essay "The Problem of the Indian" another important mechanism in which coloniality operated by showing how the racial divisions established by Europeans were intimately connected during the colonial period with a division of labor that pitted oppressed groups against each other:

> The tendency of Spaniards to settle on the coast drove away from this region the aborigines to the point that there were labor shortfalls. The viceroyalty aimed to resolve this problem through the importation of black slaves, who turned fit for the climate and the toils of the warm valleys or plains from the coast, and inadequate, in contrast, for the work of the mines, located in the cold mountain ranges. The black slave reinforced the domination of the Spaniards who, despite the Indigenous depopulation, would have felt too demographically overwhelmed with respect to the Indians who were, despite their submission, hostile and antagonistic. The Black was tasked with domestic service and crafts. Whites mixed easily with blacks, and this mixture produced one of the coastal population types

with stronger ties to Spanish culture and more resistant to Indigenous culture.[24]

As this passage makes quite clear, Mariátegui is hyperaware of the fact that the imposition of a division of labor during the colonial period along racial lines was an instrument of coloniality, since it buttressed the Spanish domination by pitting different socioracial groups against each other and prevented them from developing solidarity over their shared oppression. On one hand, black slaves were forced to perform domestic services or crafts (or work on coastal plantations), which prevented them from having systematic contact with Amerindians and pushed them to assimilate to their Spanish masters by learning their language (rather than being able to learn Quechua or Aymara by working alongside Amerindians). On the other hand, Amerindians were excluded from domestic work and forced to toil in the mines in the mountain ranges, which reinforced their geographic and social isolation.

In addition to highlighting how race was used in different ways to establish and maintain coloniality in Peru, Mariátegui in his essay "Public Education" also casts light on how class and wealth have been used to establish and maintain coloniality in Peru (and throughout the rest of Latin America) through the creation and the perpetuation of public higher education systems that silence dissenting voices, promote bureaucratization, and reward mediocrity instead of encouraging student engagement and the pursuit of academic excellence:

> The economic and political regime determined by the dominion of colonial aristocracies, which in some Hispanic American countries subsists even though it is undergoing irreparable and progressive dissolution, has placed for a long time universities in Latin America under the wardship of these oligarchies and their clients. With college education turned into a moneyed privilege, if not a caste privilege or at least a privilege of a social category associated with the interests of money and caste, universities have experienced an inevitable tendency towards academic bureaucratization. . . . Their bureaucratization fatally led to spiritual and scientific impoverishment.[25]

For Mariátegui, the problem lies with the academic bureaucratization and the scientific impoverishment of the public higher education systems in Peru (and across Latin America). Despite being traditionally considered the strongest advocate of republican and liberal principles, "the university has remained faithful to its scholastic, conservative and Spanish tradition."[26]

Finally, Mariátegui also denounces in his works (in particular, in his essay "Feminist Demands") how gender has been used to reinforce coloniality by citing those who challenge feminist demands in the name of tradition (i.e., those who argue against a woman's right to receive a formal education by appealing to traditional arguments offering an idealized portrait of the virtues of domesticity) but are really defending and perpetuating the oppression of women:

> Those who impugn feminism or its advances with sentimental or poetic arguments maintain that women should only be educated for home. But, in practice, this means that women should be educated for being females and mothers. The defense of the lyric aspect of homely life is, really, a defense of the servitude of women. Instead of ennobling and dignifying the role of women, it diminishes and demeans it.[27]

As this passage clearly shows, Mariátegui is well aware of how gender (and more specifically, the traditional gendered division of labor that assigns to women only reproductive and domestic functions) has operated to maintain a power hierarchy where women are systematically demeaned and exploited.[28] In response to this, Mariátegui pushes against coloniality by arguing for the right of women not only to be formally educated but also to work alongside men in all occupations, since "labor changes the female mentality and spirit. Women acquire, in virtue of the labor, a new notion of themselves."[29] In light of all the aforementioned passages, it is clear that Mariátegui's thought involves several resources that can be employed in contemporary decolonial projects that aim to recognize and undo coloniality, since he is sensitive to how race, class, and gender have been used to maintain colonial hierarchies and social structures. However, as I stressed in the introduction, I believe that although Mariátegui's writings can be helpful for current decolonial projects, they must not be read uncritically, as they occasionally reflect the coloniality of power that Mariátegui vehemently denounces. Thus, in the next section I will turn to a critical reading of some of Mariátegui's writings showing that although some of his thinking can be used to further decoloniality, much of it still needs to be decolonized.

Reading Mariátegui through a Decolonial Lens

As I mentioned previously, even though Mariátegui's writings occasionally demonstrate how race, class, and gender have been used to establish and maintain power hierarchies between different groups in Latin America and provide analyses that aim to dismantle the coloniality of power, he himself sometimes lapses into using these notions in ways that presuppose and perpetuate the very hierarchies that he criticizes elsewhere. For instance, in his essay "The Religious Factor" Mariátegui examines how different social groups during the colonial period reacted to the imposition of Catholicism by the Spaniards:

> In the coast, and in Lima in particular, another element came to sap the spiritual strength of Catholicism. The black slave brought to Catholic rites his fetishistic sensualism and his dark superstition. The Indian, a healthy pantheist and materialist, had reached the ethical level of mighty theocracy; the Black, on the other hand, exuded from every pore the primitivism of his African tribe.[30]

As this passage shows, Mariátegui accepts the existence of a hierarchy in which Amerindians, who are described as endorsing a "healthy pantheism and materialism" and as having achieved an "ethical level" in their religious beliefs, are considered superior to black slaves, who are characterized as being in the throes of "fetishistic sensualism" and "dark superstition." And although this hierarchy between different groups may not be biological but rather cultural or moral in nature for Mariátegui, it is nevertheless clear that Mariátegui, given the manner in which he associates primitivism with black people, subscribes to the racialist thesis that race is intrinsically important by virtue of the fact that "to be of particular race is to have a particular set of moral, intellectual and cultural aptitudes and tendencies."[31] Moreover, this characterization of black people as primitive and imbued with negative moral (e.g., sensualism) and cultural traits (e.g., superstition) is not a solitary occurrence in Mariátegui's writings. For instance, in his essay "Literature on Trial," Mariátegui writes the following when he contrasts the contributions of the descendants of black slaves to those of Chinese indentured workers brought to Peru:

> The contribution of the Negro, who came as a slave, almost as merchandise, appears to be even more worthless and negative. The Negro brought his sensualism, his superstition, his primitivism. His condition not only did not permit him to create culture, but the crude, vivid example of his barbarism was most likely to hamper such creation.[32]

Whether the "condition" of black people that prevented them from partaking in the creation of culture is a biological trait or a contingent feature and product of the material conditions they were subject to (i.e., abduction from their homeland, forced transportation across the Atlantic, labor exploitation, sexual violence) is an issue left ambiguous by Mariátegui in this passage. But what is unmistakably clear is that he acknowledges the existence of a racialized hierarchy between different human groups in which those at the bottom are endowed with negative moral and cultural traits. Moreover, even if Chinese people are positioned above blacks, for Mariátegui, insofar as he acknowledges and praises the "skill and the excellence of the small Chinese farmer" in his homeland, he also makes the following derogatory remarks about Chinese indentured workers and their descendants in Peru:

> The Chinese, in contrast, appears to have inoculated his descendants with the fatalism, apathy, and defects of the decrepit Orient. Gambling, which is an element of immorality and indolence, particularly noxious in a people more apt to trust chance than effort, is mainly encouraged by Chinese immigration.[33]

Just as ambiguous as Mariátegui's aforementioned comments about the sensualism and the superstition of blacks are his views concerning the Chinese in this passage. Indeed, it is not clear whether the fatalism, the apathy, and other defects that Chinese immigrants "inoculated" their Peruvian descendants with have a biological basis for Mariátegui or whether they are the result of certain material conditions involving wage theft, labor exploitation, housing segregation, and a dearth of healthy recreational activities. However, it is obvious that he views the influx of Chinese immigrants to Peru as a deleterious process: one that corrupts the general population through the promotion of some negative moral practices (e.g., gambling).[34] In this respect, Mariátegui is responsible for perpetuating the coloniality of power to the extent that the previous passage echoes the rhetoric of the so-called Yellow Peril, which was used to justify the exclusion of Asian immigrants in the United States and other regions of the Americas in the late nineteenth and early twentieth centuries.[35]

What explains the dissonance between Mariátegui's various pronouncements on race? Why does he move from explicitly denouncing the fact that the notion of inferior race was a Western tool to divide and oppress non-European groups to accepting and deploying racialized conceptions of certain groups that reinforce the coloniality of power? Some commentators have suggested that the obvious tensions found in Mariátegui's writings stem from his ambivalence about race.[36] Indeed, though Mariátegui maintains occasionally that race is nothing but a legal fiction, he sometimes uses the term in other ways. For instance, in other scenarios his use of the term suggests "race" is a synonym for "civilization" or "culture" as the following passage makes clear:

> What is important, consequently, in the sociological study of the categories of mestizo and Indian, is not the degree to which the mestizo inherits the qualities or defects of the progenitor races, but his ability to evolve with more ease than the Indian towards the white man's social state or type of civilization.[37]

But this use of race as synonymous with civilization or culture is not uniform in Mariétegui's writings, as there are other passages where he explicitly makes a distinction between race and culture. For instance, when he addresses the contributions of Chinese indentured workers and their descendants in Peru, he explicitly maintains "the Chinese coolie is a being segregated from his country by overpopulation and impoverishment. He grafts in Peru his race, but not his culture."[38] The botanical metaphor that Mariátegui uses here (which characterizes race as a plant graft) suggests that he considers race as having a partial biological ground or reality,[39] but this suggestion is explicitly walked back and flatly rejected just a few paragraphs later in a passage where he says that the notion of race is not biological but rather sociopolitical in nature:

Although the racial question—which has implications that lead superficial critics to improbable zoological reasoning—is artificial and does not merit the consideration of those who are engaged in a concrete and political study of the indigenous problem, the sociological question is another matter.[40]

While I agree with the critical discourse on Mariátegui that explains the tensions in his writings in terms of his ambiguity (some commentators even call it "promiscuity") with respect to the notion of race, I believe this ambiguity is not specific to Mariátegui but rather a manifestation of a struggle that he shares with others. Like many of his contemporaries (in particular, Vasconcelos and Du Bois), Mariátegui articulated a philosophical project (deeply influenced by Marxism in his case) that aimed to push back against transnational forms of white supremacy. Moreover, the project also had a national dimension insofar as Mariátegui strived to turn Peru into a genuinely independent nation by dismantling all the colonial hierarchies and social structures preserved by the republican government after independence. Through this project, he makes an honest effort in his works, much like Vasconcelos and Du Bois do, to show not only how race has been used as an instrument to divide and oppress some groups but also to provide these groups with the conceptual tools to push back against forms of global white supremacy and liberate themselves. However, Mariátegui's efforts (just as those of Vasconcelos and Du Bois) fall short, since the tools he deploys (e.g., his Marxism) to undertake his decolonial project are insufficient.

Indeed, considering that Mariátegui writes in the first paragraph of "The Problem of the Indian" that "the Indigenous question stems from our economy [since] it is rooted in the regime of landownership," it would then seem that a redistribution of land in Peru to the impoverished masses of Amerindians would be enough to ultimately achieve a full decolonization.[41] However, as some commentators such as Renzo Llorente have pointed out, this may not be enough:

> The Indians' emancipation—from the problem the Indian *has*—is essentially an economic question. But what about the problem that the Indian *is*? Race may be relatively insignificant as regards the problem that the Indian *has* but not with respect to the problem that the Indian *is*. If this is the case, Indians may well continue to represent a problem for non-Indian

Peruvians even after the former achieve their emancipation from economic oppression, and this problem may well require that non-Indian Peruvians likewise undergo an emancipation of sorts—from their attitudes and beliefs.[42]

Given that Mariátegui adopts a somewhat reductive view of the "problem of the Indian" by boiling the issue down to economics and land ownership, he exemplifies the same condition that Juliet Hooker has also diagnosed in Vasconcelos and Du Bois (and which is also our condition): despite some localized progress toward racial equality across the Americas, "We remain trapped in the grammar of race that Douglass, Sarmiento, Du Bois and Vasconcelos were grappling with in the nineteenth and twentieth centuries."[43] Moreover, for Hooker, because we remain trapped in this grammar, the traditional arguments offered to show that race is a social construction have been ineffective to undo racial hierarchies (Mariategui's work is an excellent example that vividly illustrates Hooker's claims). Thus, while Mariategui's writings present important resources to undertake decolonial projects such as the ones articulated and pursued by Anzaldúa, Lugones, Dussel, Mignolo, and several others, it is clear that they must decolonized as well. The next section will explore how this could be done in a way that respects the power and the originality of Máriategui's core revolutionary insights.

Achieving and Transcending Mariátegui's Decolonial Project

Having shown that Máriategui's writings themselves require decolonizing, I want to address now the question of how this task is best realized. However, before doing this, let me briefly discuss two particularly ill-advised approaches to tackling Mariátegui's work. One would be to dismiss his entire corpus as being tainted by racism after identifying obvious racist claims in Mariátegui's writings. This approach is problematic because it amounts to throwing the baby out with the bathwater. A second wrong-headed approach would be to selectively read Máriategui, ignoring or excising the passages in which he demeans blacks and Chinese. This is also problematic because it is "cherry picking" and thus leaves us with a truncated view of Mariátegui's thought that fails to explain why, despite attempting to dismantle the coloniality of power in a systematic fashion, he makes occasional remarks that buttress it.

In order to properly decolonize Mariátegui's thought, one needs first to acknowledge the particular historical context in which he lived and wrote. This specific context, which is the same one in which Vasconcelos and Du Bois operated, is dominated by scientific racism, which Hooker characterizes in the following terms:

> Scientific racism was the leading science of the time, articulated by the best minds of the West and disseminated in its most illustrious centers of higher learning. . . . It was a corpus of knowledge, meanings, and truths that anyone thinking about race had to contend with.[44]

If we keep in mind that the context in which Mariátegui lived and worked was dominated by the overwhelming academic prestige of scientific racism, one can then provide an explanation of the tensions found in his writings that parallels Hooker's characterization of tensions found in the works of Vasconcelos and Du Bois: "At times [they] uncritically reproduced certain claims of scientific racism and selectively borrowed from racial science, but for the most part (albeit to varying degrees) they creatively reformulated and resisted it in the service of anti-racist and anti-colonial ends."[45] Thus, a better strategy to decolonize Mariátegui consists in examining closely the specific circumstances in which his demeaning remarks about blacks and Chinese emerge. A close observation of these circumstances then suggests that Mariátegui is being deliberately ambiguous in his characterization of race in order to sow doubt in the minds of his readers or raise questions concerning the biological account of the inferior position of certain groups given by advocates of scientific racism. If this is indeed the case, one can then decolonize the thought of Mariátegui by arguing that his appropriation of some of the tenets of scientific racism is roughly similar to the efforts of an immunologist to develop an attenuated vaccine that would keep the "virus" of scientific racism alive but would also nevertheless "weaken" it to allow his readers to challenge it by generating their own "antibodies" (i.e., doubts or questions about the legitimacy of racial science). There are certainly potential shortcomings to thinking of scientific racism in terms of a kind of virus (in particular, this comparison could wrongly suggest that scientific racism is something that can be addressed through behavioral and drug therapies).[46] Yet I believe that the comparison is useful, as it enables us to capture the idea that scientific racism is not a fixed doctrine or set of ideas but rather something that has changed form (or "mutated") throughout time in order to stay alive. If we see racism as a "polymorphous agent of death" that can shapeshift as a result of changing environmental conditions, there are at least a couple of advantages. First, it allows us to think of racism (following Mariátegui) not in terms of problematic attitudes held by evil individuals but rather in terms of collective harms created and reproduced by an underlying network interrelated economic forces and social barriers.[47] Second, it enables us to argue that in contexts where scientific racism has been deprived of its "virulence," we can perhaps abandon or discard the "attenuated vaccine" Mariátegui was forced to develop. And we can continue Mariátegui's antiracist and anticolonial project by substituting his "attenuated vaccine" for a "killed vaccine"; that is, a decolonial project that not only claims that the notion of *inferior race* is a tool of domination but identifies and challenges the subtle ways in which racial hierarchies are maintained through the use of other notions acting as proxies for race.[48]

Conclusion

I have argued here that despite offering valuable resources for contemporary decolonial projects, Mariátegui's works require decolonization. I have also argued that because the historical context in which Mariátegui lived and wrote was dominated by the tremendous academic clout of scientific racism (which operated as a virus of pandemic proportions infecting every public intellectual space), the occasional remarks he makes in his writings in which he borrows from racial science are best understood in terms of his attempts to counter the overwhelming dominance of scientific racism. If what I argued for here is correct, one interesting question emerges: are other authors such as the Venezuelan sociologist and historian Laureano Vallenilla Lanz—who rejected in some of his writings the idea of inferior races while also opposing the immigration of certain ethnic groups to Venezuela—engaged in an endeavor similar to Mariátegui's? I intend to address this question in future work.

Notes

1. Ofelia Schutte, *Cultural Identity and Social Liberation in Latin American Thought* (Albany: State University of New York Press, 1993); Susana Nuccetelli,

Latin American Thought: Philosophical Problems and Arguments (Boulder, CO: Westview, 2002). In addition, Mariátegui's work has influenced, via Manuel Quijano, some prominent decolonial thinkers such as María Lugones.

2. Enrique Dussel, *Ethics of Liberation in the Age of Globalization and Exclusion* (Durham, NC: Duke University Press, 2013); and Catherine Walsh and Walter Mignolo, *On Decoloniality: Concepts, Analytics, Praxis* (Durham, NC: Duke University Press, 2018).

3. See the contribution of Phillip McReynolds to the current volume.

4. Ilan Stavans, *José Vasconcelos: The Prophet of Race* (New Brunswick, NJ: Rutgers University Press, 2011); and Juliet Hooker, *Theorizing Race in the Americas: Douglass, Sarmiento, Du Bois, Vasconcelos* (New York: Oxford University Press, 2017).

5. Mariátegui's reliance on mythmaking as a strategy for political transformation probably explains why, even though Mariátegui was quite ambivalent vis-à-vis nationalism and scientific racism, he chose to incorporate them in the narrative he created. Indeed, the most enduring myths often involve incorporating notions that human beings are ambivalent toward (e.g., death in the Epic of Gilgamesh) into a single compelling narrative with strong persuasive and emotional power. (I thank Philip McReynolds for suggesting this point.)

6. Schutte, *Cultural Identity*, 44–45. See also Melisa Moore, "Project, Prophesy, Problems: José Carlos Mariátegui's Readings of Revolution and Nation in 1920s Peru," *Delaware Review of Latin American Studies* 14, no. 2 (2013), 1–14; and Jaime Hanneken, "José Carlos Mariátegui and the Time of Myth," *Cultural Critique* 81 (Spring 2012): 1–30.

7. José Carlos Mariátegui, *7 Ensayos de Interpretación de la Realidad Peruana* (22nd ed., Lima, Perú: Biblioteca Amauta, 1978), 46: "Mientras el Virreinato era un régimen medioeval y extranjero, la República es formalmente un régimen peruano y liberal."

8. Mariátegui, *7 Ensayos de Interpretación*, 47: "La República ha pauperizado al indio, ha agravado su depresión y ha exasperado su miseria."

9. José Carlos Mariátegui, *Peruanicemos al Perú* (Lima, Perú: Biblioteca Amauta, 1970), 100–101: "En esos pueblos, el socialismo adquiere, por la fuerza de las circunstancias, sin renegar absolutamente ninguno de sus principios, una actitud nacionalista."

10. It is important to point out here that by taking this position, Mariátegui situates himself in a larger conversation in the early 1920s with other Marxist figures such as Vladimir Lenin, Leon Trotsky, and M. N. Rao regarding the form that successful social revolutions should take. In my view, his main contribution to this debate involves highlighting, along with Rao, that for countries in colonial or neocolonial conditions such as India and Peru in the 1920s, social revolutions need to be framed as nationalistic movements to be successful. (I thank Andrea Pitts for suggesting this point.)

11. Mariátegui, *Peruanicemos al Perú*, 101: "La idea de la nación -lo ha dicho un internacionalista- es en ciertos períodos históricos la encarnación del espíritu de libertad."

12. Manuel González Prada, *Nuestros Indios* (México, D.F.: Coordinación de Humanidades-UNAM, 1978), 18: "La cuestión del indio, más que pedagógica, es económica, es social."

13. Aníbal Quijano, quoted in "(Towards) Decoloniality and Diversality in Global Citizenship Education," in *The Political Economy of Global Citizenship Education*, ed. Vanessa de Oliveira Andreotti (New York: Routledge, 2014): 74–90, 76.

14. Mariátegui, *7 Ensayos*, 38.

15. Mariátegui, 49: "La solución del problema del indio tiene que ser una solución social. Sus realizadores deber ser los propios indios."

16. Mariátegui, 48: "La propagación en el Perú de las ideas socialistas ha traído como consecuencia un fuerte movimiento de reivindicación indígena; Mariátegui, 48–49: "Por primera vez el gobierno se ha visto forzado a aceptar y proclamar puntos de vista indigenista."

17. Mariátegui, *Peruanicemos al Perú*, 99.

18. Aníbal Quijano, "Coloniality and Modernity/Rationality," *Cultural Studies* 21, no. 2–3 (2007): 168–178, 169.

19. Quijano, "Coloniality and Modernity/Rationality," 171.

20. Quijano, 170.

21. Mignolo and Walsh, *On Decoloniality*, 121.

22. Mignolo and Walsh, 17.

23. Mariátegui, *7 Ensayos*, 40: "La suposición de que el problema indígena es un problema étnico se nutre del más envejecido repertorio de ideas imperialistas. El concepto de las razas inferiores sirvió al occidente blanco para su obra de expansión y conquista. Esperar la emancipación indígena del activo cruzamiento de la raza aborigen con inmigrantes blancos es una ingenuidad antisociológica, concebible sólo en la mente rudimentaria de un importador de carneros merinos. Los pueblos asiáticos, a los cuales no es inferior en un ápice el pueblo indio, han asimilado admirablemente la cultura occidental, en lo que tiene de más dinámico y creador sin transfusiones de sangre europea. La degeneración del indio es una barata invención de los leguleyos de la mesa feudal."

24. Mariátegui, 45–46: "La tendencia de los españoles a establecerse en la costa ahuyento de esta región a los aborígenes a tal punto que se carecía de brazos para el trabajo. El Virreinato quiso resolver este problema mediante la importación de esclavos negros, gente que resultó adecuada al clima y las fatigas de los valles o llanos cálidos de la costa, e inaparente, en cambio, para el trabajo de las minas, situadas en la Sierra fría. El esclavo negro reforzó la dominación española que a pesar de la despoblación indígena, se habría sentido de otro modo demográficamente demasiado débil frente al indio, aunque sometido, hostil y enemigo. El negro fue dedicado al servicio doméstico y a los oficios. El blanco

se mezcló fácilmente con el negro produciendo este mestizaje uno de los tipos de población costeña con características de mayor adhesión a lo español y mayor resistencia a lo indígena."

25. Mariátegui, 130: "El régimen económico y político determinado por el predominio de las aristocracias coloniales—que en algunos países hispanoamericanos subiste todavía aunque en irreparable y progresiva disolución—ha colocado por mucho tiempo las universidades de América latina bajo la tutela de estas oligarquías y de su clientela. Convertida la enseñanza universitaria en un privilegio del dinero, si no de la casta, o por lo menos de una categoría social absolutamente ligada a los intereses de uno y otras, las universidades han tenido una tendencia inevitable a la burocratización académica. . . . Su burocratización las conducía, de modo fatal, al empobrecimiento espiritual y científico."

26. Mariátegui, 134: "La universidad había seguido fiel as su tradición escolástica, conservadora y española."

27. Mariátegui, *Temas de Educación* (Lima, Perú: Biblioteca Amauta, 1970), 171: "Los que impugnan el feminismo y sus progresos con argumentos sentimentales o tradicionalistas pretenden que la mujer debe ser educada sólo para el hogar. Pero, prácticamente, esto quiere decir que la mujer debe ser educada sólo para funciones de hembra y de madre. En vez de ennoblecer y dignificar el rol de la mujer, lo disminuye y lo rebaja."

28. It is important to stress here several contemporary Peruvian feminist authors have expanded the critique that Mariátegui makes of female domesticity and advocated for the emancipation of women using his writings. See, for instance, Catalina Adrianzen, *El Marxismo, Mariátegui y el Movimiento Femenino* (Lima, Perú: Movimiento Femenino Popular, 1974); also see Sara Beatriz Guardia, *José Carlos Mariátegui: Una Visión de Género* (Lima, Perú: Librería Editorial Minerva, 2006).

29. Mariátegui, *Temas de Educación* (Lima, Perú: Biblioteca Amauta, 1970), 171: "El trabajo muda radicalmente la mentalidad y el espíritu femeninos. La mujer adquiere, en virtud del trabajo, una nueva noción de sí misma."

30. Mariátegui, *7 ensayos*, 176: "En la costa, en Lima sobre todo, otro elemento vino enervar la energía espiritual del catolicismo. El esclavo negro prestó al culto católico su sensualismo fetichista, su oscura superstición. El indio, sanamente panteísta y materialista, había alcanzado el grado ético de una gran teocracia; el negro, mientras tanto trasudaba por todos sus poros el primitivismo de la tribu africana."

31. In this respect, Mariátegui's thought shares important similarities with that of John Dewey in that Dewey has similar notions of primitivism and civilization with specific human groups having certain racial characteristics. For further discussion, see Thomas Fallace, *Dewey and the Dilemma of Race: An Intellectual History, 1895–1922* (New York: Teachers College Press, 2010).

32. Mariátegui, *7 ensayos*, 342, "El aporte del negro, venido como esclavo, casi como mercadería, aparece más nulo y negativo aún. El negro trajo su sensu-

alidad, su superstición, su primitivismo. No estaba en condiciones de contribuir a la creación de una cultura, sino más bien de estorbarla con el crudo y viviente influjo de su barbarie."

33. Mariátegui, 341: "El chino, en cambio, parece haber inoculado en su descendencia el fatalismo, la apatía, las taras del Oriente decrépito. El juego, esto es un elemento de relajamiento e inmoralidad, singularmente nocivo en un pueblo más propenso a confiar en el azar que en el esfuerzo, recibe su mayor esfuerzo de la inmigración china."

34. Though the systematic association between Chinese coolies and gambling was most certainly exaggerated, it is important to notice that some historians have conceded that Chinese workers did occasionally gamble. However, they have also pointed out that in light of the inhumane working conditions they were subject to, gambling was very often the only recreational outlet they had access to. In particular, see Watt Stewart, *Chinese Bondage in Peru* (Durham, NC: Duke University Press, 1951), 103.

35. See Erika Lee, "The 'Yellow' Peril and Asian Exclusion in the Americas," *Pacific Historical Review* 76, no. 4 (2007): 537–562.

36. Aníbal Quijano, "Raza, Etnia y Nación en Mariátegui: Cuestiones Abiertas," *Estudios Latinoamericanos* 2, no. 3 (1995): 3–19; Renzo Llorente "The Amauta's Ambivalence: Mariátegui on Race," in *Forging People. Race Ethnicity, and Nationality in Hispanic American and Latino/a Thought*, ed. Jorge J. E. Gracia (South Bend, IN: University of Notre Dame Press): 228–248.

37. Mariátegui, *7 ensayos*, 342: "Lo que importa por consiguiente, en el estudio sociológico de los estratos indio y mestizo, no es la medida en que el mestizo hereda las cualidades o los defectos de la razas progenitoras, sino su aptitud para evolucionar, con más facilidad que el indio hacia el estado social o el tipo de civilización del blanco."

38. Mariátegui, 341: "El cooli chino es un ser segregado de su país por la superpoblación y el pauperismo. Injerta en el Perú su raza, pero no su cultura."

39. The language of "grafting" was central to many racial scientific discourses in Latin America. For more details, see Adriana Novoa, "José Martí and Evolution: An Analysis of Nation and Race," in *Interdisciplinary Essays on Darwinism in Hispanic Literature and Film*, ed. Jerry Hoeg (Lewiston, NY: Edwin Mellen, 2009).

40. Mariátegui, *7 ensayos*, 343: "Pero si la cuestión racial—cuyas sugestiones conducen as sus superficiales críticos a inverosímiles razonamientos zootécnicos—es artificial y no merece la atención de quienes estudian concreta y políticamente el problema indígena, otra es la índole de la cuestión sociológica."

41. Mariátegui, 33: "La cuestión indígena arranca de nuestra economía. Tiene sus raíces en el régimen de propiedad de la tierra."

42. Llorente, "The Amauta's Ambivalence," 242–243.

43. Hooker, *Theorizing Race*, 200.

44. Hooker, 5–6.

45. Hooker, 6.

46. This existence of this particular pitfall has been pointed by James M. Thomas, "Medicalizing Racism," *Contexts* 73, no. 4 (2014), 24–29.

47. For more details on this conception of racism, see Leonard Harris, "What, Then, is Racism?" in *Racism*, ed. Leonard Harris (Amherst, NY: Humanity, 1999), 437–450.

48. A prominent example of this is the deployment of the notion of national origin (which functions as a proxy of race) by the Trump administration as a basis to exclude certain individuals from entering the United States.

CHAPTER ELEVEN

Distal versus Proximal

Howard Thurman's *Jesus and the Disinherited* as a Proximal Epistemology

ANTHONY SEAN NEAL

But sir, I think you are a traitor to all darker people of the world.

—Howard Thurman[1]

Signs, symbols, experiences and frameworks, this is how humans perceive the world. Attempts to describe or express the meaning of a perceived moment of experience can be affected by many factors, inclusive of displacement. The attempts or products of what gets perceived is known as the aesthetic or at least what gets perceived is perceived through the aesthetic.

—Anthony Neal[2]

Background

Framing (separating, interpreting, and representing) African American philosophy such that it speaks to the particular concerns of African Americans but also understood as a product of an African American reflective thought is always a genuine concern to those who have tasked themselves with the responsibility of explicating the ontological nature of African American philosophy, distinguishing exactly who its proponents are, and discerning its constitutive components. These tasks are also complicated by the necessity of determining its universal value or contribution such that the extension of its utility beyond the boundaries of American blackness, if any, can be illumined with demonstrable clarity.[3] Because of brevity requirements, in this chapter I will take up only the latter of these concerns: the concern of demonstrating universal value. I will also acknowledge the tasks of African American philosophy's particularity, which I find unavoidably linked to the chosen subjective form or perceptual framework.[4] In doing so, we must remember that African American philosophy is rooted in the required pronouncement of a group's humanity by those who experienced blackness in American society. This remembrance attaches two logically entailed claims: 1) the value of the African American is equal to the value of all other humans through a shared humanity; 2) the frameworks formed by the boundaries of a privileged but fragile white existence are automatically rejected whether implicitly or explicitly stated (whether by default or through conscious acknowledgment).

These two logical entailments are silently at work throughout Thurman's *Jesus and the Disinherited*, established by the declarative pronouncements of his grandmother, Nancy Ambrose. She recounted to Thurman a memory that shaped her understanding of what blackness both was and was not. She remembered the slave preacher saying, "You are not Niggers, you are not slaves, you are children of God!"[5] In this memory, the verbal transvaluation of their status was most certainly obvious, but it is what was left unsaid that is just as important. The silent partner to the transvaluation of their status is the uncompromising rejection of the status quo, which was never quite extracted from those held in bondage, and moreover, it became a compass of sorts, one that demonstrated the true understanding of the statements put forth by the slave preacher. But it is in this rejection, as I understand it, that the seedling of a universal nature of African American philosophy can be found. It is in the ability to know that the rejection of a proposition is necessary that African slaves most glaringly demonstrated their humanity.

The significance of this examination lies in its connection to the decolonial tradition within Africana philosophy, the humanist tradition in African American philosophy more broadly, and in all humanist-focused philosophic endeavors. The occurrence of the name "Jesus" in the title and the body of this treatment can be off-putting to some and misleading to most for this reason. But it was Thurman's goal, on the surface level, to clarify and expose the fallacies in African American traditions (and others) and come to an understanding of the oppressive nature of Christianity as taught and practiced in the United States. At a much deeper level of commitment, Thurman truly saw himself as speaking to the fundamental nature of human being(ness), which I take to be an intentionally lived freedom or striving intentionally toward a desired experience of freedom. The first step toward this intentionality is self-examination or reflection; the second step is the rational decision to affirm or negate a course of action. This is why Thurman proposes only two alternatives for minorities when forced to face the power of an oppressive ruling class: imitate or resist.

As stated earlier, by way of quotation and the ensuing discussion, it is through signs, symbols, frameworks, and experiences that we perceive the world. What is perceived is taken into the individual's consciousness through the perceptual framework or aesthetic. It is this perceptual framework or aesthetic that I would like to highlight, such that some understanding can be formed on just how this framework is developed. Several factors will be identified here as determinants of the aesthetic; however, these determinants are not meant to be understood as all-inclusive of the factors said to be the only ones causing the development of the aesthetic. Time and space serve as universal determinants of our aesthetic. They set the boundary and groundwork for the shaping of many other factors such as language, location, and our *Sitz im Leben* (situation in life). The subject of Thurman's analysis, the Jesus as found in the New Testament, was subjected to this type of examination. Thurman believed that it was necessary to "examine the religion of Jesus against the background of his own people, and to inquire into the content of his teaching with reference to the disinherited and the underprivileged."[6] This realization was after an epiphanic moment that occurred during a discussion in India, almost a decade after his education, his initial ministerial posts, and his first teaching appointments. This means that Thurman, like many others, formed many of his first understandings of his religious beliefs (among other formations) through frameworks that were unexamined or at least partially examined. Even in his examination, he was using frameworks that he would come to understand were not fully functional, at least for him.

What happens when the very frameworks through which knowledge is perceived are against the perceiver? How can that knowledge serve the interests of the perceiver if it is adverse? If value can be said to be gained from the reception of knowledge, to whom does the value of the knowledge received through contrary frameworks go? Howard Thurman, in a baccalaureate address to Spelman College on May 4, 1980, said the following:

> There is something in every one of you that waits, listen for the genuine in yourself—and if you cannot hear it, you will never find whatever it is for which you are searching and if you hear it and then do not follow it, it was better that you had never been born. You are the only you that has ever lived; your idiom is the only idiom of its kind in all the existences, and if you cannot hear the sound of the genuine in you, you will all of your life spend your days on the ends of strings that somebody else pulls.[7]

There are aspects of this quote that are philosophically problematic; however, Thurman's poetically creative notion of the existence of a genuine self-voice in the midst of other voices, which acts in the service of the self, was an attempt to put forth a strategic metaphor to cause the realization of the existence of distal knowledge received by the knower.

Knowledge of a moment in time, an experience, or an idea linguistically communicated is always received—when it is received—through the knower's perceptual framework. Therefore, the knower's perceptual framework must be sufficiently interrogated if the knowledge received is to be proximally located to correspond to the original phenomena or truth. In this chapter, I will show that the intent of Howard Thurman's *Jesus and the Disinherited* was to disrupt the traditional distal readings/understandings of the Jesus story, which separated the disinherited from Jesus by objectifying his being. Thus, the traditional[8] reading of the Jesus story colonizes the narrative, such that the power and value located in the movement was shifted from the underprivileged to the privileged.

I read this task of reshaping of Christianity and reforming the religion of Jesus—a task Thurman intentionally undertook—as a decolonial struggle. Thurman took this task upon himself after being asked in India why a black person would become a Christian given all that they had suffered at the hands of whites. It is in Thurman's response that he expressed the idea that the religion of Jesus was not an abstract myth; it was a religious movement that developed in a historical context. And in many ways, it was opposed to the ensuing Christian religion. In this context, the subject of the text was himself a member of the underprivileged, that is to say, the disinherited. If this is proximally situated to the original intent of the narrative, then principles that extend from this religious movement were not developed for the maintenance of power for the powerful. But they were aimed at relieving the struggle for life for the disinherited.

The performance of this type of reading offered more than mental solace to people "with their backs against the wall."[9] Mental solace is not Thurman's aim. For the disinherited, of which Thurman spoke, were not just poor but powerless. They were also very aware of the fragility of their lives. They were the dispossessed of Ralph Ellison's *Invisible Man*.[10] Survival was a tentative proposition because they had low economic worth and were also assumed to be a worthless humanity. Thurman writes that black people had low self-esteem. Life for them was spent on the margins of society. Death was certainly imminent, and even if they managed to extend their existence, it would not be desired or worthy of Nietzsche's "eternal return." Value becomes a necessary and immediate proposition upon the stratification of human existence, especially when the type of life available is attached to the individual's (or community's) lack of value.

What this reading does to mitigate these circumstances is to propose that worth as well as power should begin with the individual's determination of self(worth).

> Out of the heart are the issues of life and that no external force, however great and overwhelming, can at last destroy a people if it does not first win the victory of the spirit against them.[11]

This reading also suggests the unavoidability of this proposition:

> Was any attitude possible that would be morally tolerable and at the same time preserve a basic self-esteem without which life could not possibly have any meaning? The question was not academic. It was the most crucial of questions. In essence, Rome was the enemy; Rome symbolized total frustration; Rome was the great barrier to peace of mind. And Rome was everywhere.[12]

Lastly and most powerfully, Thurman proposes that the response to this proposition determines the conceptual world available to the respondent:

> This is the question of the Negro in American life. Until he faced and settled that question, he cannot inform his environment with reference to his own life, whatever may be his preparation or his pretensions.[13]

By putting forth these propositions, Thurman makes available a philosophically (de)colonial claim that is able to be universalized. This is not to suggest that Thurman was the first decolonial thinker or even among the first decolonial thinkers. More to the point, he should be considered during decisions of relationships between traditions of discourse. This is more a question of decolonial performance as opposed to being a decolonial performer.

There is also the question of what is left after a performance of this kind of deconstruction or the performance of the decolonial reading. Although it is unclear what exactly would remain (to do so would go beyond a proximal reading), the goal for Thurman is love or the imagined/poetic projection of the desired experience of community with the other. The last chapter of the text speaks to this desire. Moreover, I am putting forward love as the desired result of all decolonial struggle. Decoloniality does not find its end in the shifting of the power dynamic from one group to another. But to avoid the simple critique of attempting to chase too many loose ends in one short piece, I simply will define the decolonial struggle as the removal of barriers such as class, race, and condition, all of which help create the others. Once these barriers are removed then so, too, is the category of the "other." Once there is no longer a category that can be considered "other," then there is no barrier to the existence of Thurman's desired community, which is bound by love.

Returning to the subject of describing a textual reading as proximally situated, there must be a clarification of whether the term *proximal* continues its function as a locative description and if so, then the description of *proximal* is necessarily relational and must be pronounced explicitly. Therefore, in this space, *proximal* is to be understood as a locative descriptor with at least two aims. The first aim is to enhance the portrait of the material condition of the original subject(s) framed by the text. It is also locative with consideration given to the material condition of the reader, allowing for a value claim concerning the functionality of the reading with respect to the reader's own context. For example, when a reading is performed of a particular text (x) in which the description of the characters in the text places them in some real location (y), then in order for the text to have any correspondence for the reader with location (y), the reader must be allowed (and is expected to consider) the actual material conditions of individuals who lived in location (y) during the historical period (z) framed by the text (x) if any association is to be made with reality at all. This is especially true if text (x) is expected to be understood as historically accurate. *Proximal* then performs the work of a descriptor when the relationship between the material conditions of the subject/character in text (x) are as close to a 1:1 relationship with the material conditions of the actual inhabitants of location (y) as possible.

Once this comparative analysis is performed, the reader must then take the second step of performing a comparative analysis of the text and their own material conditions, existential reality, or lived situation. The goal of a proximal reading in this second reading is achievable, and the reading increases in significance; but this is only if in performing the first step of the analysis, the reader made the attempt to be as 1:1 as possible. When this is done, then the consideration given to value of the text and/or functionality in the reader's life is viewed more closely or can be said to be proximal. In essence, the possibility of many readings, both good and bad, of the text becomes very real. However, I am only concerned with those readings that can be considered as good readings in relation to their locative description. With the added value claim produced by the performance of the second step, two types of readings come to the fore: proximal with functionality and proximal without functionality.

A proximal reading without functionality simply means that the analyses have been performed, and there was an attempt made to achieve a 1:1 relationship, but the results have no relevance in the life of the reader. Take the story of Jesus's life, for example. If Jesus is to be understood as a king and always a member of the ruling class, then a proximal reading can be carried out. But there would be no relevant functionality in the life of the poor, thus rendering the text valueless. Proximal with functionality then means that once the analyses are performed, the text is functionally useful in the life of the reader. By understanding Jesus's life story as a real-life example of a poor Jew living under an oppressive regime—and being oppressed specifically because of his ethnicity and economic status—the text became tremendously functional for Thurman and others sharing his condition.

Value of Knowledge

To say that there is a value in the possession of knowledge, or to ground an argument in the inherent value of knowledge, is to also ascribe to knowledge a definition that is inclusive of a statement that portrays the usability of whatever can be said to be knowledge. This premise, although not explicitly written, is central to the major claim of the text, for it is this premise upon which Thurman's argument turns. For if this premise is found acceptable, then it would seem that the conclusion Thurman reaches necessarily follows. It is doubtful that serious readers of Thurman would have disconcerting thoughts where this premise is concerned given that Thurman obviates the ground for such disconcertion with the following:

> The significance of the religion of Jesus to people who stand with their backs against the wall has always seemed to me to be crucial. It is one emphasis which has been lacking—except where it has been a part of a very unfortunate corruption of the missionary impulse, which is, in a sense, the very heartbeat of the Christian religion.[14]

Here, Thurman demonstrates his desire to know if the religion of Jesus contained a value proposition for those with their backs against the wall or the disinherited. This query logically entails that it was possible for the religion of Jesus to say something of importance to this group. This is something I will refer to as "knowledge" with the further assumption that Thurman is looking for useful information or knowledge that could possibly be available for this group (and if available, then it is valuable).

The search for valuable knowledge with the intent to share as the solution to the peculiar problem of being black in the modern era of the African American freedom struggle[15] is the nexus that connected Thurman to others in the same struggle. That this search was published presupposes that he is speaking to a very particular group within the larger group: those who are literate. It also presupposes his assumption of the viability of this method of communicating his message. Before addressing these two presuppositions, it seems necessary to state the reason they are interesting. Certainly, Thurman was presented with the question of being a traitor, which would have provoked a response from any number of individuals. But Thurman did not just give any response. His response was written in book form. The written nature of the response says as much about Thurman as about his subject. It appears he believed the substance of his particular response to be universal; therefore, it needed to be known widely, and through a greater expanse of time, than his voice could travel.

As far as the specific propositions, which take up the concerns of target audience and the viability of the type of communication, Thurman associates two terms with this matter, creative and prognostic:

> It is a privilege, after so long a time, to set down what seems to me to be an essential creative and prognostic interpretation of Jesus as a religious subject and not a religious object.[16]

It is in much the same manner that Danielle Allen[17] refers to Plato's activity of writing when she searches for the reasons he wrote, while his master, Socrates, wrote nothing. She suggests that the concerns of both Socrates and Plato were the concepts and ideals implanted in people's souls. Plato argued, through Socrates, that they mold our characters.[18] According to Allen, "symbols are tools used to convey . . . concepts,"[19] while Aristotle puts forth that "written words are the symbols of spoken words."[20] Allen notes that Socrates "assigns philosophers the job of being symbol-makers with the authority over just and ethical symbols."[21]

However, Thurman had one problem that Plato did not face. James Haile describes it beautifully as "language is never quite enough, by itself, to express the being of the event or the moment. To this difficulty of language and expression, the American Landscape adds the problem of race and race relations."[22] Thurman was a mystic philosopher and certainly did not rely on the biblical text to substantiate his claims; however, *Jesus and the Disinherited* was his first notable work, and he chose to investigate the value proposition of the biblical story, particularly as it referred to the disinherited. His reasoning ultimately fell along two lines. First, he felt it was important to perform this type of search for himself and especially for others, as much of enduring the horrors of slavery also meant being indoctrinated with Christian principles, in particular those principles expounded upon by the apostle Paul. Christianity became a fundamental tool used to secure the structure of slavery, and it also served as an important (but not singular) constituent, shaping the perceptions of those who were enslaved. As Thurman wrote in a later work, "The religious experience may remain unique but must be completely other."[23] He put forth the formative question, "How may a [person] know [they] are not being deceived?"[24] Vincent Harding, who wrote the foreword to the 1996 edition of the text, exclaimed, "Born into the Black community of Daytona Beach, Florida, at the beginning of the century, he was carefully nurtured by a maternal grandmother who had come through the fierce crucible of slavery while leaning on the Lord."[25] Undoubtedly, if no untapped potential were to be found in the text for the disinherited, then it should be properly jettisoned. Secondly, the answer to the necessity of knowledge on this matter is that, as Thurman discovers, the empowerment of the oppressor can be found embedded solidly within the Christian text, providing for a conceptually colonized or distal reading.

If it can be said that making the connection with Quaker mystic philosopher Rufus Jones gave Thurman the vocabulary that framed his discourse concerning his mystic philosophy, then it can equally be said that Thurman's 1935 trip to India provided him with much of the subject matter with which he would engage in discourse. This simply means that being called a traitor to his race was not a subject easily shaken from his consciousness, and Thurman would abandon the subject completely—but only after he felt he had provided a sufficient response concerning his position on the matter. However, providing this sufficient response would be a lifelong struggle. Certainly, this provocation created the necessary space for Thurman's discourse; however, the need for Thurman's response, at least from his point of view, was not just to provide a satisfactory answer to the query of those in India. The need for the response rested upon the notion that Thurman's grandmother, Nancy Ambrose, had been a slave, and the black community he was a part of continued to languish under the consequences of a deeply entrenched oppressive majority culture. The query simply articulated the need for such an answer to be offered. Also, Thurman knew he was not a traitor. However, he wanted to be sure that Jesus was no traitor either.

In association with the empowerment of the oppressor, Thurman had this to say: "Most accepted social-behavioral patterns assume segregation to be normal—if normal then correct; if correct then moral; if moral then religious. Religion is thus made a defender and guarantor of the presumptions."[26] Clearly, Thurman does not allow any person or institution to escape responsibility by simply shirking their culpability in the matter. But there is a deeper ontological analysis of religion offered in this quote from *Jesus and the Disinherited*. It is often assumed by observers and practitioners alike that religion as a nominally unified concept always transcends the culture it is found in. And if this is not so of all religions, certainly it is true of the Judeo-Christian tradition. Thurman disagrees sharply with this notion and offers a counterclaim, which is that much of what is seen practiced as religion is often a reflection of the culture it comes from. Today, we live in a moment fully engulfed in the spirit of liberal religion. But in Thurman's day (this was 1949) a quote such as this one was meant to disrupt the God of segregation, the validating principle of racist reasoning, which itself was validated by the very power that enabled the white majority to oppress their fellow man. Thurman's words were as flippant as they were threatening. When Thurman intimates that the empowerment of the oppressor can be found in the text, he is essentially making the claim that there are scenarios in the text that lend themselves for use as the fundamental grounding for oppressive forces. These scenarios lead to distal readings of the text, particularly when there is no examination of the text's value in terms of functionality. This led to Thurman's reformulated reading of the text.

Distal versus Proximal

If there did exist untapped potential in the text, this type of reformulated decolonial or proximal reading method, as suggested by Thurman, is probably the only way to realize its full value. All readings of any text are subject to context. Subjecting reading to contextualization, or the filtering of text through our appetites and aversions while considering time and space, is the making of perception or the forming of a perceptual framework. *Proximal* and *distal* are originally medical terms, but as I urge their consideration in reference to a proximal and distal reading of text, I do so in connection to process philosophy, particularly as espoused by Alfred North Whitehead. He compares the retelling of an experience to mathematics, specifically the concept of approximation in reference to the study of limits. About this Whitehead wrote:

> The identification merely rests on the obvious experience of daily life. In any recasting of thought it is obligatory to include the identification as a practical approximation to the truth, sufficient for daily life. Subject to this limitation, there is no reason for rejecting any distinction between them which the evidence suggests.[27]

In this sense, then, we can consider a proximal interpretation to be an interpretation that closely considers the original context of the text but with the understanding that at best only an approximated reading is possible. This consideration should motivate the sharpening of tools to perform this activity. Distal readings perform interpretations in context with the reader's moment only. The actual tensions within the text, particularly those tensions that become the main source of conflict, receive little attention. Functionality of the text, in terms of making the human condition better, is also an unidentifiable concept within distal readings. This becomes most problematic when the reading is legitimated by such a prevailing power structure as are many orthodox readings, which in themselves presuppose a type of metaphysical understanding. According to Whitehead, "Language is thoroughly indeterminate, by reason of the fact that every occurrence presupposes some systematic type of environment."[28] Understandability is born from the acceptance of a metaphysical frame. Change arises from disagreement. "The extent of disagreement measures the extent of metaphysical divergence."[29]

Associating Thurman with the idea of a decolonized reading of a text forces the need for a demonstration of what is meant by the terms "colonized text" or a text in need of decolonization. To provide some manageability to the term, I should state that in defining the term, I am simply speaking to the manner in which I will attempt to consistently use the term in this writing. A colonized or decolonized text has to do with the balance of power in the determination of orthodox readings, function, and the value of the text. All texts are composed of symbols, metaphors, and allusions by way of logical entailment, among other literary and logical devices.

> Signs, symbols, experiences and frameworks, this is how humans perceive the world. Attempts to describe or express the meaning of a perceived moment of experience can be affected by many factors, inclusive of displacement. The attempts or products of what gets perceived is known as the aesthetic or at least what gets perceived is perceived through the aesthetic, but, what does it mean to perceive or what is perception and why don't we all perceive experiences the same?[30]

> Spoken words are the symbols of mental experience and written words are the symbols of spoken words.[31]

In understanding this proposition it must be accepted that these devices are not equal to meaning but are only tools that assist in the determination of meaning. Meaning, as such, is always outside the text and found in community, as language is necessarily communal. In terms of the status of the text with regard to colonization, when there exists a powerful and oppressive community that has determined that the text in question favors their actions (and in some ways necessitates those actions), then that text or textual reading can be understood to be colonized. Understood in this manner, colonization should also be understood to ground a certain unequal power distribution in favor of the colonizing community as opposed to humanity in total.

As such, the existence of any text, and certainly a colonized text, demands a response concerning its ability to be functional for those who are outside of the prevailing ruling or power structure. This is especially true of any text used as a guide for living or making determinations about good and evil. Does the text benefit or harm those without power? Is the text against them in the sense that it provides validation for their oppression? What can be done to alleviate this type of oppression, which has been assumed to be accredited as good by the source for determining what is good? Thurman was attempting to wrestle with these types of questions. In doing so, he was questioning the epistemological frameworks he and others had inherited while also attempting to gain ontological clarity beyond these frameworks with as much proximity to the existential conditions of the subject, Jesus, as possible. This search for functionality implies a willingness to forgo any attachment to the text if it is found to have functional value beyond the scope of providing a safe haven for those whose desire it is to oppress their fellows. The realization also exists that something of the prevailing orthodox understanding of the text must of necessity be jettisoned based upon the identification of the text as being equal to the position that validates the oppressor. I think evidence of this attitude is in Thurman's preface to the text:

> I do not pretend that I have found an answer in the pages that follow; but I am deeply convinced that in the general of my inquiry is to be found the answer without which there can be little hope that men may find in Christianity the fulfillment which it claims for its gospel.[32]

Thurman's willingness to raise such questions about the text at this point in his career speaks to the concerns he had about the importance of the value proposition the text had for those who were oppressed. Clearly, he took this question to be seminal.

Thurman's Framework and Method of Interrogation

In July of 1922 Thurman began a six-week summer session, taking two courses in philosophy: Introduction to Philosophy and Reflective Thinking.

During Thurman's time at Columbia, the philosophy department was fertile ground, in part because of the presence of John Dewey and the "young radicals," as they were called. This was "a lesser-known group of Pragmatic Naturalists," who were "mostly disciples of Dewey's reconstructed philosophy" also known as genetic history and reflective thinking.[33] It would be Edwin Arthur Burtt who would provide an introduction of Dewey to Thurman—but certainly not without pressing this knowledge together with his own intellectual grindings.

The so-called golden age of philosophy is considered to be a suitable description for this period, when philosophy was conceived of as the guide of life.[34] Philosophers, particularly at Columbia, were employing philosophical techniques to achieve solutions to the social and moral problems of their day: thus, philosophy as a guide of life. This philosophical aim was rooted in the propensity of the department at Columbia toward metaphysics. Burtt, not Dewey, recounted for Thurman in this session the process of reflective thinking as a philosophical method, a method Thurman would use throughout his life. About this method, Thurman expressed in detail the effect this philosophical style had on his writing:

> It was an analysis of the structure of reflective thinking as a process. It examined a basic methodological approach to problem-solving in all fields of investigation, from simple decision-making to the understanding and treatment of disease and the most confused patterns of human behavior. This course established for me a basic approach that I would use not only in my subsequent work as a counselor but also in thinking through the complex and complicated problems I would encounter in my personal life as a social being. As a tool of the mind, there is no way by which the value of this course can be measured or assessed.[35]

John Dewey gave a speech at the Imperial University in Japan that became an influential book, *Reconstruction in Philosophy*. In this book, Dewey proposed to bring into focus his view of the necessary direction philosophy would be conscripted to take based upon the radical changes in scientific investigation. Dewey felt that philosophy was no longer able to assume any claim to the ability to achieve objective or absolute knowledge. For him, philosophy was bound just as any other system of inquiry by the science of the day and that its methods should reflect as much. This was to be achieved, to the degree possible, by a reliance upon empirical knowledge, held in tension with the understanding that the investigator's interpretation of the relied-upon knowledge is limited to an inchoate science. From Thurman's writings, it would seem that while his metaphysical explanation for the oneness of being was intuited from an intense mystical connection to nature, he certainly used the reflective method as a way of grounding his solutions to philosophical questions in the material world. The major example put forth by Thurman is his attempt to answer the query put to him while traveling in India in 1935, which was the question of betraying all people of color by traveling abroad as a representative of the Christian church. Certainly a perplexing occurrence, this is the major question Thurman would return to again and again for the rest of his life, which is apparent in many of his subsequent writings. Constantly, the desire to live out the impulse he felt regarding the experience of community would cause him to commit to this as his life's aim. Thurman felt that he had received insight into the possibilities for community when he visited the Khyber Pass; however, it was his predilection for pragmatic solutions that would move him to accept the offer to help found the Fellowship Church in San Francisco. This opportunity created for him the ability to apply step five in the reflective method: the experimental step.

Thurman's Interrogation of the Perceptual Framework

In the past, I have jokingly described philosophy to my students as the process of violently and verbally antagonizing a subject. Most philosophers do not describe philosophy in this way; however, I find this description extremely plausible when I consider the activity of a decolonial reading of the Christian text. In this section, Thurman's work will be discussed as it pertains to the subject at hand. In *Jesus and the Disinherited*, Thurman provides a method of how he would perform a study of this nature:

> It is a privilege, after so long a time, to set down what seems to me to be an essentially creative and prognostic interpretation of Jesus as religious subject rather than religious object. It is necessary to examine the religion of Jesus against the background of his age and people, and to inquire into the content of his teaching with reference to the disinherited and the underprivileged.[36]

Here, Thurman indicates initially that his study was to be "creative and prognostic." Essentially, this study was performed to determine the usefulness of studying the person of Jesus in his experiential moment for other oppressed cultures, specifically black people in America. In order to create a robust understanding of Jesus, Thurman thought it also necessary to understand the effect of being part of an oppressed minority culture.

These are the steps to the reflective process as Thurman understood them:

1. occurrence of something felt as perplexity, difficulty, wonder—As a Christian, was he, in sense, betraying all people of color, inclusive of his Grandmother, who had been enslaved.

2. observation, designed to make clear precisely what the difficulty is . . . "I belong to a generation that finds very little that is meaningful or intelligent in the teachings of the church concerning Jesus Christ. . . . The desperate opposition to Christianity rests in the fact that it seems, in the last analysis, to be a betrayal of the Negro into the hands of their enemies by focusing their attention upon heaven, forgiveness, love, and the like. . . . It cannot be denied that too often the weight of the Christian movement has been on the side of the strong and the powerful and against the weak and oppressed."

3. occurrence to mind of suggested, solutions of the difficulty. An examination of the facts as they relate to the text and make value a judgement about their usefulness for those whose backs are against the wall.

4. reasoning out the consequences involved in the suggestions thus entertained and evaluating the suggestions by their aid. a. Grandma Nancy's Hermeneutic concerning Paul, b. view Jesus as Subject (Jew, Poor, Oppressed vs. Object (God).

5. observation or experiment to test by empirical fact the suggested solutions in the light of their implications. The Fellowship Church.

6. survey of the preceding thinking to uncovering inadequacies that might be corrected.[37]

Thurman begins the book with the following:

> Many and varied are the interpretations dealing with the teachings and the life of Jesus of Nazareth. But few of these interpretations deal with what the teachings and the life of Jesus have to say to those who stand, at a moment in human history, with their backs against the wall.[38]

In this statement of the problem, Thurman begins the process of creating a proximal framework with a view toward functionality. The bulk of this framework is derived from constitutive components. The first component rests on the ability to determine who the historical Jesus was. Thurman listed three characteristics he wanted his readers to prioritize in their understanding of who Jesus was and how his background might have played a significant role in his teachings: he was Jewish, poor, and an oppressed minority. These characteristics as put forth show Thurman to be deeply rooted in the affairs of the oppressed. The second component rests on the notion put forward by Grandma Nancy that the oppressed had the right to reject the hermeneutic of their oppressors and to create a new one that is proximal and functional—or perhaps one that rejects the text altogether. The importance of this proposition is that it unshackled the African American reading of the scripture in particular, laying the groundwork for black theologies and even more humanist contentions. These components simply point to the ability of oppressed communities, particularly the African American community of which Thurman was a part, to make their own claims about the validity and the value of the text. Decolonizing the text depends on such claims.

Conclusion

Thurman successfully makes the shift from Christianity to the religion of Jesus or love, ushering in a new path for an oppressed religious understanding based on his religious humanist concerns. He intended to demonstrate that a religion claiming to be about love should also be against oppression of any kind. In doing so, he closed the gap between the idea of revolutionary love as he understood in the message of a historical Jesus and "those who stand at a moment in human history with their backs against the wall."[39] He disrupted the distal while forming the proximal.

Notes

1. Howard Thurman, *Jesus and the Disinherited* (Boston: Beacon, 1996), 15.

2. Anthony Neal, "Freedom Gaze: Explicating the African Freedom Aesthetic," in *Displacement in Language, Literature and Culture* (Benalmádena, Spain: EDA Libros, 2018), 97.

3. Aaron W. Hughes, *Rethinking Jewish Philosophy* (New York: Oxford, 2014), 3.

4. Anthony Sean Neal, *Common Ground* (Trenton, NJ: Africa World, 2015), 1; and Neal, "Freedom Gaze," 98–101.

5. Thurman, *Jesus and the Disinherited*, 49–50.

6. Thurman, 15.

7. Baccalaureate Address to Spelman College, May 4, 1980.

8. By a "traditional" reading of the Jesus story I simply mean the prevailing narrative as Thurman understood it and also described it within the text of *Jesus and the Disinherited*.

9. Thurman, *Jesus and the Disinherited*, 7.

10. Ralph Ellison, *Invisible Man* (New York: Vintage International, 1995), 279.

11. Thurman, *Jesus and the Disinherited*, 21.

12. Thurman, 22.

13. Thurman, 23.

14. Thurman, 7.

15. Anthony Sean Neal, *Howard Thurman's Philosophical Mysticism: Love Against Fragmentation* (Lanham, MD: Lexington, 2019), vii.

16. Thurman, *Jesus and the Disinherited*, 15.

17. Danielle Allen, *Why Did Plato Write?* (Malden, MA: Wiley-Blackwell, 2013), 33–34.

18. Allen, 33–34.

19. Allen, 35.

20. Aristotle, et al., *The Categories on Interpretation*, trans. H. P. Cooke (Cambridge, MA: Harvard University Press, 1938), 115.

21. Allen, *Why Did Plato Write?*, 35.

22. James Haile, ed., *Philosophical Meditations on Richard Wright* (Lanham, MD: Lexington, 2012), xv.

23. Howard Thurman, *Creative Encounter* (Dublin: Friends United Press, 1972), 57.

24. Thurman, *Creative Encounter*, 57.

25. Thurman, *Jesus and the Disinherited*.

26. Thurman, 43.

27. Alfred North Whitehead, *Process and Reality* (New York: Macmillan, 1967), 126.

28. Whitehead, *Process and Reality*, 18.
29. Whitehead, 18.
30. Neal, "Freedom Gaze," 97.
31. Aristotle, et al., *The Categories on Interpretation*, trans. H. P. Cooke (Cambridge, MA: Harvard University Press, 1938), 115.
32. Thurman, *Jesus and the Disinherited*, 8.
33. Diane Elizabeth Davis Villemaire, *E.A. Burtt, Historian and Philosopher: A Study of the Author of the Metaphysical Foundations of Modern Physical Science* (London: Kluwer Academic, 2002), 7.
34. Villemaire, *E.A. Burtt*, 7.
35. Howard Thurman, *With Head and Heart: The Autobiography of Howard Thurman* (San Diego: Harcourt Brace Jovanovich, 1981), 44.
36. Thurman, *Jesus and the Disinherited*, 15.
37. Thurman, *Disciplines of the Spirit,* 33.
38. Thurman, *Jesus and the Disinherited*, 11.
39. Thurman, 11.

Contributors

Celia T. Bardwell-Jones is associate professor of philosophy and chair of the Gender and Women's Studies Program at the University of Hawaiʻi at Hilo. Her teaching and research include feminist philosophy, American pragmatism, critical race theory, immigration, indigenous thought, and philosophy of nature. Her work has been published in *Journal of Speculative Philosophy*, *The Pluralist*, *Transactions of the Charles S. Peirce Society*, and numerous anthologies addressing questions of decolonization, feminist philosophy, and American pragmatism.

John E. Drabinski is professor of African American studies and comparative literature at University of Maryland. His research interests are in the philosophical dimensions of the Afro-Caribbean and African American intellectual traditions. He is the author of four books, including, most recently, *Glissant and the Middle Passage: Philosophy, Beginning, Abyss.* (University of Minnesota Press, 2019).

Sergio A. Gallegos-Ordorica is assistant professor in the Department of Philosophy of the John Jay College of Criminal Justice. He received a BA in philosophy at the National Autonomous University of Mexico and an M. Phil. and a PhD in philosophy at the Graduate Center of the City University of New York. His main research and teaching interests lie in Latin American philosophy, philosophy of science, philosophy of race, feminist philosophy (particularly, indigenous feminism), and epistemology (particularly, social epistemology).

Lee A. McBride III is associate professor of philosophy at The College of Wooster (Ohio). He specializes in American philosophy, ethics, political philosophy, and philosophy of race. Recent publications include: "Racial Imperialism and Food Traditions" (*The Oxford Handbook of Food Ethics*, 2018); "Anger and Approbation" (*Moral Psychology of Anger*, 2018); and "New Descriptions, New Possibilities" (*Journal of Speculative Philosophy*, 2018).

Corey McCall was associate professor of philosophy at Elmira College in upstate New York. He is spending the 2020–2021 academic year as a Visiting Scholar at Penn State's Humanities Institute. His teaching and research focus on various conjunctions and disjunctions between Afro-Caribbean, African American, European, and American philosophical and literary traditions. He is coeditor of the edited collections *Melville Among the Philosophers* (Lexington, 2017) and *Benjamin, Adorno, and the Experience of Literature* (Routledge, 2018).

Shelbi Nahwilet Meissner (Luiseño/Cupeño) is an assistant professor of philosophy at Georgetown University, a UC Presidential Postdoctoral Fellow (Summer 2019), and a 2019 Cross Scholar of the Association of American Colleges and Universities. Meissner's work centers American Indian and Indigenous philosophy, feminist epistemology, and philosophy of language. She is an avid participant in the reclamation of 'atáaxum pomtéela//the Luiseño language.

Eduardo Mendieta is professor of philosophy and affiliated faculty at the School of International Affairs and the Bioethics Program at Penn State University. He is the author of *The Adventures of Transcendental Philosophy* (Rowman & Littlefield, 2002) and *Global Fragments: Globalizations, Latinamericanisms, and Critical Theory* (State University of New York Press, 2007). He is also coeditor with Jonathan VanAntwerpen of *The Power of Religion in the Public Sphere* (Columbia University Press, 2011), and with Craig Calhoun and Jonathan VanAntwerpen of *Habermas and Religion* (Polity, 2013), and with Amy Allen, *From Alienation to Forms of Life: The Critical Theory of Rahel Jaeggi* (Penn State University Press, 2018). He is the 2017 recipient of the Frantz Fanon Outstanding Achievements Award.

Anthony Sean Neal is associate professor of philosophy at Mississippi State University. He received his BA from Morehouse College, an M.Div from Mercer University, and his PhD from Clark Atlanta University. He is the author of *Common Ground: A Comparison of the Ideas of Consciousness in Howard Thurman and Huey Newton* (Africa World, 2015) and *Howard Thurman's Philosophical Mysticism: Love against Fragmentation* (Lexington, 2019).

Phillip McReynolds taught philosophy at the University of North Carolina at Charlotte and is the author of *The American Philosopher: Interviews on the Meaning of Life and Truth*.

Andrea J. Pitts is assistant professor of philosophy at University of North Carolina, Charlotte. Their research interests include social epistemology, critical philosophy of race, feminist philosophy, Latin American and US Latinx philosophy, and critical prison studies. Their scholarly articles can be found in *Hypatia: A Journal of Feminist Philosophy*, *Radical Philosophy Review*, *Genealogy*, *Inter-American Journal of Philosophy*, and *IJFAB: International Journal of Feminist Approaches to Bioethics*. Pitts is also the co-editor of *Beyond Bergson: Examining Race and Colonialism through the Writings of Henri Bergson* with Mark Westmoreland (SUNY Press 2019) and *Theories of the Flesh: Latinx and Latin American Feminisms, Transformation, and Resistance* with Mariana Ortega and José M. Medina (Oxford University Press 2020).

Kris Sealey is associate professor of philosophy at Fairfield University. Dr. Sealey's areas of research include the critical philosophy of race, Caribbean philosophy, and postcolonial theory. Her published articles can be found in academic journals such as *Critical Philosophy of Race* and *Hypatia: A Journal for Feminist Philosophy*. She is the author of *Moments of Disruption: Levinas, Sartre and the Question of Transcendence* (State University of New York Press, 2013). Her most recent book, *Creolizing the Nation* (Northwestern University Press, 2020), investigates the unfolding of community formations in decolonial contexts and offers Creolization as a conceptual tool through which such formations might be theorized.

Kyle Whyte is Professor of Environment and Sustainability and George Willis Pack Professor at the University of Michigan. Kyle works primarily on indigenous environmental justice, especially relating to climate change.

Index

Adams, John, 90
Addams, Jane, 5, 11, 181, 185–198, 200
Affectionate interpretation, 195
African American Philosophy, 252
Agency, 214–215
Alcoff, Linda Martín, 9, 131, 132–133, 143–147, 148, 149–150
Alexander VI, Pope, 83
Alexander, Thomas, 159
Allen, Danielle, 259
American Declaration of Independence, 87
American philosophy, 3–4, 5–6, 38–39, 51–53
Anzaldúa, Gloria, 147, 243
Appleby, Joyce, 95
Armstrong, Jeanette, 41–42
Assimilation, 93
Authenticity, 211
Awbanawben, 46–47

Bacon, Francis, 22
Baldwin, James, 111, 112
Benítez-Rojo, Antonio, 63
Bhaba, Homi, 214
Bhaskar, Roy, 144
Boles, John B., 93
Brown, John, 117
Burtt, Edwin Arthur, 264

Byrd, Jodi, 2

Care, Social Ontology of, 177–203
Carlyle, Thomas, 113, 115–119
Carrico, Richard, 44
Cavell, Stanley, 120–121
Césaire, Áime, 10, 25, 28, 68, 156, 166–167, 168–169
Chamoiseau, Patrick, 211
Christianity, 12, 20–22
Colonialism, 64–65, 68–71, 155–169
Columbus, Christopher, 19
Cook-Lynn, Elizabeth, 53
Cosmopolitanism, 101
Countermodernity, 66, 77
Creolization, 11, 205–223
  as Bricolage, 208–211
  as Liminal Dialectic, 211–217
  as Carnival/Play, 217–222
Chrichlow, Michaeline, 223
Christianity, 251–269
Culture, 27
Cupeño Uprising, 45

D'Alambert, Jean le Rond, 84
Dalton, T. C., 158
Darnton, Robert, 85
Davidson, Donald, 137, 143, 148
De Caro, Mario, 138–140
Decolonial Philosophy, 29, 37–38

276 | Index

Decolonization, 6, 7, 11, 23–24, 43–57, 67, 234–245, 255–256
Deconstruction, 256
Delaney, Martin, 70
Dewey, John, 5, 10, 39, 155–169, 229, 264
Diderot, Denis, 84
Dotson, Kristie, 133
Douglass, Frederick, 73, 122–123
Du Bois, W. E. B., 5, 9, 63, 69, 73–74, 76, 111–130, 242–243, 244
Dumm, Thomas, 124–125
Dussel, Enrique, 5, 148, 243

Ehrenreich, Barbara, 178
Ellison, Ralph, 74, 255
Emancipation, 94
Emerson, Ralph Waldo, 2, 9, 111–130
Enlightened Reader, 84–85
Environmental Justice, 43
Episteme, 18, 162
Experience, 253–254

Fallace, Thomas, 10, 156–157
Fanon, Frantz, 1, 24, 25, 26, 69, 162
Feminism, 143–147, 238
   Indigenous, 49
   Latina, 131–150
Ferdinand, King of Aragon, 19
Forbes, Curdella, 217
Foucault, Michel, 23–24, 164
Frye, Marilyn, 143
Fuller, Mary, 86

Gamio, Manuel, 236
Gandhi, Mohandas, 27
Gilroy, Paul, 66, 71–72
Glissant, Édouard, 63–64, 69, 75, 77
Globalization, 177
González Prada, Manuel, 232–234
Goodchild, Maria, 41
Gooding-Williams, Robert, 114, 120

Gray, Francis C., 90
Gregory, Dick, 111

Haile, James, 259
Harding, Vincent, 259
Hall, Stuart, 213
Hamilton, Charles, 70
Harris, Leonard, 39
Hegel, G. W. F., 159
Higher Education, 50–53
Hochschild, Arlie, 178, 179, 199
Hooker, Juliet, 125–126, 243, 244
Hull House, 196–197
Humanism, 26, 252–253
Hunt, Sarah, 54–55

Immigrants, 192–194
   Chinese, 240–242
Imperialism, cultural, 7
India, 28, 260
Indigenizing, 55–56, 231–239
Indigenous Peoples, 26, 38, 39, 43–47, 112, 163

James, Denise, 39
Jefferson, Thomas, 8, 83–109
Johnson, Mark, 159
Juan, Jorge, 8, 84, 85, 90, 96–100

Kant, Immanuel, 8, 83, 85, 100–103
Kittay, Eva Feder, 11, 179–180, 182–185
Knepper, Wendy, 209–210, 211, 213
Knowledge, 253–254

La Condamine Expedition, 96
La Condamine, Charles-Marie de, 84, 97
Lake, Danielle, 39
Lamming, George, 217
Land, 38–39, 40–44
Langer, Susanne, 169

Last, Angela, 167–168
Le Bon, Gustav, 233
Lissak, Rivka Shpak, 195
Livingston, Alexander, 5
Locke, Alain, 27, 73–74
Locke, John, 20
Llorente, Renzo, 242–243
Lovelace, Earl, 11, 205–223
Lugones, María, 21, 26, 206, 213, 243

Mackinnon, Catherine, 143
Madison, James, 95
Manguel, Robert, 85
Manichean, 27
Maracle, Lee, 37, 42
Mariátegui, José Carlos, 11–12, 229–250
Marshall, John, 95
Martinez, David, 47
Martinez, Jacqueline M., 9, 131, 133–137, 147–148
Marxism, 231–234
Mbembe, Achille, 67
McKenna, Erin, 5
McKittrick, Katherine, 163
Middle Passage, 208
Mignolo, Walter, 148, 234–235, 243
Modern Science, 22–23
Mohanty, Shandra, 24, 26
Moraga, Cherríe, 147
Moya, Paula L. M., 9, 131, 137–143, 147, 149
Murdoch, H. Adlai, 206
Murray, Albert, 74–75

National Association for the Advancement of Colored People (NAACP), 156–157
Nationalism, 232–233
Native Americans, 92–93 (*See also* Indigenous Peoples)
Necropolitics, 67

Newton, Huey, 70
Normativity, 137

Ontology, 76, 146–147
  Social Ontology, 177–203
Ortega, Mariana, 149

Pappas, Gregory, 165
Parreñas, Rhacel Salazar, 178–179
Paul, 259
Peden, William, 87
Peirce, Charles Sanders, 134–137
Peircean Semiotics, 135–137
Peterson, Merrill D., 87
Philippines, 177–203
Plato, 120, 259
Poetics, 163–164
Pratt, Mary Louise, 85, 86
Pratt, Scott L., 5, 39
Pullman Strike (1894), 187–188
Putnam, Hilary, 137, 138–143, 144, 148, 149

Qualitative Thought, 165–166
Quijano, Aníbal, 234–235
Quine, W. V. O., 132–133, 137

Rabliauskas, Sophia, 40–41
Ramos, Juanita, 147
Reading, 83–109
  Distal vs. Proximal, 251–269
Reconstruction in Philosophy, 69, 155–169
Religion, 239
Rejection Politics, 54–55
Resistance, 39, 44–45, 65, 208
Robinson Crusoe, 163
Rojas, Aristides, 236
Rorty, Richard, 143–147
Ruíz, Elena, 149

Scientific Racism, 244–245

Schutte, Ofelia, 148, 198, 231
Settler colonialism, 5, 26
Shiva, Vandana, 22
Shklar, Judith, 121
Siegfried, Charlene Haddock, 39, 186–187
Situatedness, 135–136
Slavery, 4, 8, 68, 72–73, 76, 86, 93–94, 103–104, 112, 119, 162, 259
Socrates, 259
Spencer, Herbert, 233
Smith, Harrison, 89
Smyth, Heather, 208
Society for the Advancement of American Philosophy (SAAP), 39
Sorel, Georges, 231–234
Sound, 71–75
Sy, Christine, 41

Taino People, 19
Tecumseh, 37
Tecumseh, 46
Thurman, Howard, 251–269
The West, 63–79
Thurman, Howard, 12, 251–269
Toypurina, 45
Tradition, 73–74
Trujillo, Carla, 147
Trump, Donald J., 124

Tuck, Eva and Yang, K. W., 26, 28, 37
Ture, Kwame, 70
Turtle Island, 38

Ulloa, Antonio de, 8, 84, 85, 90–92, 96–100

Vallenilla Lanz, Laureano, 245
Value, 255
  Of knowledge, 257–261
Veriamontes, Helena Maria, 137
Vasconcelos, José, 230, 242–243, 244

Warda, Arthur, 102
Washington, Booker T., 69, 117–119
Welchman, Jennifer, 158
Weir, Alison, 180
Wells, Ida B., 124
Washington, George, 95
Whitehead, Alfred North, 261
Whitehead, Deborah, 155
Whitman, Walt, 86
Williams, Michael, 144
Wills, Gary, 87
Wolfe, Patrick, 2
Worldmaking, 65
Wynter, Sylvia, 10, 23, 26–27, 155–169, 214–215

www.ingramcontent.com/pod-product-compliance
Ingram Content Group UK Ltd.
Pitfield, Milton Keynes, MK11 3LW, UK
UKHW041916140426
5217IPUK00013B/183